NIRVANA
The Recording Sessions

NIRVANA

The Recording Sessions

ROB JOVANOVIC

soundcheck books

the stories behind the sounds

First published in paperback in Great Britain in 2012 by
Soundcheck Books LLP
88 Northchurch Road,
London,
N1 3NY
www.soundcheckbooks.co.uk

ISBN: 978-0-9566420-6-6

Book design: Benn Linfield (www.bennlinfield.com)

Printed and bound by the CPI Group (UK) Ltd, Croydon, CR0 4YY.

www.soundcheckbooks.co.uk

Question:

"Is there something you would like Nirvana to be remembered for?"

Kurt Cobain:

"Writing good music, good songs. That's all I could say, because that's more important than anything else."

Contents

Introduction

There have been many books about Nirvana. They were (and still are) such a powerful musical force that there will probably be many more. Most of the books have concentrated on the amazing life of Kurt Cobain. Some have also talked about the music. This book concentrates on the music.

From Kurt Cobain's initial noise-making as a teenager in 1982 (using a suitcase as a drum kit) to Nirvana's final session in January 1994, this book details each session, each track at each session and (where possible) each version of each track at each session. Research has taken in the many studios that the band used and the producers and engineers that worked with them on those sessions.

A discography is also included to assist in tracking down some of the harder-to-find recordings as well as details of all of the band's videos, TV and radio sessions and a concert history too. The book shows the progression from the early grunge of *Bleach*, through the power-punk glories of *Nevermind,* to the twisted majesty of *In Utero* before ending with the haunting beauty of the *MTV Unplugged* session. This is a quite breathtaking legacy from a band that lasted such a short time; their first and final albums were released just four years apart.

I'm now lucky enough to have been given the chance to update my original book which was published almost a decade ago. Since that edition there have been a slew of 21st Century releases including the *With The Lights Out* box set, *Sliver* compilation, *Live at Reading* concert, and expanded versions of *Bleach* and *Nevermind,* all of which have added many tracks to the session history, which itself has grown by eight sessions due to new information that has come to light. So delve in and re-live the recording history of the most important band of the 1990s.

Rob Jovanovic
Nottingham, England

Reading Guide

As no accurate records were kept of the majority of Nirvana's studio recording sessions, it's difficult to be 100% accurate about what was recorded when. From testimony given by those who were there and from trawling the band's interviews on the subject, I have been able to put together as close a record of Nirvana's recording history as possible. That covers one part of the problem

What is more difficult to pin down are the recordings made as home demos and during rehearsal sessions. As well as the dearth of documentation on these sessions, there is the added problem for the avid researcher that few of these stand out sufficiently in the memories of those present to be precisely placed. In recent years more and more of these have become officially available, but even then there is discussion about the correct dates and venues of each take.

In this book, each session is numbered and labelled using {x} for every session from 1982 to 1994. TV shows are sub-noted {Tx}, radio shows are numbered as {Rx} and miscellaneous non-Nirvana sessions are {Mx}.

By a similar token, all individual songs are numbered and noted as [x]. To differentiate between versions of these songs on TV, or radio sessions, live and video performances they keep their number but have T, R, L and V added to the reference as follows – [Tx], [Rx], [Lx] and [Vx]. Where, for instance, several different TV performances were made of a particular song they become [Txa], [Txb], [Txc], etc, etc.

The songs performed on the *MTV Unplugged* show are given their own letter, [Ux], as they were both performed on TV as well as being released as tracks on a live album and also as a DVD.

Don't worry if you find this too complicated; this system is for the fan that really wants to hunt down every instance of a particular song; simply ignore the brackets after every entry and just read the text if your interests lie with the narrative, which is a fascinating story in itself.

Each session, TV show, radio session and the like has a self-explanatory set of introductory information where you can find the date, venue and band members present (and what they played) as well as details of any producer or director involved. Then each song recorded at that session is listed and details are given of where it has been officially released. If a song is listed in the session summary in bold type it is discussed in more detail below the session summary; if it is discussed but is listed as 'not officially released' it means that recordings of the track are available only if you look hard enough.

Early Sessions

Aberdeen, Washington, did not have a lot going for it in the late 1960s and early 1970s. In February 1967, Kurt Cobain was born into the relatively small (population 19,000) logging community that was often cold, more often wet, and in the midst of a slippery descent into unemployment, widespread alcoholism and suicide. As the jobs went, so did the people, looking elsewhere for work or a way out of another kind. It wasn't a community that you thought would spawn a punk rock band. This was widely accepted as redneck territory.

By his early teens at the start of the 1980s, Cobain was starting to get a liking for punk. He managed to do this by getting his hands on old copies of *Creem* magazine, various fanzines that showcased pictures of the Sex Pistols, and a handful of seven-inch singles. He briefly had guitar lessons in 1981 (the same year in which he met local band the Melvins) and soon began thrashing away at some crude self-penned attempts at songs.

"I took lessons for a week" said Cobain. "I learned how to play 'Back in Black' by AC/DC, and it's pretty much the 'Louie Louie' chords, so that's all I needed to know. I never did pay the guitar teacher for that week either. I still owe him money. I just started writing songs on my own. Once you know the power chord, you don't need to know anything else." He'd become rebellious after the divorce of his parents in 1975 and he used music as an outlet for his pent-up emotions. "I was ashamed of my parents," he told *Guitar World*. "I desperately wanted to have the classic, typical family. I wanted that security, so I hated my parents for quite a few years because of that."

Kurt kept diaries, artwork and lyrics in a series of notebooks for a few years and by 1982, at the age of 15, he was fit to burst with musical ideas, even if these were initially limited in their scope. He used an aunt's 4-track tape deck to record his first batch of songs during a Christmas vacation. Even at this embryonic stage his punk ethos was apparent. His Aunt Mari recalled his response when she offered him the use of her computer for his earliest recordings: "I want to keep my music pure," he replied.

By his next 'sessions', at the age of 17, Kurt had dropped out of school and was in the midst of bouncing from one low rent apartment to another, while occasionally sleeping rough or dossing down in a car. He was also writing prodigiously and among his many known songs from these early days we have tantalizing reports of tracks called "Spam", "Hitchhiker" and "Class of '85", but no documentation of where and when these tracks were actually recorded, if at all.

Cobain started making dub tapes of these early demos and circulating various versions amongst friends, but it is impossible to document exactly what he did or when he did it. What we do know is that he gave a copy of his early *Fecal Matter* demo to a fellow Aberdonian, a bass player called Krist Novoselic, who was suitably impressed.

Krist was of Croatian parentage and had moved to Aberdeen, WA, aged 16 – he'd been born in Los Angeles in 1963. After a short spell living back in Croatia he returned to Aberdeen and fell in with Cobain. In 1986, after having ideas of becoming a covers band for money, they began weekly practice sessions with drummer Aaron Burckhard. Their first show as a trio took place in March 1987 at a Raymond, WA, house party; soon after they played their debut radio session and in early 1988 they recorded their first studio session. Through 1987 they played under the names of Skid Row, Ted Ed Fred, Throat Oyster and Bliss. By now they had already changed drummers a couple of times and Melvins' drummer Dale Crover was in the seat.

Kurt's song writing between 1985 and the end of 1987 paved the way for both Nirvana's first album and his recognition as a gifted musician and lyricist. He hadn't had it easy, never living in the same place for long, being broke for most of the time and battling to keep to his punk ideals from the outset.

NIRVANA

The Recording Sessions

Session number

{1}

Venue: Mari Earl Fradenburg's house, Seattle, WA.
Date: December 1982
Producer: none
Players: Kurt Cobain (guitar, bass, vocals, suitcase as drums)

Tracks recorded:	Available on:
Unknown tracks	not available – known as the 'Organized Confusion' tape.

During a Christmas vacation break at his Aunt Mari's in Seattle, Kurt made his first documented recordings. On the trip, Kurt had taken his first electric guitar which his uncle Chuck Fradenburg had bought him for his fourteenth birthday the previous February. Mari Earl is Kurt's mother's younger sister and had been relatively close to Kurt since he was a small child (she was just thirteen years older than Kurt). She had made a living as a singer-songwriter and her encouragement had a huge impact on Kurt's early musical experimentation. Details are sketchy at best and the 'session' has only been documented from the hazy recollection of Mari many years later. She recalled that, "Most of what I remember about the songs was a lot of distortion on guitar, really heavy bass, and the clucky sound of the wooden spoons. And his voice, sounding like he was mumbling under a big fluffy comforter, with some passionate screams once in a while. Musically it was very repetitious." Kurt used Mari's TEAC 4-track tape deck to record himself and the resulting tape has since become known as the 'Organized Confusion' tape.

Organized Confusion was also the name Kurt gave to a fantasy punk band that he dreamed of forming around 1982-83; he even made himself a t-shirt bearing this imaginary band's name. Whether a copy of this tape exists to this day is unknown as it has never been circulated among collectors. Occasionally copies have been reported but in each case the tape has turned out to be a fake.

Session number

{2}

Venue: Dale Crover's house, Aberdeen, WA.
Date: 1985
Producer: none
Players: Kurt Cobain (guitar), Shawn Murray (vocals),
        Steve Shillinger (drums)

Tracks recorded:	**Available on:**
Unknown	not available

Just one of a number of ensembles Kurt Cobain put together during the mid-1980s so that he could say he was in a band. In reality it was just various groups of beer-drinking friends having a laugh together. They used Dale Crover's house to practice in, while Crover was playing drums on tour. Greg Hokanson, Steve Newman and Bob McFadden were some of the others who would also be drafted in and out over the coming years as Cobain tried to find a combination that fitted his idea of a real band.

Session number

{3}

Venue: Mari Earl Fradenburg's house, Seattle, WA.
Date: December 1985
Producer: none
Players: Kurt Cobain (guitar, vocals), Dale Crover (drums)

Tracks recorded:	Available on:
Sound Of Dentage [1]	not available
Commercials [2]	not available
Bambi Slaughter [3]	not available
Made Not Born [4]	not available
Unknown #1	not available
Unknown #2	not available
Unknown #3	not available
Unknown #4	not available
Unknown #5	not available
Spank Thru [5]	*Sliver* **compilation album**
Unknown #6	not available
Buffy's Pregnant [6]	not available
Unknown #7	not available
Downer [7]	not available
Unknown #8	not available

Three years had passed since the first documented Cobain recordings had taken place at his Aunt Mari's house in Seattle. In the intervening time he had begun playing with Dale Crover and Greg Hokanson in the latter's bedroom. Information about these 'sessions' exists mainly because of a short-lived internet website circa 2000-01. Dale Crover had allowed a friend to copy this tape, known as the *Fecal Matter* tape, which the trio planned on calling their band, and this friend then posted some information about it online.

Crover had played drums with the Melvins, but in this line-up he played bass, with Hokanson on drums. The trio played a few gigs but when they traveled to Seattle to use Mari's 4-Track recorder again, Hokanson dropped out leaving just Cobain and Crover.

Mari set the boys up in her music room and left them to it. Over two or three days they worked on fifteen songs, only seven of which have known titles (see above), putting down the basic tracks then adding vocals afterwards, as Mari remembers well, "They set up in my music room and they'd just crank it up. It was loud. They would just put down the music tracks first, then he'd put the headphones on and all you could hear was Kurt Cobain's voice screaming through the house!" As Hokanson was not around, Crover reverted to drum duties, with Cobain on guitar and both of them adding vocals.

The only songs known to have been progressed further to any sort of real release were the early version of "Downer" [7] which was reportedly slower than the later take (an instrumental version was also recorded at this time and so Kurt's vocals may have been added subsequently) and "Spank Thru" [5] which was recorded several times before being released on the *Sub Pop 200* compilation album. A track called "Suicide Samurai" [119] was mentioned in the Charles Cross book *Heavier Than Heaven* as being from this session but no other documentation has surfaced to confirm this.

Spank Thru [5]

Opening the song in a deep voice that belied his age, Cobain almost talks the listener through his tale of teenage masturbation before screaming and coughing his way through the chorus. In a later interview Krist Novoselic claimed that hearing "Spank Thru" [5] on this demo tape is what inspired him to ask Kurt to start a band with him.

"Bambi Slaughter" [3] also see session {5}
"Spank Thru" [5] also see sessions {6}, {7}, {10}, {12}
"Downer" [7] also see sessions {6}, {7}

Session number

{4}

Venue: Novoselic's house, Aberdeen, WA.
Date: 1986
Producer: none
Players: Kurt Cobain (drums), Steve Newman (bass),
       Krist Novoselic (vocals, guitar)

Tracks recorded::	Available on:
Unknown	not available

In another of Cobain's short-lived mid-decade projects, he decided that a Credence Clearwater Revival covers band might be a way of making money from the local country rock fans in town.

This was the first collaboration between Cobain and the lanky Croat Novoselic. The latter was going by the Americanized spelling of his name at this time, Chris rather than Krist. After just a half-dozen sessions, the trio finally disbanded after Cobain and Newman started a fight using planks of wood and a vacuum cleaner.

Session number

{5}

Venues: Cobain's house, Aberdeen, WA and Tracy Marander's house, Olympia, WA.

Dates: various 1987-88

Producer: none

Players: Kurt Cobain (guitar, vocals)

Tracks recorded:	Available on:
Bambi Slaughter [3]	**not officially released**
Beans [8]	*With The Lights Out* **box set**
Black And White Blues [9]	**not officially released**
Clean Up Before She Comes [10]	*With The Lights Out* **box set**
Cracker [aka Polly] [11]	*With The Lights Out* **box set**
Sad [aka Sappy] [12]	**not officially released**
Don't Want It All (aka Spectre, Seed, Misery Loves Company) [13]	*With The Lights Out* **box set**
About A Girl [14]	*With The Lights Out* **box set**
The Montage Of Heck [15]	**not officially released**
The Montage Of Heck **edit [15a]**	**not officially released**

Not a session as such, but here are grouped together a collection of known, and circulated, recordings from 1987-88. David Fricke writing in *Rolling Stone* compared these recordings to John Lennon's mid-1970s Dakota musings and Bob Dylan's early 1960s hotel room recitals, but in fact Cobain's home demos are much more bi-polar and threatening than either of the greats he was likened to. At the same time these songs manage to hint at the noise-fests that were to follow and also show the gentler, but no less harrowing, side of Cobain's song writing with the likes of "Cracker" [aka "Polly"] [11]. It's likely that there are many more recordings that have never slipped out into the public domain because during this period Kurt was making numerous home recordings and demos while all the time improving his song writing and lyrics.

As is shown within the Cobain *Journals*, Kurt changed the titles of songs frequently during these early days and the titles listed above carry the names of the songs that were used originally, with their more common and better known titles in brackets. Many of these songs were recorded at Tracy Marander's apartment at 114½ Pear Street, Olympia, WA, while she was out at work, a situation that even worked itself into some lyrics. Kurt moved in with Marander in the autumn of 1987, but exact recording dates are unknown and most likely were never documented. When a number of these takes were included on the 2004 box set *With The Lights Out*, the dating of the songs caused considerable debate amongst fans. Even song titles were argued over.

It can be seen that Kurt had continued working on some of the songs from the very earliest recordings at Aunt Mari's five and six years previously, although what changes he'd made cannot be known for sure. "Bambi Slaughter" [3] dates from the *Fecal Matter* demos in 1985. Using what can only be assumed to be a basic 4-track unit, though it seems like an even more basic boom-box, Kurt is accompanied only by his guitar and sometimes has double-tracked his voice on various songs.

Bambi Slaughter [3]

There is now considerable doubt whether or not the home recording demo from 1988 known as "Bambi Slaughter" [3] is in fact another track altogether. The song listed here opens with the lines "Hey the love of two / A desire is what's for you" and lasts just 1:30 with an understated chorus of "hey, hey, hey". Charles Cross is quoted in *Heavier Than Heaven* as saying that the *Fecal Matter* (session {2}) version of "Bambi Slaughter" [3] contains a lyric that addresses the story of someone pawning their parents' wedding rings, and no mention of those lyrics survives in this take. It is possible that the same tune or melody was used in both songs, but more likely is the assumption that this take is a new as-yet-unidentified Cobain composition that dates later than the 1985 *Fecal Matter* tapes.

Also see session {3}

Beans [8]

More of an indulgence than a song, this track features eighty seconds of Kurt at his obnoxious best. Singing in a high-pitched voice (probably through a vocal distortion device) Cobain sings of eating some beans while plucking away at an acoustic guitar. Later on he supposedly wanted to use this snippet to close out *Bleach*, but Sub Pop nixed the idea saying that he sounded like 'a retard'. Undated when included on *With The Lights Out*, but almost certainly from this period.

Black And White Blues [9]

This guitar-only instrumental was for a while thought to be a fake, but has since been accepted as an original Cobain performance, though the origin of the tune is unknown. Available only on bootlegs, it was given its title as some thought it might possibly be a Huddie Ledbetter (Lead Belly) cover. However it has more of a jazzy feel than a blues one and brings to mind the 1930s guitar expertise of someone like Django Reinhardt. No other recordings of this track are known.

Clean Up Before She Comes [10]

If ever a song was a snapshot of Kurt's life at any point then this is it. While girlfriend Tracy Marander would be out at work she would sometimes leave lists of what chores Kurt should do before she came home. With this in mind the title is pretty obvious as Kurt sings of living in, and cleaning up, 'a dusty dump'. Lyrically the words don't really vary much from these refrains, while musically he repeats a simple guitar motif. There has been speculation that Kurt re-recorded this demo in 1994 shortly before his death.

Also see session {40}.

Cracker [aka Polly] [11]

An early Nirvana set list shows the songs "Seed" [13], "Cracker" [11] and "Sad" [12] listed with Kurt's notation "Mellow 4-track shit" alongside them. Bootleggers put two and two together and it has become generally accepted that "Cracker" became "Polly" [11], "Sad" became "Sappy" [aka "Verse Chorus Verse"] [12] and that "Seed" became "Misery Loves Company" [13] via "Spectre" (see below). This could be erroneous as

"Polly" [11] contains the lines "Polly wants a cracker" and also "Have a seed" – so in theory it could have had the early titles of "Cracker" or "Seed". To throw more confusion into the mix, Charles Cross claims that the early working title of "Polly" [11] was "Hitchhiker".

Whatever the original title, this is the first known recording of "Polly" [11] and shows that Kurt was writing subtle, understated but menacing songs as early as 1987. Though forty seconds shorter than the *Nevermind* version (see session {19}), the acoustic guitar part and vocals in this demo are pretty much identical. Kurt picked up on the narrative for the song by reading a newspaper report (in June 1987) about a young girl that was kidnapped, raped and tortured with a blowtorch. The lyric is particularly effective as it is sung from the point of view of the rapist.

Also see sessions {15}, {19}, {26}

Sad [aka Sappy] [12]

Again the supposed original title for this demo comes from the set list mentioned above. The *Journals* show that at one time Kurt had two completely different songs titled "Sappy" [12] and "Verse Chorus Verse" [62] the lyrics to which are shown on opposite pages of the book. Again confusion abounds over the naming of these early songs as it was commonly reported that the unlisted Nirvana track on the *No Alternative* compilation CD in 1993 was entitled "Verse Chorus Verse"; it is in fact the same song known here as "Sappy" [12]. This track [12] can be easily identified by the opening lines of "And if you say your prayers / you will make God happy", while the released version opens with "And if you save yourself / You will make him happy." This home demo features only Kurt's unusually low voice, singing a pretty much completed lyric, and his finger-picking on an electric guitar. This song was worked on at many subsequent sessions and a speeded-up, full band version was eventually released in 1993 as mentioned above.

Also see sessions {16}, {19}, {26}

Don't Want It All [aka Seed, Spectre, Misery Loves Company] [13]

A bizarre twenty-second intro (which is missing from many bootleg versions) opens with a noise best described as 'electronic gurgling' before the song proper starts. The painfully slow guitar part is dragged over some primal sounding percussion. The alternative titles of "Spectre" (maybe someone thought the vocal sounded 'ghostly', which it does) and "Misery Loves Company" (maybe a joke as the singer sounds pretty depressed) both seem to be figments of a bootlegger's imagination. No other attempts at this song are known.

The version included on *With The Lights Out* opens with a belch and is titled "Don't Want It All" which is a line in the song.

About A Girl [14]

"About A Girl" [14] was a major step forward in Kurt's song writing development. He catches a Beatle-esque melody on his solo guitar and sings with a heartbreaking voice. It's a song that he wrote for his girlfriend Tracy Marander, a fact that he never admitted directly to her but she discovered later through friends. Dated from the summer of 1988, this version has different lyrics to the *Bleach* version, opening up with "Don't leave a note to me / I do promise to agree", another reference to the lists of chores that Tracy would leave for Kurt to do while she was out at work (see also "Clean Up Before She Comes" [10] sessions {5} and {40}). Other lines that were later scrapped include "I do live in constant fear / I do wonder why I'm here" which could be a reference to Tracy's threat's to kick Kurt out if he couldn't find, and hold down, a job.

See also sessions {13}, {41}

Montage of Heck [aka The Landlord] [15] edit [15a]

The spring of 1988 saw Kurt playing with sound collages like never before. Here he assembled a thirty-five minute collection of TV clips, vinyl samples, spoken-word snippets and original clips of self-penned material (as well as the sound of someone passing water and then flushing the toilet, which then blends into the sound of birds singing in the trees!). He also created a shorter version, known as "The Edit" [15a] which lasted a little under ten minutes. This edit includes many of the original clips and what sounds like Krist Novoselic exclaiming "The landlord is a piece of shit from hell!"

Among the many tracks sampled and messed with are the Beatles' "A Day In The Life", "Taxman" and "Being For The Benefit Of Mr Kite", Simon & Garfunkel's "The Sounds Of Silence", Cher's "Gypsies, Tramps & Thieves", Donny Osmond's "Go Away Little Girl", John Denver's

"Rocky Mountain High", Dean Martin's "Everybody Loves Somebody", The Jackson Five's "ABC" and Led Zeppelin's "Whole Lotta Love", as well as many clips from religious broadcasts, children's programs and cartoons like *The Flintstones*. If nothing else it proves that Kurt had quite an eclectic record collection.

Later Kurt took another sample of sounds for use as the intro to "Love Buzz" [27], see session {9}.

Session number

{6}

Venue: Dale Crover's bedroom, Aberdeen, WA.
Date: January 1988
Producer: none
Players: Kurt Cobain (guitar, vocals), Krist Novoselic (bass), Dale
      Crover (drums)

Tracks recorded:	Available on:
If You Must [16]	not available
Downer [7]	not available
Floyd The Barber [17]	not available
Paper Cuts [18]	not available
Spank Thru [5]	not available
Hairspray Queen [19]	not available
Aero Zeppelin [20]	not available
Beeswax [21]	not available
Mexican Seafood [22]	not available
Pen Cap Chew [23]	not available
Anorexorcist [24]	**not available**
Raunchola [25]	**not available**
Gypsies, Tramps & Thieves [26]	**not available**
Gypsies, Tramps & Thieves [26a]	**not officially released**

Again this tape is not currently available. However, the above track
listing is accepted as an accurate record because the same internet
source that produced the *Fecal Matter* information (session {3}) is in
possession of a copy given to him by Dale Crover. Crover, Cobain and
Novoselic started the year with some serious practicing spread over the
first three weekends in January (1-3, 8-10 and 15-17). Kurt had booked
an afternoon session (session {7}) at Jack Endino's Reciprocal Studio
in Seattle and wanted to be as prepared as possible when they entered

the studio because time was money. The original plan was to record all thirteen of the above tracks but in reality they only managed the first ten. It's not known if the above tape includes takes from different nights or from one single practice. Two of the practiced songs which were not recorded at the Endino session (session {7}) have been played live and copies from these shows are in circulation (see below) as is a demo of the Cher song "Gypsies, Tramps & Thieves" [26], but with Krist, not Kurt, on lead vocals. The date of this version is unverified but it may well have been from these early 1988 demos.

Anorexorcist [24]

Though time ran out to demo this at the Endino session (session {7}) they did play it live at a show in Tacoma, WA, the same evening. It had also been played live on the KAOS radio show (radio session {R4}) in April 1987. Some bootleggers have mis-titled this as "Suicide Samurai" and until the *Fecal Matter* tape becomes available it is unknown if this is a version of the song mentioned by Charles Cross ("Suicide Samurai" [119]) from 1985 or simply a mistake. The live versions of this song feature a semi-breathless Cobain singing in a manner reminiscent of his "Negative Creep" [33] vocals over a driving drum and bass combo. This breaks down at 0:55 to a slow grungey interlude before picking up again. The lyrics are pretty unintelligible (in the April 1987 version) and most likely unfinished at this point. The live track lasted about 4:20.

Raunchola [25]

The second song planned for the Endino session (session {7}) that was dropped because they ran out of time, it was nonetheless worked on throughout January 1988 and included on the above tape. The only known recording of this track is from the Tacoma, WA, show on January 23, 1988. Krist Novoselic had described it as a "really, really raunchy song" and so bootleggers gave it the title "Raunchola". Kurt opens singing "If it's a hard, cold beat / You can go dance every night" and seems to have a completed lyric for the song, though musically (at least in this live version) it is little more than a thrash jam. Kurt also gets to let go on some top notch howling during the chorus.

Gypsies, Tramps & Thieves [26] With Krist on lead vocals [26a]
This is a raucous run through of the famous Cher song which had
been a Top 10 hit in November 1971. Krist's vocals are erratic, to say
the least, and he swings from screeches and hollers to parts where he
is struggling manfully to stop himself from bursting into laughter. If
this take is from the Crover practices it sounds like Dale is playing his
percussion parts on a biscuit tin lid and the whole thing has the air of a
Weird Al Yankovic spoof.

Bleach

The sessions for what would become Nirvana's debut album were spread over a year. When they started they didn't even have the name 'Nirvana' but what they did have was a handful of demos to record and a different drummer. Sub Pop, the label that would give them their break, wasn't yet a fully operational outfit and they were all pretty much broke. Kurt had saved a small amount of money to pay for the initial session (session {7}) and later in the year, for the final *Bleach* sessions (session {13a–f}), they got extra guitarist Jason Everman to foot the bill. He didn't even play on the album though he was credited as doing so. All sessions for the album took place at Reciprocal Studios in Seattle under the guidance of Jack Endino. Recording Nirvana's debut releases did his career no harm either.

Kurt was already taking his music seriously and insisted on a number of rehearsals before the January 1988 session {7}. He'd honed a number of songs to record from his quickly growing repertoire. The plan was to record a tape of demos to send to his favorite punk labels like Touch 'n' Go and SST. Producer Jack Endino passed on a tape to Sub Pop though, and the rest is history. Dale Crover left to be replaced by Nirvana's first 'permanent' drummer, Chad Channing, and the new trio cut a debut single, "Love Buzz" [27], in the summer of 1988 – a cover of a song by an obscure Dutch band of all things. Then they reached an agreement with Sub Pop for an album, re-cut some of their songs and had a concentrated effort to finish the album between December 1988 and January 1989. The resultant record, *Bleach*, led the grunge movement and put Seattle's burgeoning rock scene firmly on the global map.

This scene had the Sub Pop label at the heart of it. Bruce Pavitt had started his Subterranean Pop fanzine back in 1979 and had produced cassettes to be given away with his publication. This gradually gathered momentum and in April 1988 Pavitt linked up with Jonathan Poneman to launch a 'real' label (they had put out quarterly EPs since late 1987) and shortened the title to Sub Pop.

By the time Sub Pop approached Nirvana to work on a single, the band had switched drummers from Dale Crover (who moved to California with the Melvins shortly after session {7}) to Dave Foster, briefly back to Aaron Burckhard and then finally to Chad Channing. Nirvana would re-record some of the tracks that Crover had played on, but three of his tracks – "Downer" [7], "Floyd The Barber" [17] and "Paper Cuts" [18] – would make the album.

For some people, especially those that went back to buy it after hearing *Nevermind* (30,000 copies of *Bleach* were sold before the follow-up album, almost four million have been sold worldwide since), *Bleach* was a difficult album to listen to; abrasive, uncompromising and punk-metal, whereas *Nevermind* was punk-pop. *Bleach* did have some 'pop' moments though, as "About A Girl" [14] and "Love Buzz" [27] proved, but the overriding sound was heavy, sludgey, grungey. It was released in June 1989 with a Sub Pop press release that was meant to be tongue-in-cheek, but turned out to be pretty accurate: "Hypnotic and righteous heaviness from these Olympia pop stars. They're young, they own their own van and they're going to make us rich!"

Bleach sold well for a relatively unknown band, and reached the indie Top 10 in the UK before its infinitely more successful follow-up arrived. Nirvana was on the way.

Bleach reviews:

Select:	"...you can destroy furniture to it." 4/5
NME:	"This is the biggest, baddest sound that Sub Pop have so far managed to unearth." 8/10
Q:	"Ultimately the bulldozer riffing wins out." 3/5 (reviewed October 2000)
Kerrang!	"... the sound of four snuffy, bum-fluffy delinquents with $600 saved and the urgent need to make some noise."

Original US versions track listing:
Blew / Floyd The Barber / About A Girl / School / Love Buzz / Paper Cuts / Negative Creep / Scoff / Swap Meet / Mr Moustache / Sifting
Original UK versions track listing:
Blew / Floyd The Barber / About A Girl / School / Paper Cuts / Negative Creep / Scoff / Swap Meet / Mr Moustache / Sifting / Big Cheese

1991 and later versions track listing:
Blew / Floyd The Barber / About A Girl / School / Love Buzz / Paper
Cuts / Negative Creep / Scoff / Swap Meet / Mr Moustache / Sifting / Big
Cheese / Downer

2009 anniversary edition track listing:
Same as 1991 onwards versions plus the whole of the 9 February show
at the Pine Street Theatre, Portland, OR. (see Live Tracks on Official
Releases).

Bleach

1989
Cassette

Sub Pop SP34a	US	
Tupelo TUPMC6	UK	

LP

Sub Pop SP34	US	initial 1000 on white vinyl with free poster
Sub Pop SP34	US	pressing of 1001-2000 with free poster
Sub Pop SP34	US	various color vinyl

Tupelo TUPLP6	UK	initial 300 on white vinyl
Tupelo TUPLP6	UK	nos. 301-2300 on green vinyl
Tupelo TUPLP6	UK	
Waterfront DAMP114	Australia	on red, yellow or blue vinyl
CD		
Sub Pop SP34b	US	2 extra tracks
Tupelo TUPCD6UK		

1990

Cassette		
Sub Pop SP34a	US	
Tupelo TUPMC6	UK	
CD		
Sub Pop SP34b	US	
Tupelo TUPCD6	UK	

1991

Cassette		
Geffen GFLC19291	UK	
LP		
DGC/MCA 25002	Japan	with obi strip
CD		
DGC/MCA MVCG93	Japan	with obi strip
Geffen GFLD1929	UK	
Geffen GED24433	Australia	

1992

Cassette		
Sub Pop SP34a	US	remastered
Geffen GFLC19291	UK	remastered
LP		
Waterfront DAMP114	Australia	limited to 500 copies green vinyl/cloth bag
CD		
Sub Pop SP34b	US	remastered
Geffen GFLC19291	UK	remastered
Geffen MVCG-93	Japan	13 track album

19

2002
LP

Sub Pop 9878700341	UK	

CD

Rhino 5186561462	UK	20th Anniversary 25 track edition

2003
CD

DGC WPCR-11525	Japan
Geffen UICY2003	Japan

2009
LP

Sub Pop 034	US

Double LP

Sub Pop SP834	US	remastered
Sub Pop SP834	US	digipak

CD

Sub Pop 70834	UK	
Sub Pop 5051865614623	UK	remastered

2012
LP

Sub Pop SP034	US

Packaging notes:

The cover photo of the band was taken at an Olympia gig by Tracy Marander and shows (left to right) Cobain (foreground), Novoselic, Crover and Everman. The inner sleeve shot is a Charles Peterson photo from the February 25, 1989 show at the University of Washington (the limited edition poster was also shot at this show). On CD sleeves, the photo of Kurt falling backwards onto the drums is another Peterson photo from a show at Raji's in Los Angeles on February 15, 1990. As he often did, Kurt lists himself as 'Kurdt Kobain' on the sleeve, Krist uses 'Chris Novoselic', Chad Channing and Dale Crover are listed as drummers and Jason Everman is named as extra guitarist because he paid for the sessions! The 2009 re-issue included a 52 page CD-sized booklet, mainly of pictures, and a fold-out cardboard CD sleeve.

Session number

{7} The Recording So

Venue: Reciprocal Studios, Seattle, WA.
Date: January 23, 1988 [11.30a.m. – 6 p.m.]
Producer: Jack Endino
Players: Kurt Cobain (guitar, vocals), Krist Novoselic (bass), Dale
Crover (drums, backing vocals)

Tracks recorded:	Available on:
If You Must [16]	*With The Lights Out* box set
Downer [7]	*Bleach*
Floyd The Barber [17]	*Bleach*
Paper Cuts [18]	*Bleach*
Spank Thru [5]	not officially released
Hairspray Queen [19]	*Incesticide*
Aero Zeppelin [20]	*Incesticide*
Beeswax [21]	*Incesticide*
Mexican Seafood [22]	*Incesticide*
Pen Cap Chew [23]	*With The Lights Out* box set

"This band called, completely out of the blue," says Jack Endino. "They
said, 'We wanna come up to Seattle. We're from Aberdeen, we're living
in Olympia right now and we're friends with the Melvins and we've got
Dale from the Melvins playing drums with us just for the session and
we wanna come up and just record some songs'." Endino wasn't about
to turn a session down, even if Reciprocal was the cheapest studio in
Seattle, so they booked in for six hours at $20 per hour. Endino was also
a Melvins fan so the mention of Dale Crover's name made him more eager
to work with this band. Although they'd played under several monikers,
Endino took the booking under the name 'Kurt Kovain'. The trio loaded
their equipment into a friend's campervan and set off for Seattle.

On January 23, 1988 Kurt Cobain entered a recording studio for the first time shortly before noon. They unloaded their rag-tag assembly of equipment and began setting up. Kurt's Univox guitar with Univox humbucking pickups, a Randall amp for Dale and Krist's bass, about which Endino recalls, "the bass cab was a big 2x15 that in the early days was always missing one wheel."

They were ready to record as many demos as possible in their allotted time. They had booked just six hours to record because of a gig commitment that night in Tacoma and a lack of money, so things had to go smoothly. Although Kurt was nervous and excited, he was also serious about doing things properly. Endino was impressed by their professionalism, as he told the BBC: "They didn't screw around in the studio, they just wanted to get it done. I mean you don't record and mix ten songs in one afternoon unless you are very, very focused and they were very focused. Most of the music was done in one take. So that in itself impressed me enough." They did slip a little though as they had twelve songs ready to go but ran out of time and money. In fact the final song they attempted, "Pen Cap Chew" [23], cut out part way through because the tape ended and they couldn't afford the $30 for a new roll.

Starting at noon, each song was done with a run through and then one take, in most cases, and recorded on the 8-track set up. By three in the afternoon the basic recording was done; Endino immediately set about producing a rough mix of the session for the band to take home with them. This must have been a sight to behold as the band tried unsuccessfully to squeeze into the tiny control room which barely held a couple of people at the best of times, especially with the towering Novoselic present. The rough mix was completed shortly before 6 p.m.

The bill came to $152.44: Endino charged them only for five hours of studio time at $20 per hour and $30 for one roll of tape and taxes. Cobain handed over his savings and grasped the tape. Then it was time to head to Tacoma. Tracy Marander remembers Kurt sitting in the van, clutching the tape with a big smile on his face. When the band left, Endino was impressed enough to stay behind and do a second mix for himself – this is the tape that he would later pass on to Sub Pop. "It was Kurt's singing that stood out," he says, "He screamed with such passion, just something about his voice was arresting."

The Tacoma gig at the Community World Theater went well and an interesting bit of trivia shows up if you inspect the set list for that night. They played the ten songs from the afternoon's session, in order, with Anorexorcist [24] and Raunchola [25] as songs eleven and twelve in their set. These are the two songs they ran out of time for at Reciprocal that afternoon and for those two tracks it was their last chance for fame, as they were subsequently dropped and never recorded.

If You Must [16]

In hindsight it might seem strange that the first song Kurt chose to record in a professional studio was one that he would soon come to hate so much. Not long after recording this session, Kurt wrote to Crover explaining that "The first song on the demo is no longer played, it is sickening and dumb. Destroy it, it is evil. In the likes of Whitesnake and Bon Jovi." True to form, there is no record of this song being attempted again. The song itself is a hypnotic piece with ringing guitars and a steady beat. Kurt sings his first lyric which confronts the very act of song writing, "Write some words / Make them rhyme / Thesis or storyline / Set the mood / Something new / Is it me? / Or my attitude?" It builds into a screaming, howling climax and Kurt gives it his all, especially over the noisy middle-eight. The song seems quite polished at this early stage and despite the somewhat misguided worries that it might be reminiscent of a metal-hair band it would probably have fitted quite well with the other songs on *Bleach*.

Also see session {6}

Downer [7]

"I was trying to be Mr Political Punk Rock Black Flag Guy. I really didn't know what I was talking about" admitted Cobain. This track was a full-throttle sonic assault with what would become a Nirvana trademark, the quieter verse followed by a fast shouted chorus. Kurt's claim about his attempts at singing a political rant are upheld with the lines "Sickening, pessimist, hypocrite, master / Conservative, communist, apocalyptic, bastard." This was one of two songs that Dale Crover added backing vocals to. This version was used by the band even after Crover had been replaced on drums by Chad Channing. Though not included on initial versions of *Bleach* it was later inserted as the final track and also on the *Incesticide* compilation.

Also see sessions {3}, {6}

Floyd The Barber [17]

Kurt showed off two interesting facets of his song writing on this song – his ability to sing about vivid characters that he had dreamt up and also to be able to take a comfy cultural icon (in this case a TV show) and twist it into his own graphic nightmare world. *The Andy Griffith Show* ran on US TV between 1960 and 1968 and featured Griffith as Andy Taylor and the characters Barney, Aunt Bea, Opie and Floyd. In the song, Kurt sings of going for a haircut at Floyd's but the visit soon turns nasty as he is strapped to the chair ("Barney ties me to the chair / I can't see, I'm really scared") before being shaved, tortured and ultimately killed ("I sense others in the room / Opie Aunt Bea I presume / They take turns and cut me up"). They later attempted the song again with Chad Channing on drums (session {13}) but preferred this earlier version with Dale Crover. Endino re-mastered the track before its inclusion on *Bleach*.

Also see sessions {6}, {13}

Paper Cuts [18]

One of the slower tracks on *Bleach*, it tells another horror story from the victim's perspective. This one was loosely based on a true story (or urban myth) about a local Aberdeen drug dealer who befriended an abused child that had been locked up in a dark room with shredded newspaper for a toilet. Kurt addresses these horrors directly: "At my feeding time / She'd push food through the door / I crawl towards the cracks of light / Sometimes I can't find my way." The lyric also seems to contain elements that address either Kurt's relationship with his mother, or maybe he sings only of the victim and the victim's mother – "The lady whom I feel maternal love for / Cannot look me in the eyes." Again this is the take that was used on *Bleach*.

Spank Thru [5]

An epic of Nirvana's early repertoire, this song confronted Kurt's masturbatory experimentations in graphic detail. The song was later re-recorded with Chad Channing (session {10}) but never issued on a

Nirvana release (the second version was given to Sub Pop to use on the *Sub Pop 200* compilation). After some 'sound effects' that leave little to the imagination the jaunty tune kicks off with a late–1970s sounding guitar riff leading to the devastating verse of "I can cut it / I can taste it / I can spank it / I can beat and ejaculate it", then in a line not for the faint hearted he proclaims "Sticky boredom with a book / I can make it do things you wouldn't think it ever could." Thanks for sharing that with us, Kurt! Cobain also puts in a nifty guitar solo towards the end.

Also see sessions {3}, {6}, {10}, {12}

Hairspray Queen [19]
This song had previously been heard on the KAOS radio performance of April 17, 1987 and is one of the longest tracks of this session coming in at a little over four minutes. Featuring a very new-wavy guitar part and ultra–bouncy bass line, Cobain interweaved a mixture of different vocal styles over the top. He screams, he sings in a high-pitched voice and he croons in a classic rock style. This take was used on *Incesticide* in the original band-mix of the session.

Also see session {6}

Aero Zeppelin [20]
Based tongue-in-cheek around the band names Aerosmith and Led Zeppelin, this is a riff fest that Kurt cheekily described as "Christ!? Yeah, let's just throw together some heavy metal riffs in no particular order and give it a quirky name in homage to a couple of our favorite masturbatory 70s rock acts." Possibly the heaviest of the songs attempted that afternoon, the lyric considers the retro feel of some of the Seattle bands of the time ("How a culture comes again / It's a clone of yesterday / And you swear it's not a trend / Doesn't matter anyway") and shows views about the music business that Kurt would hold onto for all of his life ("You could shit upon the stage / They'll be fans they'll be fans... All the kids will eat it up / If it's packaged properly"). Again this song was used in its original quick mix form on the *Incesticide* album.

Also see session {6}

Beeswax [21]

A stifled laugh (or maybe it's a sneeze) opens proceedings which quickly turn to a heavy, descending guitar riff. Kurt's vocals are at best hard to decipher and at worst totally unintelligible. The heavy riffs and Crover's vicious pounding of the drums don't help matters when it comes to listening to the words. Again this was used in rough mix form on the *Incesticide* compilation.

Also see session {6}

Mexican Seafood [22]

A swift, but very melodic, guitar line opens out into a strange song that seems to be about a urinary infection which might have been obtained from eating the delicacy in the title! "Oh well it hurts when I / It hurts when I pee" sings Kurt for the chorus. A full version of the lyric, which includes references to a whole list of nasty ailments and afflictions, was included in the *Journals* published in 2002. The whole song lasts less than two minutes and was used on *Incesticide* in the original quick-mix form.

Also see session {6}

Pen Cap Chew [23]

As explained above, this song was a victim of a reel of tape lasting only about 32 minutes and it cut out as the tape came to an end. The song, which was never worked on again, was a slow grinding trudge that speeded up occasionally and addressed some of the political issues that Kurt had ranted about on "Downer" [7] – "Waste your time by saving worthless gullibles / Kill a politician and then wear his clothes / This decade is the age of rehashing / Protest and then go to jail for trespassing." The entire song must have been quite a long one as it was faded out ("[it] has a fade ending that I did just for their amusement" says Endino) but still almost reached three minutes in length. The title came from the couplet that came after the tape ran out but was sung in concert and said "Has your conscience got to you for accidents? / Is this why unknowingly you eat your pens?"

Also see session {6}

Session number

{8} The Recording Ses

Venue: Novoselic's house, Tacoma, WA.
Date: May 1988
Producer: none
Players: Kurt Cobain (guitar, vocals), Krist Novoselic (bass), Chad
       Channing (drums)

Tracks recorded:	Available on:
Unknown	not available

In the six months following on from the debut session, the Nirvana
drum stool became something of a merry-go-round. Dale Crover moved
to San Francisco with the Melvins, thinking that bands from the
Northwest would never make it; then Dave Foster briefly filled in before
Chad Channing took over the sticks on a permanent basis in May 1988.
Channing had been introduced to Cobain and Novoselic after a show
and they asked him to join them for a jam session in the basement of
Novoselic's house.

It went well and he was asked back again, for a total of half a dozen
sessions, but he was never actually told he was a member of the band,
though when they returned to the studio a few weeks later he was the
drummer of choice.

Session number

{9}

Venue: Reciprocal Studios, Seattle, WA.
Date: June 11, 1988
Producer: Jack Endino
Players: Kurt Cobain (guitar, vocals), Krist Novoselic (bass), Chad
Channing (drums)

Tracks recorded:	Available on:
Love Buzz [27]	Love Buzz single, *Bleach*

Chad Channing's first session with the band was on this date to record
a debut single for Sub Pop. "We had our particulars," said Channing,
"but it was also relaxed and loose. Everyone was feeling really inspired.
It was the first record for everybody. It was a lot of fun."

Jonathan Poneman was keen for the band to put out some vinyl as
part of the Sub Pop Singles Club. He suggested the cover version that
was then a memorable part of the Nirvana live set – "Love Buzz" [27].

The song had originally been a hit for Dutch band Shocking Blue.
Their other claim to fame had been their number one single "Venus"
in 1970, which must be a lucky song as it was also a number one
hit on both sides of the Atlantic for all-girl singing trio Bananarama
in 1986. Krist Novoselic had come across the track and played it for
Cobain who instantly took a liking to it. When Poneman suggested they
record it, with Sub Pop picking up the studio costs, Cobain was torn
between finally getting a single issued and the fact that it would be a
cover rather than one of his original compositions. The lure of finally
getting a single out won through and they headed back to Seattle and
Reciprocal Studios.

The five hour session was expected to be plenty long enough to record
the single, a suitable b-side and maybe another track or two – after all,
they had managed to record and mix ten songs in a similar time frame

28

last time out. Things were more complicated than that though and only "Love Buzz" [27] was recorded in the session.

Love Buzz [27]

It's easy to hear why this track was a favorite at early Nirvana shows. It starts out with Novoselic's intriguing mid-paced solo bass guitar playing a semi-psychedelic, Turkish or middle-eastern sounding riff. This is joined after 0:07 by Channing's drums and this combination is then crashed into by Kurt's guitar at 0:15, thus creating a memorable opening to their debut single. The finished track, lasting about three-and-a-half minutes, is the perfect power-pop single, but Kurt had other ideas about how he wanted to open the song.

Cobain had taken along one of his sound collage tapes and wanted to tag a section of one of these on to the beginning of the song. He originally had a twenty-second snippet opening the song, though Sub Pop later insisted it be shortened to the final ten seconds that survived, and also inserted another one as a noise break mid-way through. "Since all eight tracks were full on the master tape," explains Endino, "we had to plug the studio cassette deck into the board like a virtual ninth track, and each time I ran through the mix, Kurt had to press 'play' on the cassette deck at the right instant so that the stuff would be blended into the mix I was doing. When we later went to re-mix 'Love Buzz' for the album Kurt forgot to bring that cassette, so those noises are absent."

Also see session {11}

Session number

{10}

Venue: Reciprocal Studios, Seattle, WA.
Date: June 30, 1988
Producer: Jack Endino
Players: Kurt Cobain (guitar, vocals), Krist Novoselic (bass), Chad
      Channing (drums)

Tracks recorded:	Available on:
Spank Thru [5]	Sub Pop 200 compilation
Big Cheese [28]	**Love Buzz single, *Bleach***
Blandest [29]	***With The Lights Out* box set**

With "Love Buzz" [27] at the last session taking longer than expected,
the band re-booked with Endino to record three more songs including a
re-recording of "Spank Thru" [5]. A second five-hour session {11} took
place and two tracks were undertaken.

Big Cheese [28]
Kurt Cobain had always hit out at authority figures and when Sub Pop
boss Jonathan Poneman started suggesting which songs to record and
which to re-record, Kurt decided it was time to pen a song in his 'honor'
– hence this song. When "Blandest" [29] fell by the wayside, "Big
Cheese" [28] was picked as the b-side for "Love Buzz" [27]. Later this
ominous sounding track was added to versions of *Bleach* too.

Also see sessions {11}, {18}

Blandest [29]
This simple but catchy song was originally meant to be the b-side for
"Love Buzz" [27]. However the band were, for some reason, unhappy
with the track and instructed Endino to record over it – which he did.
The idea was to re-record it at a later date but they never got around

to it. "When they were planning *Incesticide*" says Endino, "Krist called me up and wanted to know if I remembered 'Blandest' and if there was a tape of it anywhere. I told him no – you guys told me to erase it!" Luckily for collectors, a copy has circulated from a band member's personal tape of the session otherwise the song would have been lost forever.

Session number

{11}

Venue: Reciprocal Studios, Seattle, WA.
Date: July 16, 1988
Producer: Jack Endino
Players: Kurt Cobain (guitar, vocals), Krist Novoselic (bass), Chad
      Channing (drums)

Tracks recorded:	Available on:
Big Cheese [28]	*Bleach*
Love Buzz [27]	Love Buzz single, *Bleach*

After hearing the tapes from the previous two sessions (sessions {9} and {10}) that he'd paid for, Jonathan Poneman asked the band to re-record the vocals for "Love Buzz" [27]. So on this, their third visit to Reciprocal in five weeks they did just that and also completed the final mixes for that track, and for "Big Cheese" [28]. All work this day was completed in three hours.

Session number

{12}

Venue: Reciprocal Studios, Seattle, WA.
Dates: September 27, 1988
Producer: Jack Endino
Players: Kurt Cobain (guitar, vocals), Krist Novoselic (bass), Chad
    Channing (drums)

Tracks recorded:	Available on:
Spank Thru [5]	*Sub Pop 200* compilation

With the tracks for the debut single in the can, the final task of the summer was to polish up a song for the *Sub Pop 200* compilation. Accordingly the band spent two hours mixing "Spank Thru" [5] from an earlier session (session {10}). Jack Endino also included backing vocals of himself in the finished mix.

Also see sessions {3}, {6}, {7}, {10}

Session number

{13a to 13f}

Venue: Reciprocal Studios, Seattle, WA.
Dates: December 24, 1988 to January 24, 1989
Producer: Jack Endino
Players: Kurt Cobain (guitar, vocals), Krist Novoselic (bass), Chad
     Channing (drums)

Tracks recorded:	Available on:
About A Girl [14]	*Bleach*
Big Long Now [30]	*Incesticide*
Blew [31]	*Bleach*
Blew (alt. version)* [31a]	**not officially released**
Mr Moustache [32]	*Bleach*
Mr Moustache (alt. version)*	**not officially released**
[32a]	
Negative Creep [33]	*Bleach*
Paper Cuts (backing vocals) [18]	*Bleach*
School [34]	*Bleach*
Scoff [35]	*Bleach*
Sifting [36]	*Bleach*
Sifting (instrumental)* [36a]	**not officially released**
Swap Meet [37]	*Bleach*
Floyd The Barber [17]	not available

After Sub Pop released "Love Buzz" [27], thoughts turned to recording an album. The label had no money to advance them, but the band wanted to go ahead anyway. They had some new songs to record and also planned to use some of the songs from the first Endino session (session {7}), but this time with Chad Channing drumming. As recording of the album began there was no contract but, on Krist Novoselic's insistence, the two parties entered into an agreement on January 1, 1989. The band had to stump up for the studio costs for the sessions and an old friend of Channing's, a guitarist by the name of Jason Everman, came up with the $606 required, as previously mentioned. In return the band listed him as second guitarist on *Bleach*, even though he didn't play a note on it. Later he would tour briefly with the band.

Session number

{13a} December 24, 1988

Starting on Christmas Eve the recording was spread over six sessions stretching into January The five-hour Christmas Eve session was used as a chance to experiment with some different guitar tunings, fiddle about with Channing's drum set-up and run through some of the new songs, so new that the lyrics weren't finished and in some cases not even started. Around ten songs were begun in this session which ended just past midnight. "Floyd The Barber" [17] was tried out but the band decided the previous take with Dale Crover drumming (see session {7}) was better and so, to save on tape costs, they recorded over it. The same fate befell other takes on this first day of recording, mainly because Kurt was unhappy with his vocal performances. The following songs are the ones that survive from December 24.

Swap Meet [37]

One of the first songs recorded at the session, the band tuned down to D for this love story of a Swap Meet couple (a Car Boot couple to UK readers). "They make a living off of arts and crafts / The kind with seashells, driftwood, and burlap / They make a deal when they come to town / The Sunday swap meet is a battle ground." The driving guitars and bass carry the song along, while the choruses give Chad Channing the chance to show off his drumming skills. Like "Floyd The Barber" [17] this is Kurt's take on local community life. He'd probably witnessed many swap meets in Aberdeen, maybe even picked up a second hand record or two at them, but unlike "Floyd The Barber" [17] he doesn't put a horrific spin on the story, settling for giving the characters a sad air of desperation in their simple lives. Cobain was working on this track right up to its recording. Chad Channing remembered that Cobain was still writing lyrics for it as they traveled to the studio.

Blew [31a]

Having already tuned down to D for "Swap Meet" [37] the band prepared to record this second track and, forgetting the previous down-tuning, they took the key down further to C, mistakenly thinking it was to D. After recording it they asked Endino if they should re-do it with the 'proper' tuning but he suggested they keep it as it was. As well as sounding musically different (with the alternate tuning and a different guitar solo), this take was also totally different lyrically. Kurt was still writing lyrics up to, and even during, the sessions, and this version has a first verse and chorus that was dropped from the *Bleach* version – "We were in a garden wasting time / And we were in love and like to blew / We were in a garden like to blew / And if you wouldn't mind I would like to choose". The original chorus was "See it, believe it, need it, is it sane / Is there another reason for your name / Is there another word that is your name". The final version was lyrically much simpler.

Mr Moustache [32a]

This title came from a cartoon strip that Kurt drew to illustrate his idea of the typical macho red-necked Northwestern male. This early take had only mumbled sounds for most of the lyric and just gave the band a chance to thrash through the tune as a practice. Musically it is pretty much the finished song. A tape of this take has subsequently been circulated among collectors.

Sifting [36a]

Another early take with no lyrics, this instrumental run-through lasted 5:20 and has been bootlegged. One notable difference from the final version is the inclusion of a long guitar solo using a 'wah wah' pedal from 2:59 to 4:15.

Session number

{13b}, {13c}, {13d}

December 29, 30 and 31, 1988

The bulk of recording for the album took place over the last three days of 1988 with five-hour sessions on December 29 and 30 and a 4½ hour session on New Year's Eve. Kurt was still working on the words, even after the five-day break over Christmas, as Jack Endino told the BBC: "I'd say, 'So OK, are we ready to cut vocals on this song?' and he'd say, 'Wait a minute, let me finish the lyrics' and he'd be furiously scribbling and he'd go, 'OK, I've got the lyrics.' It was that easy for him. He could come up with lyrics pretty instantly. It was fun recording these guys. The lyrics gave me a good laugh more than once. They were very good-natured about it."

Cobain agreed that the words were not his main priority at all, "Not much thought went into it at all. It's pretty obvious. I didn't care about lyrics at all at that point. I didn't have any appreciation for them. I'd never thought of a song because of its lyrics at that point." This approach is perhaps best demonstrated on "Negative Creep" [33] and "School" [34] which comprise of just a few words that are repeated over and over. The equipment used for the session was pretty much identical to that used a year previously (see session {7}) with the exception of the Randall amplifier that was away being repaired. Endino brought in his own 1968 Fender Twin to use instead.

Big Long Now [30]

This was the only completed song to be cut from *Bleach*. At over five minutes long Cobain thought (correctly) that the last thing the album needed was a long, slow, plodding track. A slow, clanging guitar introduces the song, then cymbals and bass build a crescendo up to fifteen seconds where the beat picks up. Kurt's ethereal vocal floats in. "It's not cold enough" he sings to add to the feeling of desolation.

Throughout, the song stays at the same pace, though the middle-eight has more of a restrained shouty vocal before the whole thing slowly winds down to a crawl and fades into gentle feedback. Later, this take was used on the *Incesticide* album.

Blew [31]
Chosen as the band's debut UK single at the end of 1989, Bruce Pavitt insisted that this track open *Bleach*. The finished song showcases the quieter verse/screamed chorus that the band used many times later. Krist Novoselic opens with a bass solo that moulds with the heavy guitar riffs to set up a churning basis for Kurt's half-spoken, half-sung first verse, before he screams out the chorus. The lyric was completely re-vamped from the initial take of the song on December 24, 1988
Also see session {13a}

Mr Moustache [32]
Using the completed lyrics (that had been sung in earlier live shows) this was a tidier take than the Christmas Eve 'experiment.' The song hurtles along at a furious pace: "Yes I eat cow / I am not proud" Cobain intones in this serenade to the average red-necked listener.

Negative Creep [33]
One of the fastest and most aggressive songs on the album, it also features probably the fewest number of words with just four lines repeated over and over in its 2:55 duration. The stop-start chugging melody helps make it memorable despite the lack of lyrical interest. Whether the subject of the song is Cobain or another character is unknown.

School [34]
Drawing on memories of school that weren't that long ago, Kurt sings another super-sparse lyric with just three lines repeated this time: "Won't you believe it, it's just my luck", "No recess" and "You're in high school again" was all he felt like saying. He does add a stinging guitar solo though which breaks up an otherwise uninspiring rock-out.

Scoff [35]

This song could be aimed at either the narrator's parents or girlfriend. Where "Negative Creep" [33] admitted shortcomings, "Scoff" [35] was more defiant: "In my eyes I'm not lazy / In my face it's not over / In your room I'm not older / In your eyes I'm not worth it." Musically it's pretty representative of Nirvana at the time, a heavy drum beat pounds out a path for the stinging guitars to follow with Kurt screaming across the top.

Sifting [36]

By the time they got to the end of *Bleach*'s second side many critics were growing a little tired of all the slow grunge. "Sifting" [36] was probably just one too many of those kind of songs. The band had proved that they could do this type of track beyond doubt and it added nothing to the album.

About A Girl [14]

Though this song had been around for the best part of eighteen months, the band had not attempted it at any of the earlier sessions. Kurt had anticipated the problem of having too many long, slow songs on the album and was keen to get the pop-rock of "About A Girl" [14] included somewhere. "*Bleach* seemed to be really one-dimensional," he later admitted. "It just has the same format. All the songs are slow and grungey and they are tuned down to really low notes and I screamed a lot. But at the same time as we were recording we had a lot more songs like 'About A Girl'." Musically it is a straightforward band version of the original song but the lyric had been updated since the summer 1988 take.

Also see session {5}

Session number

{13e} and {13f}

January 14, and 24, 1989

The final two sessions for *Bleach* (lasting five and five and a half hours respectively) were used to overdub, re-record vocals, and mix the album. Backing vocals were also added to "Paper Cuts" [18] from an earlier session (see session {7}). This track was also remastered before being included on the album.

After making his debut in a February 1989 show in Olympia, WA, Jason Everman was finally an active member of the band as they toured sporadically during the spring. In June, *Bleach* was finally released by Sub Pop and the band had their one and only recording session with Everman, who didn't last long and played his final show on July 18. September saw another session to record songs for a planned EP before they embarked on their first overseas tour to Europe. On this jaunt they played in nine countries over a two month period. At the end of the tour, Krist married his girlfriend Shelli Dilley. Only a small number of new songs surfaced during this period, but that was about to change in a hurry.

Session number

{14}

Venue: Evergreen State College, Olympia, WA.
Date: June 1989
Producer: Greg Babior
Players: Kurt Cobain (guitar, vocals), Krist Novoselic (bass), Chad
Channing (drums), Jason Everman (guitar)

Tracks recorded:	Available on:
Do You Love Me [38]	*Hard To Believe*
Dive [39]	*With The Lights Out* box set

There is very little information about Jason Everman's only session with Nirvana. The only song released from the session is the Kiss cover "Do You Love Me" [38]. It's also known, via a very poor video recording, that "Dive" [39] was recorded at this session and though it's likely that there may have been others, they have yet to surface.

Do You Love Me [38]
A pretty straight run through of the Kiss song from their 1976 *Destroyer* album, recorded for inclusion on the tribute album *Hard To Believe*. The double guitar attack does give the take a more authentic Kiss sound and Krist Novoselic adds some suitably anguished backing vocals. Towards the end the whole thing fragments with everyone trying to get a word in while the music breaks down to some screaming feedback before a shout of "Fucking turn it off!" Which they do.

Session number

{15}

Venue: Music Source Studios, Seattle, WA.
Dates: September 1989
Producer: Steve Fisk
Players: Kurt Cobain (guitar, vocals), Krist Novoselic (bass), Chad
      Channing (drums)

Tracks recorded:	Available on:
Been A Son [40]	*Blew* **EP**
Stain [41]	*Blew* **EP**
Even In His Youth [42]	*Incesticide*, *With The Lights Out* **box set**
Polly [11]	*With The Lights Out* **box set**
Token Eastern Song [aka Junkyard] [43]	*With The Lights Out* **box set**

Details on these sessions are sketchy at best. It took place in September, but no one is sure if two or three night's work went into them. Three sessions were booked but recollections vary as to whether they were all used. Part of the confusion arises because Music Source Studios is a fairly up-market Seattle facility that usually caters for movie soundtrack work and radio advertisements, not rock music. Compared to Reciprocal it was a palace, a 24-track palace at that. The studio's bread-and-butter work took precedence during the day so rock sessions were done at night, sometimes very late at night. The first evening was used to lay down the basic tracks, with the second night used for vocals and mixing. Five songs were completed, though only two received an official release.

The idea was to record some tracks for a European EP release of *Blew*, which was to have been released to promote the forthcoming

European tour. As things turned out, the tour was over before it was issued. The equipment used by the band was now in a bad way having taken a beating on tour, which didn't help and Cobain was unhappy with much of the work. Steve Fisk recalls that Chad's drums were "held together with two rolls of duct tape." Some songs were re-tried almost eighteen months later – see session {24}.

"It was a very cheap, quickie session," recalls Fisk, "They didn't record quick, they did a lot of trying it again. There's five songs on one reel. There probably is not a lot of multiples. There might be bits and pieces. There was no money. It was recorded on some used tape that was lying around. Sub Pop was broke."

Been A Son [40]
This initial take is the one included on the *Blew* EP. Kurt wrote this song in reaction to his father Don Cobain's pressuring of him to be a more 'typical' sports-loving son and Kurt's idea that Don would have preferred his sister to have been a son. It wasn't the only song in this session that addressed Kurt's relationship, or lack of, with his father. Like the other recordings here, the song writing had progressed from the grinding epics of *Bleach* to a more punk-pop sound; catchier and more melodic but not necessarily lightweight. It's also one of the first Nirvana songs with real harmony vocals – "Total Lennon harmonies, right out of Rubber Soul" says Fisk. Another highlight was Novoselic's crunchy bass solo at 1:12.

Also see session {41}

Stain [41]
Another of the newer, faster songs, though Kurt wrote only one verse for it, which he sings three times in total. "I'm a stain", he howls in another reference to how he feels his father sees him. Later this take was also put on the *Incesticide* compilation.

Even In His Youth [42]
This original version of the song was not used and the band re-recorded it in 1991. This take had a different intro with a fuzzy guitar turning to a screech and battling the drums before the bass line kicks in (at 0:11) to help the familiar melody start up. Again Kurt is looking at

his father for song writing inspiration "Daddy was ashamed", he cries. Kurt seems unsure of the lyric at some parts and his vocal performance generally isn't up to his usual standard which is probably why the song was shelved for the time being.

Also see session {24}

Polly [11]

Though Kurt had written and demoed this quite a while before, this was the first time the song had been recorded with a band. After a false start, this arrangement features Kurt singing the opening verse with just a single electric guitar and some light percussion from Chad. Then at 0:19 it explodes with guitars. The overall effect, though pleasing, seems to be missing something. The power of the lyric is certainly lost in this format, so it was a good thing that when it was recorded for *Nevermind* the band chose to revert to the original, simpler, acoustic arrangement.

Also see sessions {5}, {19}, {26}

Token Eastern Song [aka Junkyard] [43]

Given the title it's not surprising that this song, like "Love Buzz" [27], has a slightly eastern feel to it. This effect is created by a heavy groove provided by Chad and Krist, over which Kurt's swirling guitars are applied. Played live on a few occasions this is one of two known studio attempts to get it down on tape. The chorus, which gave rise to the alternative title "Junkyard", was, according to Jack Endino, "Born in a junkyard" sung over and over. Close listening gives favour to the alternate theory that Kurt is actually singing "Hold it in your gut" though. Whichever one it is, this was a promising song that could have been a fine addition to the Nirvana roster.

Also see session {24}

Blew

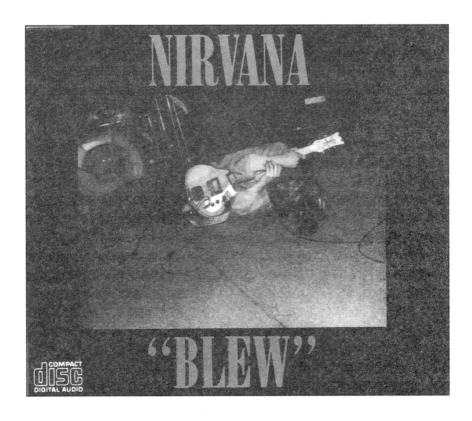

12" vinyl
Blew [31] / Love Buzz [27] / Been A Son [40] / Stain [41]
Tupelo TUPEP8 1989   UK

CD
Blew [31] / Love Buzz [27] / Been A Son [40] / Stain [41]
Tupelo TUPCD8 1989   UK

Session number

{16}

Venue: Reciprocal Studios, Seattle, WA.
Dates: January 2 and 3, 1990
Producer: Jack Endino
Players: Kurt Cobain (guitar, vocals), Krist Novoselic (bass), Chad
       Channing (drums)

Tracks recorded:	Available on:
Sappy [44]	*Sliver* compilation

The first sessions of the New Year saw the band return for ten hours work with Jack Endino. Things were certainly getting slower, the seven hours on the 2nd and three hours the following day didn't even afford enough time to complete the one song they attempted – "Sappy" [44]. Endino recalls that this session "pretty much sucked and is still in a Sub Pop vault somewhere. I don't think this version has been bootlegged. Nothing else was recorded or attempted at that session."

In 2004 this take was finally revealed as a track on the *Sliver* compilation CD. *Sliver* was marketed as a single CD which contained the best of *With The Lights Out*, but this track was one of three from *Sliver* which weren't included in the box set. Instead it was used as an incentive for hardcore fans to buy both.

Also see sessions {19}, {26}, {34}

Nevermind

Like *Bleach*, the sessions for *Nevermind* were spread out over a full year. Also like *Bleach*, the band that started the recording process went through numerous changes before settling on the line-up that would finish the album. A third similarity was that the initial sessions were a race against time, but while the first *Bleach* session was crammed into a single afternoon (session {7}), the preliminary *Nevermind* sessions were crammed into a week (session {19}). But that was where the comparisons ended. The step up from *Bleach* to *Nevermind* was outstanding both musically and commercially. The way *Nevermind* took off would change the lives of all connected to it forever.

The initial plan had been to record another album for Sub Pop. Jonathan Poneman had heard the work of promising new producer Butch Vig on a Killdozer album (*12 Point Buck*) and liked what he heard. Poneman approached Vig who agreed to do a week's worth of sessions with Nirvana as they passed through on tour. "I wanted to work with Sub Pop because I thought they were a cool label," says Vig. Kurt Cobain had a few new songs, though probably not enough for a full album yet. He did have the title *Sheep* that he wanted to use, though.

Vig and the band worked well together, but tensions were starting to surface between Cobain and Channing. After eight songs had been recorded, the band went back on tour and continued until the middle of May. By June, Channing was out of the band. Cobain claimed it was because Channing "wasn't a very powerful drummer", while Channing said it was down to "creative differences". The truth is somewhere between the two. Cobain wanted Channing to hit harder and the drummer tried to adapt to suit Cobain's requests, but it wasn't enough.

Over the summer, things were relatively quiet on the surface. With no permanent drummer, Nirvana borrowed Mudhoney's Dan Peters for a one-song session with Jack Endino (see session {20}) and then hired Dale Crover back from the Melvins to play a week-long stint supporting Sonic Youth. Peters would play one show in September and then Dave Grohl from Scream stepped into the breach on a suggestion from Buzz

Osbourne. Cobain was immediately impressed with Grohl, describing him as the best drummer he'd ever heard. Grohl made his live debut with Nirvana in October at a show in Olympia, WA.

While spending much of the summer home from tour, Kurt and Krist had been busy dubbing copies of their Madison session and sending the tapes to as many major labels as they could think of. This had sparked a lot of interest. "We knew we wanted to sign with a major label," says Novoselic, "We felt everyone else, like Dinosaur Jr and Sonic Youth, had all signed to majors and we thought that was a good way to get some cash. And Sub Pop was always on the brink of bankruptcy. Always."

The new trio worked at a couple of sessions here and there but made sure that Sub Pop didn't pay for them. This was to make sure that the company didn't have any hold over the tapes (see sessions {20} and {25}). In early 1991 they agreed a deal with Geffen that paid an advance of $287,000. Sub Pop was paid off to the tune of $75,000 ($37,000 of which came from the band's advance, but still leaving them with a cool $250,000). Sub Pop was also entitled to two percent from sales of the next two Nirvana albums, which would turn out to be quite a windfall.

Ready to work on their major label debut, the band lobbied hard to have Butch Vig produce again. Other, more experienced, producers were put forward by Geffen (Don Dixon, Scott Litt and David Briggs were mentioned among others), as the label felt Vig was too inexperienced for such a project, but the band got their way and the album was recorded with Vig in Los Angeles during the late spring of 1991 (see session {26}).

Costing a mere $135,000 to record (studio hire, mastering and Vig's fee – though he later renegotiated) *Nevermind* soon changed the musical landscape of the 1990s and managed to cross over into the mainstream, something that had been unthinkable only a few months earlier. It was released in September 1991 with modest expectations from both the band and label. Krist Novoselic said, "We wanted to do as good as Sonic Youth. We totally respect those people and what they've done. We thought we'd sell a couple of hundred thousand records at the most and that would be fine." The initial pressing was just under 50,000 copies and within a few weeks they had sold out. If Geffen had been better prepared, and pressed more copies, the album would likely have reached the US number one spot well before it actually did (in January 1992). When they finally re-pressed and got the albums into the shops it sold three million copies in the first four months.

A large part of the early success was the MTV airplay of the lead-off single "Smells Like Teen Spirit" [59]. When people heard (and saw on TV) this wondrous five minutes of unadulterated punk rock hooks, they would invariably buy the album. In January 1992 this snowball of public acceptance took *Nevermind* to number one in the US charts – knocking off Michael Jackson's *Dangerous*. "I went from working in Tower Records to being set up for the rest of my life," says Dave Grohl, "I went out and bought a BB gun and a Nintendo. The things that I always wanted as a kid."

"I think *Nevermind* did change the music business to an extent" says Butch Vig, "It killed the whole metal-hair band scene in the US and every label wanted to sign a Nirvana clone. I think we realize now they had something that nobody else had. It changed my life. I went from working as an obscure engineer/producer to having every single label call me up. It opened up a lot of doors, but I've also come to realize that I'll probably never work on an album that has that kind of critical and commercial success again. I'm really lucky and also proud to have worked on it. Like any great music, it becomes intertwined with a certain time period in your life. It touched a lot of people in a lot of ways."

"I have thought about it and I can't come to any logical conclusions at all" said Cobain in 1992, "I don't want to sound egotistical but I know it's better than a majority of the commercial shit that's been crammed down people's throats." To date the album has sold over fifteen million copies worldwide.

1991
Cassette

Geffen DGCC 24425	US	promo without 'hidden' track Endless Nameless [67]
Geffen DGCC 24425	US	without 'hidden' track Endless Nameless [67]
Geffen DGCC 24425	US	
DGC GEC 24425	UK	
Geffen CC24425	Germany	
Geffen MVXZ12	Japan	

LP

Geffen DGC 24425	US	
DGC DGC 24425	UK	
DGC MVJG-25001	Japan	

CD

Geffen DGCD 24425	US	without 'hidden' track Endless, Nameless [67]
Geffen DGCD 24425	US	
DGC GED 24425	UK	
DGC MVCG-67	Japan	
GED DGCD24425	Germany	

1992
LP

Geffen GEO236	Czech Republic	picture disc

1996
LP

Mobile Fidelity Sound Lab MFSL1-258	US	remastered

CD

Ultra Disc UDCD666	US	gold audiophile
Mobile Fidelity Sound Lab UDCD690	US	gold

1997
LP

Simply Vinyl SVLP 038	UK	180gm

1998
LP

Simply Vinyl SVLP0038	UK	180g vinyl

2004
CD in 12" sleeve

Universal Music UICY-95014	Japan	limited edition

UMD

Eagle Vision EU30069	US	(All regions) for the Sony Playstation

2005
DVD

Eagle Vision EV 30069-9	US	Classic Albums series NTSC format
Eagle Vision EREDV436 UK		Classic Albums series PAL format
Eagle Vision RV0296	Australia	Classic Albums series PAL format

2007
LP

Universal Music UIJY 9009	Japan	200gm

CD

Universal Music UICY 93358	Japan	limited edition

2009
LP

Simply Vinyl SVLP 038 UK		
Universal Music B001266-01	US	180gm

Nevermind: 20th Anniversary edition
2011
LP

Geffen 602527851983	UK	limited edition

Double LP

DGC B0015884-01	US	

4xLP

Geffen 0602527779041 UK		

CD

Geffen 602527851983	UK	limited edition
Geffen 0602527779089 UK		

Double CD

Geffen 0602527779034	UK	deluxe edition
DGC 27777903	Australia	2CD+DVD

53

DGC B0015885-00	US	4CD + DVD
DGC B0015885-00	US	
Geffen 0602527779058	UK	super deluxe edition
DVD		
Eagle Vision EREDV436	Germany	Classic Albums series PAL format
Double SHM-CD		
Universal Music UICY-15120	Japan	
4xSHM-CD+DVD		
Universal Music UICY-75124	Japan	super deluxe edition

Initial versions (approx. 50,000 copies of the CD) track listing:
Smells Like Teen Spirit [59] / In Bloom [48] / Come As You Are [60] / Breed [46] / Lithium [45] / Polly [11] / Territorial Pissings [64] / Drain You [51] / Lounge Act [65] / Stay Away [66] / On A Plain [57] / Something In The Way [63]

Later pressings include "Endless, Nameless" [67] after approximately ten minutes of silence at the end of the last listed song, "Something In The Way" [63].

2011 2CD Deluxe Edition track listing:
CD1: Smells Like Teen Spirit [59] / In Bloom [48] / Come As You Are [60] / Breed [46] / Lithium [45] / Polly [11] / Territorial Pissings [64] / Drain You [51] / Lounge Act [65] / Stay Away [66] / On A Plain [57] / Something In The Way [63] / Endless, Nameless [67] / Even In His Youth [42] / Aneurysm [54] / Curmudgeon [69] / D-7 [100] / Been A Son [L40] / School [L34] / Drain You [L51] / Sliver [L50] / Polly [L11] CD 2: (Smart Studios, 'Boombox' and BBC live sessions) In Bloom [48] / Breed (Imodium) [46] / Lithium [45] / Polly [11] / Pay To Play [49] / Here She Comes Now [47] / Dive [39] / Sappy [12] / Smells Like Teen Spirit [59] / Verse Chorus Verse [62] / Territorial Pissings [64] / Lounge Act [65] / Come As You Are [60] / Old Age [61] / Something In The Way [63] / On A Plain [57] / Drain You (Live) / Something In The Way (Live)

2011 4CD Super Deluxe Edition track listing:
CD1 and CD2 same as Deluxe Edition above.
CD3: "Devonshire Mixes" Smells Like Teen Spirit [59a] / In Bloom [48a] /Come As You Are [60a] / Breed [46a] / Lithium [45a] / Territorial

Pissings [64a] / Drain You [51a] / Lounge Act [65a] / Stay Away [66a] / On A Plain [57a] / Something In The Way [63a]
CD 4: "Live at the Paramount". Jesus Doesn't Want Me For A Sunbeam [L108] / Aneurysm [L54] / Drain You [L51] / School [34] / Floyd The Barber [17] / Smells Like Teen Spirit [L59] / About A Girl [L14] / Polly [L11] / Breed [L46] / Sliver [L50] / Love Buzz [L27] / Lithium [L45] / Been A Son [L40] / Negative Creep [L33] / On A Plain [L57] / Blew [L31] / Rape Me [L71] / Territorial Pissings [L64] / Endless, Nameless [L67]
Recorded at the Paramount Theater, Seattle, WA, on October 31, 1991.
Super deluxe edition DVD includes film of the Paramount show as listed above, plus the promo videos for Smells Like Teen Spirit / Come as You Are / Lithium / In Bloom.

Packaging notes:
Kurt Cobain had initially wanted a photo of a woman giving birth underwater as the cover photo. Geffen vetoed this idea as it would have been too graphic. Geffen art director Robert Fisher suggested that they tone it down to a picture of a baby underwater. He hired underwater photography specialist Kirk Weddle to take the cover photo at a children's pool in Pasadena. Weddle used the infant son, Spencer, of his friend Renee Elden. The whole shoot took about ten minutes as the baby started to cry. Renee was paid $250 for the use of Spencer. The band was happy with the shot and Cobain suggested incorporating the dollar bill on the fishing line, which was added later.

The inner sleeve had excerpts of words from each song on the album and a couple of lines that did not appear on the album too ("The second coming came in last and out of the closet / At the end of the rainbow and your rope"). Cobain took the photo for the back cover and if you look closely at the 'meat collage' behind the toy monkey, you can see a small picture of the band Kiss. Cobain's photo was credited as being by Kurdt Kobain. Talking about the back cover Cobain told *Nevermind It's An Interview* (a CD of Nirvana interviews), "It's just a rubber monkey that I've had for years. I was in a Bohemian photography stage, you know, taking a bunch of weird, arty pictures, and that's one of them. It's a collage that I made many years ago. I got these pictures of beef from a supermarket poster and cut them out, and made a mountain of beef

55

and then put Dante's people being thrown into hell climbing all over it. That's pretty much it." The band photos were snapped by Cobain's friend Michael Lavine, as was the dollar bill that was added to the front cover.

The 20th anniversary super deluxe edition of the album housed four CDs and one DVD in one 12"x12" hardback book inside a slip-case. The package included a 90-page book with photos and memorabilia and a fold-out poster.

Nevermind reviews

Select: "... this, their second album, realizes all the promise of their first." 4/5

Melody Maker: "Nirvana have opted out of the underground without wimping out of the creative process."

Q: "the trio have created precisely the record their former label, Sub Pop, strived for ..." 4/5

Rolling Stone: "*Nevermind* finds Nirvana at the crossroads – scrappy garageland warriors setting their sights on a land of giants." 3/4

New York Times: "That crunching noise heard in record stores across the country last week was the sound of Nirvana's 'Nevermind' (Geffen) stepping on just about every other album."

Vox: "... here is the first truly inspired band of the '90s ..." 9/10

Nevermind: 20th Anniversary edition reviews:

Guardian: "... it's an abrasive, combative performance that reminds you of their extraordinary might."

USA Today: "20 years later, '*Nevermind*' still smolders."

Session number

{17}

Venue: The Dutchman, Seattle, WA.
Dates: March 1990
Producer: none
Players: Kurt Cobain (guitar, vocals), Krist Novoselic (bass), Chad
      Channing (drums)

Tracks recorded:	Available on:
Unknown	not available

Located at 101 South Spokane Street in industrial south Seattle, The
Dutchman was a multi-room venue which various local bands used for
storage and practice. Originally a restaurant dating back 70 years, the
building burnt down in 2009. Nirvana used the venue during the spring
of 1990 to try out some new songs (one of which was "In Bloom" [48])
and to practice before playing shows on the way to the sessions in
Madison, WI. (Session {19}).

Session number

{18}

Venue: Evergreen State College, Olympia, WA.
Date: March 20, 1990
Producer: none
Players: Kurt Cobain (guitar, vocals), Krist Novoselic (bass), Chad
       Channing (drums)

Tracks recorded:	Available on:
School [34]	not officially released
Big Cheese [28]	not officially released
Floyd The Barber [17]	not officially released
Lithium [45]	**not officially released**

Kurt hadn't just spent time recording and sampling for sound collages, he had done similar work interspersing film and TV clips with random pieces of Super 8 footage that he'd shot over the years. On this occasion he wanted to film the band while this visual collage was screened behind them. They snuck into the university's TV studios and the band ran through three tracks from *Bleach* and a new song called "Lithium" [45]. The footage has never been released.

Lithium [45]
The version played here is certainly embryonic lyrically, though the rest of the song is very similar to the final version. Because of the venue, and its less-than-perfect sound set up, the drums have a real echo to them. Kurt sings many of the lines from the final cut but sometimes in a different order. The quiet verse/screamed chorus motif is certainly well in place even if it is somewhat overpowered at times due to the acoustics. This was an early sign of the great things to come.

Also see sessions {19}, {26}, {27}

Session number

{19}

Venue: Smart Studios, Madison, WI.
Dates: April 2 to 6, 1990
Producer: Butch Vig
Players: Kurt Cobain (guitar, vocals), Krist Novoselic (bass), Chad
 Channing (drums)

Tracks recorded:	Available on:
Imodium [aka Breed] [46]	*Nevermind* Deluxe
Dive [39]	Sliver single, *Incesticide*, *Nevermind* Deluxe
Here She Comes Now [47]	*Heaven And Hell Volume 1*, *Nevermind* Deluxe, *With The Lights Out* box set
In Bloom [48]	*Sub Pop Video Network 1*, *Nevermind* Deluxe
Lithium [45]	*Nevermind* Deluxe
Polly [11]	*Nevermind* Deluxe
Sappy [44]	*Nevermind* Deluxe
Pay To Play [49]	*DGC Rarities Volume 1*, *Nevermind* Deluxe, *With The Lights Out* box set

After playing the first gig of a fifteen-date tour in Chicago, Nirvana bundled into their van and drove straight over to Madison, Wisconsin, arriving at around 3 a.m. on Monday April 2. The Midwest doesn't just have bitingly cold winters; spring can be pretty mean too. This was one of those springs. Nirvana were due to play a show in Madison on Saturday 7th before driving to Minneapolis for another gig on the 9th. In the meantime they had five days to record. They had spent almost all of the last three weeks of March working up new songs and practicing for the upcoming tour at the Dutchman practice complex in Seattle. This is where "In Bloom" [48] had first come to light. "We had all this stuff kicking around" says Novoselic "and then two weeks before the session began we'd rehearse every day just to put the songs together. The first time we played 'In Bloom' it was way different than the way it came out – it sounded like a Bad Brains song." This approach was becoming the norm for Nirvana and by the time they reached Madison they still had some unfinished songs and songs without lyrics.

Stylistically the new songs were very different to *Bleach*. Gone were any signs of the over-heavy, ponderous anthems that characterized much of that album. Instead they had a bunch of three-minute pop gems which they played with a fuzz pedal and let Kurt scream over. This was a combination that Butch Vig was blown away by. Vig, a future member of the band Garbage, had been chosen to produce the week's sessions ahead of the much-used Jack Endino and other 'name' producers such as Scott Litt. He had already worked with Nirvana's ally Tad, and with others on Sub Pop's list of 'up and coming' bands. He was considered to be 'up and coming' in his own right. Vig wasn't sure what to expect from the sessions as he recalled "I wasn't totally crazy about *Bleach* the first time I heard it. Except I really loved 'About a Girl' [14]. The funny thing was, I remember Jonathan Poneman saying, 'If you saw Nirvana here in Seattle, it's like Beatlemania. And they're going to be as big as the Beatles!' And I'm thinking to myself, 'Yeah, right.'"

Smart Studios had been born after Vig met Steve Marker at the University of Wisconsin. The pair started to experiment with recording techniques in the early 1980s. In 1983 they moved into a warehouse space and pooled their funds to the tune of $2,000 – enough to buy an eight-track tape machine and a couple of microphones. In 1987 they moved again to East Washington Avenue and Vig's reputation as a producer began to grow as he produced records for bands on influential indie labels like Touch and Go and Twin/Tone.

Vig wanted to help the band replicate its live sound and one of his ideas to achieve this was to put sheets of plywood down on the studio floor, therefore making the room more 'active'. The recording process was relatively straightforward. Vig recalls that the sessions were "very simple and had very few overdubs." The band used their own equipment with the exception of Cobain, who Vig convinced to use the producer's

60

own Fender Bassman amplifier on "Lithium" [45] and "In Bloom" [48]. Vig's Yamaha snare drum was also used (it was the same one that was used on the Smashing Pumpkins album *Gish*.) The recordings were 16-track and Vig was assisted by Doug Olson. "Butch is quite an open minded guy," says Olson. "So the environment if someone is working with him is generally one open to suggestions." The atmosphere at Smart was laid back. Novoselic would be talkative and joke around with Vig, asking him lots of questions, but Cobain was withdrawn. Channing claims that Cobain was nervous about the incomplete nature of some songs and he spent a lot of time in the corner of the studio with his notebook, feverishly scribbling away. "[Kurt] would be totally engaged, then all of a sudden a light switch would go off and he'd go sit in the corner and completely disappear into himself," said Vig. "I didn't really know how to deal with that."

The band had initially planned to put down an entire album's worth of material in the week, as they were comfortable with some songs having toured with them for a while. Others had only been practiced and were incomplete. They soon realized that this plan wasn't realistic. Cobain had problems with his voice and the band took a day off at the mid-point of the already hurried sessions to let him rest his tender vocal chords. Cobain was also unhappy with some of Channing's drumming and spent time behind the drum kit himself demonstrating how he wanted things played.

Five of the songs that were worked on here later made it to *Nevermind*, although only one track, "Polly" [11], was used directly from these sessions. The other tracks that were re-recorded for *Nevermind* were done so because of the June 1990 departure of drummer Chad Channing. The band didn't want to release an album with the ex-drummer on it and decided to re-do several of these songs with a new one. The final released versions of the songs on *Nevermind* would show basic arrangements that were unchanged from these initial sessions.

Imodium [aka Breed] [46]
Although this is named after a treatment for diarrhea (Kurt saw Tad Doyle, of Seattle grunge band Tad, taking this while on tour) the lyric doesn't seem to have any connection to the title. This take opens with a burst of feedback that is quickly swamped by the tidal wave of guitar and

drums building the tension, and then an energetic bass line to create an overpowering sonic blast. The lyric was very simple, just a single verse and chorus each sung twice, and a guitar solo was thrown in before the final chorus. Butch Vig decided to be a little bit creative during the mixing. He let the opening guitar burst flood from one channel and the bass from the other while later on he switched the guitar solo from channel to channel to keep the listener off-guard.

Also see sessions {26}, {26a}, {27}

Dive [39]

"We wrote ['Dive'] together" says Krist Novoselic, "He [Cobain] had that guitar riff and I added the bass riff, so I guess it turned into a bass song." And what a bass song it was. Close in style to the songs from *Bleach*, Dive quickly became a live favorite with its heavy mosh riffs, while Cobain gave a vigorous vocal performance. This song had first been attempted with Jason Everman back in June 1989 (session {14}), but this is the earliest known studio recording to have leaked out.

Also see session {14}

Here She Comes Now [47]

Unlike the two-minute Velvet Underground original, this cover version was stretched out to more than five minutes. The gentle keep-it-like-the-original feel is broken mid-way through the take as the amps are switched on to full and a fuzzy guitar screams into life. Kurt sings the title over and over doing his best, if unconventional, Lou Reed impersonation before the take twists into an extended instrumental jam.

Also see session {19b}

In Bloom [48]

Initially known by the title "Knows Not What It Means", this song had been tried out live in Chicago immediately before these sessions. This take featured some jazzier drumming from Channing that was simply out-pounded by Dave Grohl when they later re-recorded the song (see session {26}). Butch Vig did some 'creative' editing on this track before mixing it, as Novoselic explained: "When we were listening to it we said 'ah, this bridge isn't so hot.' So Butch just took out a razor blade and cut the bridge out of the sixteen-track master, and then threw it in the garbage."

Also see sessions {26}, {26a}, {27}, {41}

Lithium [45]

At least seven takes of this song were recorded at Smart, and three of them have been leaked to collectors over the years. Two of the takes are clearly introduced (by Doug Olson) as "Lithium, take six" and "Lithium, take seven" while the third version has a slightly different guitar arrangement.

Take six has a very gentle opening (with Kurt strumming an acoustic guitar) before bursting into the familiar loud chorus, but with a slight variation as Kurt screams "Yeah-hey" instead of the better known "Yeah-yeah." Lithium is used as a medication when treating certain mental conditions and this is reflected in the line "I've found my friends / They're in my head." Apart from the variation in the chorus, the lyric is almost complete apart from the odd word here and there.

Take seven also opens with an acoustic guitar, but it's more prominent in the mix, otherwise this is very similar to take six. The third, un-introduced, version of this song has an electric guitar played during the opening verse, but is otherwise similar to the other two. All three of these takes fade out at the end rather than bringing the song to a definite conclusion. This is just one of the many minor adjustments made to the song when it was recorded for *Nevermind* – the tweaking of the chorus and simplification of Novoselic's bass line were others (see session {26}).

Also see sessions {18}, {26}, {27}

Polly [11]

"Kurt just sat in there and did it on his acoustic guitar," says Butch Vig. "We recorded Polly in half an hour flat. I just recorded it with an AKG microphone." The simplest and quietest song on *Nevermind*, Polly is the only track from these sessions to be used directly on the album. Late one night Cobain just sat and strummed away on his battered old $20 acoustic guitar which had duct tape to hold the tuning keys in place. Krist Novoselic played along and the vocals, and Channing's cymbals, were overdubbed later. Channing sat in a tiny room, just big enough for him and a single cymbal. An enduring mistake occurred when Cobain made a false start, coming in too early with "Polly said" at 1:54, then stopping before picking up the vocal line at the correct moment. The producer and band decided to leave the glitch in because they thought it sounded good. Cobain liked the error so much he later reproduced his mistake when the song was played live.

Also see sessions {5}, {15}, {26}

Sappy [aka Verse Chorus Verse] [44]

A further attempt at the oft-tried song brought up another dead end. The softer guitar and busier percussion still wasn't to the band's liking. Cobain's solo at 1:44 lasts for thirty seconds and is a subtle variation from the other takes of it at different sessions.

Also see sessions {5}, {16}, {26}

Pay To Play [49]

This marks the only time that Nirvana released an early version of a song with a different working title to the finished article. This song was re-recorded as "Stay Away" [66] in Los Angeles (see session {26}). The title is taken from the sometimes-used club policy of letting a band play at the venue only if it purchased tickets to then resell under their own steam. The energetic guitar riff is supposedly taken from one of the unnamed songs on the *Fecal Matter* tape (see session {3}). The band may have allowed this version to be issued under a different title as it was changed on numerous levels. This track best displays the differences in Chad Channing's and Dave Grohl's drumming styles and this version breaks down into a feedback fest at the end. The lyric was tweaked quite a bit too – here Cobain sings a first verse of "Monkey see monkey do / Walk around follow you / Pull it out keep it in / Have to have poison skin" which is markedly different to the "Stay Away" [66] version.

Also see "Stay Away" [66], session {26}

Session number

{19a}

Venue: Smart Studios, Madison, WI.
Dates: April 11 to 13, 1990
Producer: Butch Vig

Mid-way through the week after the departure of the band, Butch Vig sat down to produce a mix of the seven original songs recorded at Smart. This took him three days. The band had taken a rough copy of the session when they'd left the previous weekend which they later used as a demo tape to send to major labels over the summer.

Session number

{19b}

Venue: Smart Studios, Madison, WI.
Date: June 8, 1990
Producer: Butch Vig

Tracks mixed:	Available on:
Here She Comes Now [47]	*Heaven And Hell Volume 1*

Butch Vig finally mixed "Here She Comes Now" for the Velvet Underground tribute album *Heaven And Hell Volume 1*. Jonathan Poneman had taken the tape of this track at the end of the week in which it was recorded and Vig only got the chance to mix it four months later.

Session number

{20}

Venue: Reciprocal Studios, Seattle, WA.
Date: July 11, 1990
Producer: Jack Endino
Players: Kurt Cobain (guitar, vocals), Krist Novoselic (bass), Dan
       Peters (drums)

Tracks recorded:	Available on:
Sliver [50]	Sliver single, *Incesticide*

With Chad Channing out of the band, Mudhoney's Dan Peters was the next in line. "Chad wanted to express himself in a way that really didn't gel with the band," says Krist Novoselic. "Chad really compromised his style to suit the band. I don't think he was happy doing that and it was a good departure. It worked well for everyone."

The new trio wrote "Sliver" [50] and put it down on tape three days later. They managed the short-notice recording by nipping into Reciprocal while Tad, who were recording there, were on a dinner break. "He looked like he was going to be in our band," says Novoselic of Peters. "And that was just another case of compromising his style for our band. He was going to go out and buy a bigger drum set and you know you can really hear his style, it's just Mudhoney – those snare rolls. That was when the future of Mudhoney was uncertain and there was all this 'Are Mudhoney going to break up?' Dan saw an opportunity to join our band. We love Dan as a person and we love his drumming. If Dan were to have joined our band it would've been certain that Mudhoney was finished, and we didn't want to be responsible for that."

Sliver [50]
Using Tad's equipment (except for the guitars) the make-shift Nirvana line-up recorded the song in under an hour. "It was done so fast and raw and perfect that I don't think we could capture that again if we

decided to re-record it," said Cobain. "It's just one of those recordings that happened and you can't try to reproduce it." "Sliver" was a perfect choice for a single. In just two and a quarter minutes, Cobain manages to tell the story of being dropped off by his parents at his grandparents for the night for mashed potatoes and ice cream, but then starting to cry, demanding "Grandma take me home!" Later he wakes up in his mother's arms. All of this domestic drama is perfectly accompanied by the framework of a melodic bass line and some steady drumming by Dan Peters. "It was written in a day and it came together in an hour," said Peters.

Also see sessions {21], {41}

Session number

{21}

Venue: Reciprocal Studios, Seattle, WA.
Date: July 24, 1990
Producer: Jack Endino
Players: Kurt Cobain (guitar, vocals)

Tracks recorded:	Available on:
Sliver [50]	Sliver single, *Incesticide*

Two weeks after the initial Sliver session, Cobain visited Reciprocal to record his vocals for the song, he also added some more guitar work and then Jack Endino mixed it. The whole process was completed in one day. The vinyl issue had a telephone conversation between Jonathan Poneman and Krist Novoselic tagged onto the end of the track lasting about 45 seconds. This was removed from the CD single and *Insecticide* versions.

Also see sessions {20}, {41}

Sliver

1990
7" vinyl
Sliver [50] / Dive [39]
Sub Pop SP73   US   initial 3000 on blue vinyl
Sliver [50] / Dive [39]
Sub Pop SP73   US   various color vinyl

1991
7" vinyl
Sliver [50] / Dive [39]
Tupelo TUP25   UK   initial 2000 on green vinyl

12" vinyl
Sliver [50] / Dive [39] / About A Girl [L14]
Tupelo TUPEP25   UK   various color vinyl
CD
Sliver [50] / Dive [39] / About A Girl [L14] / Spank Thru [L5]
Tupelo TUPCD25   UK

Session number

{22}

Venue: 'rehearsal space', Seattle, WA.
Date: August 1990
Producer: none
Players: Kurt Cobain (guitar, vocals), Krist Novoselic (bass),
        unconfirmed drummer

Tracks recorded:	Available on:
Drain You [51]	**not officially released**

During August, Nirvana supported Sonic Youth on a series of West Coast dates. Dale Crover filled in on drums for these shows, which were around the time of this early demo of "Drain You" [51]. Though unconfirmed, it is very likely that Crover also played drums on this jam session. Soon afterwards Dave Grohl was known to be practicing with the band and Dan Peters was told he was no longer needed. "Rehearsals were always a sullen time, never fun," Peters told *Mojo*. "It was the only time I'd ever played music with people who were just acquaintances, not full-on buddies."

Drain You [51]
Krist Novoselic is heard talking before the song kicks off. This take is pretty lazy compared to the finished article with a very sloppy Cobain solo and unfinished lyrics (one incomplete verse and rearranged chorus). Charles Cross (in *Heavier Than Heaven*) claims that this song was originally titled "Formula". A twenty-second clip of another, unidentified, track is tacked onto the end of this take.

Also see sessions {26}, {26a}, {27}

Session number

{23}

Venue: various venues, Seattle, WA.
Date: late 1990
Producer: none
Players: Kurt Cobain (guitar, vocals), Krist Novoselic (bass), Dave
    Grohl (drums)

Tracks recorded:	Available on:
Pennyroyal Tea [52]	unconfirmed
Unknown demo [53]	**not officially released**
Others	unconfirmed

Through the tail end of 1990 the band worked on many tracks at
rehearsal spaces in and around Seattle. It's known that "Pennyroyal
Tea" [52] dates from around this time (though no recordings have been
leaked) and others have also been mentioned but not confirmed.

Unknown demo [53]
This two-minute instrumental is said to date from late 1990. Krist
Novoselic's intriguing bass line opens the song and is joined at 0:04 by
a roaring guitar and heavily hit drums (which suggests Dave Grohl is
playing). The song is similar in structure and style to both "Drain You"
[51] and "Sliver" [50]. It's unknown if it was ever progressed.

Session number

{24}

Venue: Music Source Studio, Seattle, WA.
Date: January 1, 1991
Producer: Craig Montgomery
Players: Kurt Cobain (guitar, vocals), Krist Novoselic (bass), Dave
   Grohl (drums)

Tracks recorded:	Available on:
Aneurysm [54]	Smells Like Teen Spirit single, *Nevermind* Deluxe, *With The Lights Out* box set
Oh, The Guilt [55]	not officially released
Radio Friendly Unit Shifter [58]	not officially released
On A Plain [57]	not officially released
All Apologies [56]	not officially released
Even In His Youth [42]	Smells Like Teen Spirit single, *Nevermind* Deluxe
Token Eastern Song [43]	not officially released

To keep Sub Pop from getting their hands on any new songs they recorded (the band hadn't quite signed with Geffen yet) they drove from their New Year's Eve show in Portland, Oregon, back to Seattle to use the studio for free. As it was New Year's Day and their soundman, Craig Montgomery, knew someone who worked at Music Source, they were allowed in without charge. Montgomery had been asking for the chance to record a session with them and now he had leverage to be able to do so.

This session, the first studio one with Dave Grohl, was at a studio usually used for recording commercials and the band weren't too impressed with the results, but they did finish two songs that later made it out as b-sides.

Aneurysm [54]

An extended instrumental opening (lasting 1:20) goes through three phases before Kurt starts singing. When he does, the lyric to this track is short but still manages a few references to using heroin – "Over do it and have a fit", "Come on over and shoot the shit" and "She keeps it pumping straight to my heart" are all seen as subtle, or maybe not so subtle, junkie comments.

Oh, The Guilt (55]

This is an early instrumental run through of the song that would later be recorded for a split single with the Jesus Lizard.

Also see session {28}

Radio Friendly Unit Shifter [58]

Two years before being recorded for *In Utero* (see session {34}), the instrumentation for this song was clearly in place and sounds tight and well practiced. Grohl's drumming is a noticeable highlight and shows why Cobain was immediately so impressed. While not exactly the same as the released version, it is pretty close and lacks only Cobain's vocals.

Also see session {34}

On A Plain [57]

While Montgomery might have been an accomplished soundman, he had a bit of learning to do as far as being a studio engineer was concerned (though all involved agreed that the studio was not conducive to recording a rock record). Here the vocals are buried so far in the mix they are virtually drowned out. What can be heard though is that the song is pretty much complete, including the bridge, and, apart from a raggedy ending, it was almost ready to go.

Also see sessions {25}, {26}, {26a}, {27}

All Apologies [56]

Some commentators will be surprised to hear that the lyric for this song is almost identical to the finished version two years before it was recorded for *In Utero* (see session {34}). Many thought that the line "In the sun / I'm married" was referring to Cobain's marriage to Courtney Love on a Hawaiian beach in February 1992, but here it is being sung thirteen months before they would wed. Musically it is quite different to the final version with a jaunty acoustic guitar carrying the melody along, and a tambourine prominent in the mix.

Also see sessions {34}, {35}

Even In His Youth [42]

The version on this tape misses the very start of the take and so it's unknown if the original feedback introduction was still being used, it may have been edited out. It was released on the "Smells Like Teen Spirit" single later in the year.

Also see session {15}

Token Eastern Song [43]

As well as being almost completely instrumental, this take is musically radically different than the original demo (see session {15}) recorded with Steve Fisk. This version still features some of the twirling, 'eastern' sounding guitars, but has an aggressive stop-start feel (partly due to Grohl's heavy drumming) with some call and response guitar parts. In the mix, Cobain alternates between some fast jangly, pick-ups and the heavy riffs that dominate the song. This is the last known attempt at this track and it was never released.

Also see session {15}

Hormoaning

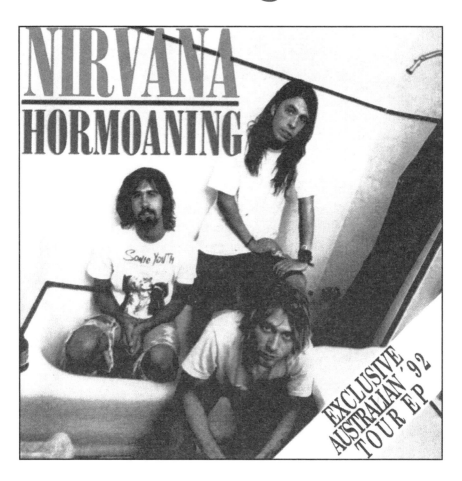

1991
12" vinyl

Geffen GEF2171	Australia	5,000 copies - some on blue vinyl

Cassette

Geffen GEFC21711	Australia	5,000 copies

CD

Geffen GEFD21711	Australia	5,000 copies

1992
CD
Geffen MVCG17002   Japan

2011
12" vinyl
Geffen B0015411-01   UK & US   limited edition
Track listing:
Turnaround / Aneurysm / D-7 / Son Of A Gun / Even In His Youth /
Molly's Lips

Session number

{25}

Venue: 'barnyard' rehearsal space, Tacoma, WA.
Date: March 1991
Producer: none
Players: Kurt Cobain (guitar, vocals), Krist Novoselic (bass), Dave
    Grohl (drums)

Tracks recorded:	Available on:
Smells Like Teen Spirit [59]	*With The Lights Out* box set,
	Nevermind Deluxe
Verse Chorus Verse [62]	*Nevermind* Deluxe
Lounge Act [65]	*Nevermind* Deluxe
Come As You Are [60]	*Sliver* compilation,
	Nevermind Deluxe
Old Age [61]	*Nevermind* Deluxe
On A Plain [57]	*Nevermind* Deluxe
Territorial Pissings [64]	*Nevermind* Deluxe
Something in the Way [63]	*Nevermind* Deluxe

While preparing to travel to Los Angeles to record *Nevermind*, the band set up at a Tacoma practice space ("this old barn where we rehearsed" – Krist Novoselic) to rehearse and took the chance to record some of their new songs so that Butch Vig could hear them before they started the formal recordings. This was the venue that prospective producers Don Dixon and David Briggs had been taken to earlier in the year before the band finally decided to work with Vig. The practice space was set up for a friend's band; "This thing had a studio in it," said Dave Grohl, "Everything was carpeted with this brown shag carpet. He even had stage lights in there and a massive PA that he just did not know how to use." They also wrote new material during this time, as Grohl explained, "We came up with so much stuff where we'd go, 'God, this is the best thing we've ever done!' Then we'd forget how to play it. So many songs got thrown away until we finally said 'Maybe we should start recording them on a cassette.'"

The tape they sent to Vig arrived just as he was about to leave for the West Coast and was pretty poor quality. In fact it was so poor that he struggled to hear the songs properly. What he did manage to pick out was the first demo of a song called "Smells Like Teen Spirit" [59] and another new tune titled "Come As You Are" [60]. "The whole thing was unbelievably distorted," recalls Vig, "You could kinda hear a little bit of the hooks and things and I could hear the "hello, hello, how low" [from "Smells Like Teen Spirit" [59]), I could hear a little bit of that and hear the riff in "Come As You Are" and between the songs they were goofing around and going, 'How's that sound Butch?' and 'This is Dave,' and Dave would play like a really sloppy drum solo. The thing I noticed was that the new songs were much better crafted and hooky." Despite the unprofessional nature of the tape, Vig was enthused about the upcoming session and he had every right to be.

"The boombox recordings are some of the coolest stuff for hardcore fans," said Butch Vig as they were released as part of the 20th anniversary of *Nevermind* remasters. "They sound superlow-fi and dirty and trashy, really primal."

Smells Like Teen Spirit [59]
This early take of Nirvana's most famous song is a long way from the polished anthem that would take the world of music by surprise later in the year. The recording quality is low, the performance is refreshingly rough and only short snippets of recognizable lyrics are sung as the take approaches six minutes in length. The whole effect is more authentic and Cobain's heartfelt screamed choruses carry more menace.

Also see sessions {26}, {26a}, {27}, {41}

Lounge Act [65]
From these demos, this track is the closest to the finished article, sounding like an nth generation dub of the *Nevermind* version.

Also see sessions {26}, {26a}, {27}

Come As You Are [60]

A sparse take of this breakthrough track. Without any overdubbing or vocal trickery, the song has a more heartfelt vibe and the band gives a great, seemingly live, performance.

Also see sessions {26}, {26a}, {27}, {41}

Old Age [61]

This Nirvana demo briefly surfaced on an internet site before being removed. Anyone who was quick to download it obtained a portion of the song lasting just over a minute with Kurt Cobain on vocals. Many observers placed the origin of the recording at these pre-*Nevermind* practices, but there was no proof that it was so. The recording was less distorted than the tape described by Butch Vig so it might have been a different session altogether.

Hole recorded a version of this song for *Live Through This* in September 1993 though it was not used on the album. It did surface on Hole's *Beautiful Son* (USA) EP in 1993, the "Violet" (UK) CD single in 1995 and on the *My Body The Hand Grenade* compilation CD in 1997. The opening of Hole's version of this song is identical to the opening of their song "Credit In The Straight World" which was included on the *Live Through This* album in 1994.

More recently a four-minute version was issued on the *Sliver* compilation, the *Nevermind* re-issues and a later version from the *Nevermind* sessions proper

Also see session {26}

On A Plain [57]

Twenty seconds of discussion about the opening of the song precedes this take which, though rough around the edges, is relatively close to the final version apart from the expected lyrical changes.

Also see sessions {24}, {26}, {26a}, {27}

Territorial Pissings [64]

Free of the Krist Novoselic vocal intro, this take howls straight into action. Cobain's vocals seem close to the final album version and Dave Grohl's unforgiving drumming carries the whole thing along at break-neck pace.

Also see sessions {26}, {26a}, {27}

80

Something in the Way [63]

Stripped of the string accompaniment, the song sounds even more like a late night plea for help, with just sparse percussion and plodding bass line to play against Kurt Cobain's vocal and guitar performance.

Also see sessions {26}, {26a}, {27}

Session number

{26}

Venue: Sound City Studios, Los Angeles, CA.
Dates: May 2 to 19, 1991
Producer: Butch Vig
Players: Kurt Cobain (guitar, vocals), Krist Novoselic (bass), Dave
     Grohl (drums)

Tracks recorded:	Available on:
Smells Like Teen Spirit [59]	*Nevermind, With The Lights Out* box set
In Bloom [48]	*Nevermind*
Come As You Are [60]	*Nevermind*
Breed [46]	*Nevermind, With The Lights Out* box set
Territorial Pissings [64]	*Nevermind*
Drain You [51]	*Nevermind*
Lounge Act [65]	*Nevermind*
Stay Away [66]	*Nevermind*
On A Plain [57]	*Nevermind*
Lithium [45]	*Nevermind*
Endless, Nameless [67]	*Nevermind*
Polly [11]	*Nevermind*
Something In The Way [63]	*Nevermind*
Old Age [61]	*With The Lights Out* box set
Song In D [68]	not officially released
Sappy [aka Verse Chorus Verse] [12]	not officially released
Verse Chorus Verse [62]	*With The Lights Out* box set

Nirvana and Butch Vig traveled to Los Angeles in late April to rehearse before entering the studio. They set up in a North Hollywood practice space and moved into the Oakwood apartments not far from Sound City Studios. This was the last chance the band had to finalize arrangements and recording details before heading into the studio. It would save a lot of time and money to be as prepared as possible. "Krist and Dave have a big part in deciding on how long a song should be," said Cobain, "and how many parts it should have. So, I don't like to be considered as the whole songwriter, but I do come up with the basis of it. I come up with the singing style during practice and I write the lyrics usually minutes before we record." Despite this modesty, Cobain is listed as the solitary writer on all of the album's songs, except for "Smells Like Teen Spirit" [59].

They spent the last week of April running through the new songs and Butch Vig dropped by a few times to hear some of them for the first time. "We did some arranging in the rehearsal room," says Vig, "Teen Spirit was quite a lot longer, for instance. Most of the songs were fine the way they were. With some it was just a question of tightening things up if they were too long. Even in rehearsals when they started playing ["Smells Like Teen Spirit" [59]] their guitar and bass rigs were so loud, so unbelievably loud and Dave didn't have any mics on him or anything and the drums were equally as loud in the room. And I remember literally standing up and starting to sweat and pacing around the room because the song was so powerful and so amazing and so hooky ... I didn't even know what Kurt was singing at that point."

In early May they relocated to Sound City Studios, although in 1991 it was falling behind the times. Every other big studio on the West Coast seemed to be going digital, but not Sound City. This was the venue for the recording of such albums as Neil Young's *After The Goldrush* and Fleetwood Mac's *Rumours*. Krist Novoselic remembers it "being kind of dumpy", but it was big, had the Neve board that they required and was cheap (only $500 per day). The band supplemented their equipment with a selection of hired instruments. Dave Grohl hired an entire drum kit (at a cost of $1500) from the 'Drum Doctor' whose own Ross Garfield came in to help set them up. Vig acted as engineer as well as producer and had some help from house engineer Jeff Sheehan when it came to setting up the equipment. A selection of amps were also hired – a Vox

AC30 and a Fender Bassman. Kurt used his Mosrite with a Mesa Boogie amp, Krist used a pair of Gibson Ripper basses – one blonde and one black. "I didn't play to E," explains Novoselic, "I tuned down to D flat, with all the strings tuned down one and a half steps."

The main studio was pretty big, certainly much larger than any of the previous studios that Nirvana had recorded in. Butch Vig: "The drums were in the centre of the room with Kurt off to one side and Krist off to the other. So we could use an ambient mic in the kick drum, we built this drum tunnel made of bass drum cases glued together, which came out about eight feet into the room."

The average day would begin with the band arriving at around 3p.m. and working for eight or nine hours until around midnight. They'd then take off to party or maybe head down to Venice Beach were they'd stay until the sun came up before heading back for some sleep. One night Krist was stopped for drunk driving and was jailed for most of the next day before label staff could procure his release.

Starting on Thursday May 2, the basic tracks were recorded over a period of ten days. "Smells Like Teen Spirit" [59] was the first song recorded, as Dave Grohl recalls: "The first two days it was just Krist and me messing around. Kurt came in on the third day, and we did the song ["Smells Like Teen Spirit"] in one take. Then he sang three vocal tracks. That was it." By June 11, the basic tracks were done and the drums returned to the rental shop. With these songs complete, it was obvious that this was going to be a very different album to *Bleach*. The songs were more concise and the arrangements more melodic. "I think we've been focusing on dynamics a lot more on this record," said Kurt Cobain. "With the *Bleach* album everything was just straight ahead and simple and it becomes boring to play that kind of music all the time so we decided to break things down with our songs. I mean, we showed signs of doing that on *Bleach*, but I think we're way more focused now with both of the elements of soft and pretty and hard and aggressive."

"We'd work from noon and then we'd go to Venice Beach at night to see the sun come up," recalled Krist Novoselic. "It was a magical time."

The days flew by as song after song was quickly rattled off, often within just two or three takes. At least fifteen songs were tracked, all with the maximum amount of energy, especially from Cobain. "We wanted to capture the raw energy of the band but with optimum performance," says Dave Grohl. "Almost every track on that record, he [Kurt] blew his voice out by the end of the take," adds Butch Vig. "I'd say 'let's try one more take' and his voice would be shot." Sometimes the singer just didn't want to sing or play it again, and Vig had to turn psychologist to get Kurt to change his mind. He'd tell Kurt that John Lennon had double-tracked his vocals if Kurt didn't want to, it was the kind of story that would get Kurt to come round. If it was OK for John Lennon then it must be OK for Kurt Cobain. Vig told the BBC how he managed to get the best from the singer: "That was the hardest thing, probably just getting Kurt, motivating him, to push him a little bit. To push him beyond where he thought he could go, because a lot of times he would only want to do things once and it may not have been his best performance and so you had to figure out a way to get him to do a better vocal take or go back and play a guitar part and try to make it just sound better or locked into the band better or come up with a little melodic thing that sits in the track better."

When the band ran out of its allotted time in Sound City's studio A, and Ozzy Osbourne moved in to record a segment for MTV, they moved over to the smaller studio B for overdubs and last minute vocal work. "Kurt was very moody," says Vig. "I knew that from the Smart Studio sessions. He was very difficult to figure out because he could be in an elated mood, ready to play, then half an hour later he'd just sit in a corner and not say anything to anybody. Sometimes it would bring the session to a halt. He would be totally uncommunicative. I found out right away that Kurt didn't like to sing a lot. I would record him warming up and if I was lucky I would get three more takes out of him. He likes to slur the words and sometimes it took me several passes to figure out what he was singing. But that's part of what made his singing special. He gave those words some magic, in that you don't always know what he was saying. I would then pick one as the best and then take certain bits from the other tracks. That was it. He was that good."

Smells Like Teen Spirit [59]
It's very rare in popular music that a song comes along and defines a generation. One that changes a decade. A song that people remember where they were the first time they heard it. The Beatles and the Sex Pistols have songs in this category and with this song Nirvana joined

85

their ranks. If Nirvana were the right band in the right place, then this was their right song at the right time. Like many things in Kurt Cobain's life, this song was shrouded in irony. It was after all, Cobain's disgust of the whole bottling of teen angst as a cultural commodity to provide MTV with neatly-packaged sound bites that he was wailing against. To cap it all his song was taken up by MTV and used to place him at the center of all that he hated. Even the video, that aped MTV's average corporate offerings, was put into heavy rotation.

The song was named after a slogan that had been written on the wall of Cobain's apartment. Cobain's friend Kathleen Hanna (of the band Bikini Kill) helped him trash his bedroom one night in a fit of good-natured angst and she wrote 'Kurt smells like teen spirit' across the wall. She meant it as a reference to a brand of deodorant, but Cobain, unaware of the product, thought it was a compliment about his revolutionary views. He didn't find out until the song had been recorded. Later he claimed that it was his attempt to write a song in the style of the Pixies and that he'd borrowed a riff from Boston's "More Than A Feeling" (a song that they sometimes covered live and even mixed into "Smells Like Teen Spirit" on occasion).

The recording of the song was probably the easiest of the Sound City sessions. The drum and bass parts were recorded very quickly and Cobain's guitars were added afterwards. "Kurt had a hard time doing the guitar intro and then clicking onto a clean effect in the verse" says Butch Vig, "It was a foot pedal called a Small Clone. It had this watery effect, the same one we used in "Come As You Are" [60]. He couldn't get the timing of it. I said 'We'll go back and overdub it later.' That pissed him off. He wanted to play it live all the way through. The little ad-libs after the chorus were actually at the end of the song. I suggested putting those in at the end of each chorus as a bridge into the next verse. And I remember Kurt sitting down with the acoustic and he had a couple of variations of the melody and the verse he was singing and we picked the one that was best. Kurt said before playing it, 'I don't know where I should go with this vocal melody.' He was strumming an acoustic guitar and played me two melodies. I said, 'I like it when you drop down low because there is more of a dichotomy of notes in the verse'. But most of the songs were fairly finished. I don't know whether they played them live, but I know that they did practice a lot. It wasn't like 'what are you playing here'. They knew. Chris had figured out his bass lines, and the

86

drum patterns for the most part were worked out, and Kurt had a pretty good idea of what he wanted to do. But he had a couple of lines in some that he was still working on."

Because of the fame that the song enjoyed, the lyric would become a source of much speculation and discussion. "We were lucky with the vocal," recalls Vig. "I kept the warm-up and he did three other takes. Then I spent a lot of time doing a composite version. Each verse has a different feel to it but it also needed a certain continuity to it. The 'hello, hello' and the choruses are double-tracked. Kurt's voice sounds great double-tracked." In light of how Cobain ended his life, the spotlight would be thrown on the song's opening line of "Load up on guns and bring your friends" and much was made of the fact that he slurred his words to the point of being unlistenable to some. This point was highlighted on the band-approved Weird Al Yankovic spoof single "Smells Like Nirvana" where the comedian sings "What is this song all about / Can't figure any lyrics out / How do the words to it go? / I wish you'd tell me, I don't know." Cobain explained that lyrics were not his major consideration when writing a song; it was music first, lyrics second. "I don't like to make things too obvious, because it gets stale if it's too obvious" he said, "We don't mean to be really cryptic or mysterious. I think that different, or weird, or spacey, lyrics paint a nice picture. It's the way I like art."

Also see sessions {25}, {26a}, {27}, {41}

Breed [46]

The band was still referring to this song under its original name of "Imodium" right up until recording. Then it was suggested to make the change, as Imodium was a patented pharmaceutical and could cause copyright complications. The basic techniques employed on the Smart version were kept on this take – the slowly building crescendo at the start and the switching between channels of Cobain's guitar solo. Again Cobain plugged his guitar directly into the mixing desk. He sang several takes, but the initial one was used as he got worse with every take because of the effort he was putting in. "For the bass distortion we turned the amp up really loud and in the mix we also overloaded the board," explains Vig, "We didn't use any pedals, just overloaded the channels. We went for a Ramones-type panning. Guitar hard right,

drums hard left. A lot of Kurt's solos had a simple melodic sensibility and he would record them very quickly"
Also see sessions {19}, {26a}, {27}

Come As You Are [60]

Though this track is very different from the album opener, "Smells Like Teen Spirit", it does nevertheless use the 'formula' of quiet verse/ loud chorus that was to become the band's trademark. It is viewed as a landmark in Nirvana's recording history in that it was the first time that they allowed a producer to really step in and influence the way a song was arranged. It also showed the amount of trust they had in Vig and his techniques, with Krist Novoselic claiming "He told us what to do." Vig also added a lot to the production of the song. First he triple-tracked the bass in an attempt to make it sound like a twelve-string guitar; then he double-tracked Cobain's vocal: "The vocal was a first take. He sang it brilliantly all the way through, then I asked him to do another. I didn't plan to double-track him but the second take was great and the phrasing was so similar. He said, 'We don't want to do that.' I said, 'Let's live with it and see if we get used to it.'"

"The lines in the song are really contradictory," said Cobain in 1992, "You know, one after another. They are kind of a rebuttal to each line, and they're just kind of confusing I guess. It's just about people and what they're expected to act like."

Killing Joke threatened to take court action against Nirvana over the song claiming its guitar riff was taken from their song "Eighties" but the suit was thrown out at an early stage.
Also see sessions {25}, {26a}, {27}, {41}

In Bloom [48]

Using the same arrangement from the Smart sessions (see session {19}), the band re-recorded the song and picked up some extra style with Dave Grohl's backing vocals. "[Grohl was] having to sing about a step higher than he could sing," recalls Butch Vig, "his voice would break and we'd all be laughing hysterically. We worked a lot on Kurt's voice. We tried a lot of mics and ended up using a Neumann microphone that brought out the flaws in his voice that I was so enamoured with, the raspiness and growliness." Grohl also brought a more powerful drum performance to the take. At times he was pounding the drums so hard he had to change the drum heads on a take-by-take basis. As well as double-tracking the vocals Cobain double-tracked his guitar in the chorus, putting each one through a different amplifier for the fuzzed effect that it afforded.

"I don't like macho men" said Cobain. "You know, I don't like abusive people. I guess that's what that song is about. It's an attack on them." The song turns on people who "like to sing along" to a song even though they are ignorant of what they are singing. Keeping Cobain's previous quote in mind, it became even more ironic that this song became a sing-along crowd favorite! The band thought this might be the opening single from the album; it was eventually the fourth single, released in 1992, reaching the UK Top 10 and #5 in the US.

Also see sessions {19}, {26a}, {27}, {41}

Territorial Pissings [64]

Krist Novoselic gets this two-and-a-half minute thrash rolling by singing directly in to the guitar pickup of Cobain's Fender Jazzmaster. The words he's singing are from "Get Together", a hit for the Youngbloods (a 1960s folk rock group from Boston, MA) and were added at the suggestion of Butch Vig: "I think I suggested we should put something kind of odd in there. Kurt asked him to sing it 'joyously terrible'." The bass and drums were completed in a single take, with Cobain plugging his guitar (for three takes), in true punk fashion, directly into the board rather than playing through an amp. The result is the closest to a punk-sounding song on the album. It was initially called "The Punk Song" on the session sheets until Cobain chose the final title.

Lyrically Cobain was at a loss to explain. "I really didn't know what I was trying to say. There's no point in my even trying to analyze or explain it," he said. He addresses a number of subjects including being an outsider ("When I was an alien"), feminism ("Never met a wise man / If so it's a woman") and paranoia ("Just because you're paranoid / Don't mean they're not after you").

Also see sessions {25}, {26a}, {27}

Drain You [51]

A straightforward love song (or at least as straightforward as Nirvana songs could get), it took a while to record. "Instead of concocting a guitar solo," remembers Butch Vig, "every time Kurt did a vocal he would run to the side of the room at that part of the song and pick something up – squeaky ducks, percussion things or an aerosol. We just left them all in on the mix." This strange assortment of sounds can be heard in and out of the mix during the fifty-second break that begins at 1:36. The result was one of Cobain's favorite songs. Vig cut Cobain's three vocal takes together to use in different parts of the song. These vocals open the song with a simple guitar riff before the song detonates at 0:07.

Also see sessions {22}, {26a}, {27}

Lounge Act [65]

Krist Novoselic has a field day on this track as his melodic bass line leads off the song. Butch Vig says, "We struggled a bit on this one. Five or six takes. We changed a few of the fills. Kurt plays this through the AC30 and then added some Bassman guitars when the guitar picks up. I love the melodic hook on this. A very quick vocal." Musically this track contains one of the undeniable melodies on the album, even when Cobain turns it up a notch for the second verse at 1:32.

Cobain and Novoselic thought they sounded like a cocktail bar band on this one – hence the title. Cobain explained that the song was about "having a certain vision and being smothered by a relationship and not being able to finish what you wanted to do artistically because the other person gets in your way." This 'other person' may well have been ex-girlfriend Tobi Vail because, as Charles Cross reported, Kurt wrote her a letter (unsent) at the time of *In Utero* that said in part, "Every song on this record is not about you. No, I am not your boyfriend. No, I don't write songs about you, except for "Lounge Act", which I do not play, except when my wife is not around."

Also see sessions {25}, {26a}

Stay Away [66]

This re-working of "Pay To Play" [49] (see session {19}) included a number of lyrical changes. "Kurt changed the lyrics when he went in to sing it," says Vig. "That surprised me, I thought the original lyrics were good." As well as changing most of the verses he added "God Is Gay" at the end of the song, which amused those present at the session.

90

"We thought [it] was extremely funny," recalls Vig. "[it] caused a fair amount of controversy among the right-wingers when it came out, who held it up as an example of why music should be censored."

Also see sessions {26a}, {27}

On A Plain [57]

While many of the songs had been written and well rehearsed before getting to Los Angeles, this was not one of them. Musically it had been practiced, but Kurt was still writing the lyric in the studio. This slap-dash approach even made it into the actual words he sings and became a central theme. The song opens with him admitting, "I start this off without any words." Later he asks: "What the hell am I trying to say", then he sings of his own self-editing, "It is now time to make it unclear / To write off lines that don't make sense" before closing with the extra effort of "One more special message to go / And then I'm done then I can go home".

The track was Krist Novoselic's favorite song on the album. "That's a total Kurt Cobain talent shining right there," he recalled. "Somebody who knew what a song was and had a knack for hooks."

Butch Vig called it "A great pop song. A really new one. It took a few takes to get it." The pop nature of the song was enhanced by Dave Grohl's ethereal backing vocals that shape and close the track. Vig wanted to use more of Grohl's vocals on the track but Cobain disagreed. "We did another mix with Kurt's and Dave's 'ooh' backing vocals continuing after the end," recalls Vig, "but Kurt thought it was too poppy. Kurt wrote the lyrics right before he sang them. The line 'Don't quote me on that' was an in-joke that week. Everyone would say 'But don't quote me on that!'" The band gave this song its live debut at an impromptu show at the infamous LA club Jabberjaw on May 29.

Also see sessions {24}, {25}, {26a}, {27}

Lithium [45]

"Lithium" had been recorded on at least two other occasions, with the Smart session seeing quite a few takes, but still the band had trouble recording it. Eventually it would all be worth the extra effort, as it was later voted as the fans' favorite all-time Nirvana track. The recording ran over multiple days, becoming the longest time that they had spent

91

on a single song at the same session. It was proving hard to keep to the precise tempo required through the verses, so Dave Grohl recorded the drums using a click-track. Butch Vig: "It was a bit of a struggle to do because the band kept speeding up for some reason, from where the tempo started out and it wasn't a good speeding-up, sometimes it's cool if tracks take on an edge as the song develops, but in this particular case it just started losing the groove. So we suggested a click-track for Dave and he was like 'I dunno if I've ever played with one', which can totally screw people up. He was amazing at it, he just put it on and went 'I can play with this' and then they did a couple of takes with it and nailed it." The bass was added later (Novoselic: "I did some work on that bass line, I enriched the bass playing a little more but that was about all we changed"), then two guitar parts were mixed in, the slow verse, and loud chorus. Butch Vig again: "After we got the sound, he'd only need one or two takes. Doing vocals he would sing so hard and passionately that he would not be able to speak for about ten minutes afterwards. Some days that would be all I would get out of him. He would sing three or four takes of one song and wouldn't be able to talk."

Cobain used the lyric to address some views on religion, in this case his own views, but many of his songs were sung 'in character' as he explained: "Most of the music is really personal as far as the emotion and experiences that I've had in my life, but most of the themes in the songs aren't that personal. They're just stories from TV or books or movies or friends. But definitely the emotion and feeling is from me. I think there's a large percentage of people who are born without the ability to detect injustice. Those are people who usually turn to religion. I don't think it's their fault, I don't blame them, I have pity for them."

Also see sessions {18}, {19}, {27}

Endless, Nameless [67]

The difficulty that the band had in recording "Lithium" [45] actually caused the breakdown that led to the recording of this 'track'. After a frustrating day of trying to get "Lithium" [45] down correctly, Cobain exploded in a fit of anger. The band started a semi-spontaneous jam (they hadn't planned on playing it then but they had played variations on it before) which turned nasty with Cobain eventually smashing his guitar (the Mosrite or a Fender depending on who you ask). "They started

92

playing that jam which became 'Endless, Nameless'," recalls Butch Vig, "and I was just like 'roll the tape' and you could tell he [Cobain] was really pissed about something. I mean it was scary to see because the veins in his neck were literally popping out he was screaming so hard and in the middle of the song he totally smashed his guitar up... and of course it wound down until they had trashed everything."

Cobain was adamant that this track should be used as a hidden track on the CD version of *Nevermind*. He wanted a long gap of silence after "Something In The Way" [63] that would lull listeners into a false sense of security thinking that the album had finished. This quiet would be broken when "Endless, Nameless" [67] appeared like a ghost from their CD players.

The use of this hidden track caused some problems though, as it was missed out from the original mastering session and so the first pressing (luckily only around 50,000 copies) was one track short. The mistake was soon rectified and subsequent versions of the CD had it in place.

Krist Novoselic's bass opens the jam, with Cobain's guitar cutting swathes of distortion across the channels. Dave Grohl pounds some discordant rhythms around the mess and Cobain screams some inaudible words before the whole thing manifests into a melody at 0:44. More severe vocals burst forth at 1:08 and the noise/melody exchange sweeps to and fro. The last four minutes are a slow, impenetrable, descent into chaos.

Also see session {27}

Polly [11]
The guitar, bass and vocals all came from the Smart sessions (see session {19}), just Dave Grohl's percussion and some backing vocals were recorded here. It was a song that would soon cause a stir, but Kurt defended it by saying "There have been a few complaints from people who say it glamorizes rape, but I just tried to put a different twist to it. It's definitely not a pro-rape song."

Also see sessions {5}, {15}, {19}

Something In The Way [63]
As 1991 was a time when vinyl hadn't yet been completely killed off, Cobain had planned to end each side of the record with a gentle acoustic

93

song. "Polly" [11] was pencilled in to close side one. Right at the end of the sessions Cobain presented this track to his band mates. He had written most of it at the end of 1990 but had kept it to himself and had not even shown the band how to play it at rehearsals for some reason. Now, around May 9, they tried to record a band version of it but were unhappy with the results, though they later managed this successfully in radio sessions.

Butch Vig: "We spent most of a day trying to record it as a band, working out different drum parts. Kurt came into the control room and said, 'I can't get into this at all.' I said, 'How do you hear it then?' and he sat down on the couch and was hardly mumbling the vocal, playing the guitar so quietly. So I said, 'Everybody shut up,' turned the fans and everything off and brought a couple of mics into the control room.

I sent a message out to the lobby and said don't anyone come in or bother us, we're recording in the control room. And he recorded that there and I literally felt like I had to hold my breath for three and a half minutes or however long he sang it. That's the whole basis of that song, the intimacy... I knew we needed to embellish the track a little more but keep it fairly understated. He kind of laid on the couch and I gave him an acoustic mic and a vocal mic and he recorded it in the control room. Then he put the harmonies on and we went back and did the bass, which Chris [Krist] found very hard. We then recorded the drums in studio B. It almost killed Dave to play so quietly."

That night they all went out to a party where they ran into Kirk Canning (the husband of Dee Plakas from the band L7). It transpired that Canning played cello and they asked him to come by Sound City the next day to work with them on this track. In just two takes, Canning managed to bring a beautiful simplicity to the album that was later revealed in full when they recorded a session for MTV's *Unplugged* program in 1993.

For years it was believed that the song concerned a time when Cobain, as a teenager, was so down on his luck that he actually had to sleep under a bridge in Aberdeen, WA. This story was later shown to be an exaggeration on the singer's part. "He hung out there, but you couldn't live on those muddy banks, with the tides coming up and down. That was his own revisionism," says Krist Novoselic.

Also see sessions {25}, {26a}, {27}

94

Old Age [61]

As the snippet that was leaked onto the internet proved (see session {25}), Kurt had written this song by early 1991. Butch Vig commented that it was played at the Sound Studio sessions: "He [Cobain] had one other he was playing on acoustic, it was kinda bluesy. I asked, 'You want to try and put that down on tape?' And he said, 'No, it's not really done.' And one of the songs I think Kurt may have given part of the chord progression to Courtney for one of the Hole songs, or at least there's a little bit of a nod from it. "Old Age", I think."

Also see session {25}

Song in 'D' [68]

Never released, finished, or indeed, properly titled – this song is something of a mystery. The only references to it have come from Butch Vig, who said, "They had about fifteen songs that they were working on. And I thought we were going to at least try and record all of them. There were a couple that we recorded that Kurt never finished the lyrics on. One was called 'Song in D', it was really catchy. I was hoping he would finish the lyrics 'cause it would have been another amazing song. It had a kind of R.E.M. feel to it."

Verse Chorus Verse [aka Sappy] [12]

The band made yet another attempt to record this troublesome song at Sound City. They tried a couple of takes, but Cobain called an end to it saying he wasn't into it and it was again shelved.

Also see sessions {5}, {16}, {19}, {34}

Verse Chorus Verse [62]

Just to confuse matters, Cobain so liked the title "Verse Chorus Verse" he applied it to another song that he tried out at these sessions. Butch Vig confirms that this is very different to the 'other' "Verse Chorus Verse" [12] Here it was recorded with a rough vocal take, Cobain overdubbed some guitars and then it was apparently abandoned and has never been heard outside of this studio.

Also see session {25}

95

Session number

{26a}

Venue: Devonshire Studios, Los Angeles, CA.
Dates: May 20 to 28, 1991
Producer: Butch Vig

Tracks mixed:	Available on:
Smells Like Teen Spirit [59a]	*Nevermind* Deluxe
In Bloom [48a]	*Nevermind* Deluxe
Come As You Are [60a]	*Nevermind* Deluxe
Breed [46a]	*Nevermind* Deluxe
Lithium [45a]	*Nevermind* Deluxe
Territorial Pissings [64a]	*Nevermind* Deluxe
Drain You [51a]	*Nevermind* Deluxe
Lounge Act [65a]	*Nevermind* Deluxe
Stay Away [66a]	*Nevermind* Deluxe
On A Plain [57a]	*Nevermind* Deluxe
Something In The Way [63a]	*Nevermind* Deluxe

The recording sessions at Sound City were taking longer than expected so Butch Vig started doing some basic mixes while recording was still continuing. As soon as the band was done at Sound City, Vig moved to Devonshire Studios in Burbank. As the recording sessions had overrun, Vig had less time than he wanted to do the mixing, and no time to take a break to rest his ears before starting work again. He also had the band hanging around while he tried to work. Kurt Cobain would wander in and start moving the faders, wanting it to sound more like Black Sabbath (Ozzy Osbourne was actually working at the studios at the same time).

"We only did a few backing vocal tracks and rough mixes of all the songs," says Vig, "I did mix a couple of the songs there with the band, but we weren't happy with them." As time started to run out though, there was a general feeling that he had burned out on the album and that a fresh pair of ears should be brought in to mix the final sequence.

Cobain had wanted Vig to bury the vocals and take the 'high-end' off the guitars – thus making the record sound muddy, much as *Bleach* had done. Vig argued against this and pointed out that Cobain's voice should be well up in the mix as it was such an emotional force on the recordings.

"We just went round and round again," says Vig. "I think it was smart to get Andy Wallace to come in with a fresh perspective." Vig's versions of the album tracks were eventually issued two decades later with the deluxe 20th anniversary release of *Nevermind*.

"Smells Like Teen Spirit" [59a] is a much 'cleaner' mix of the track where the guitars sound more Garbage-like (Garbage the band, that is) on the verses. "In Bloom" [48a] and "Come As You Are" [60a] are closer to the final release, though the drums sometimes sound crisper and more 'poppy'. "Breed" [46a] allows Kurt Cobain's lead guitar to flutter through to the front of the mix before being pulled back into the crunch of the chorus. The chorus of "Lithium" [45a] is changed by the guitar sound while "Territorial Pissings" [64a] drops the Novoselic introduction completely. "Lounge Act" [65a] has a little bit of atmospheric echo hovering around before the song's intro creeps into the mix, but otherwise is similar to the album version. On "Stay Away" [66a], Vig lets Dave Grohl's drums dictate the intro ahead of the bass line while the vocal outro of "On A Plain" [57a] is given some electronic effects which don't necessarily blend with the rest of the song, or album. "Something In The Way" [63a] gently closes the album without any hidden tracks.

Session number

{27}

Venue: Scream Studios, Studio City, CA.
Dates: June 1 to 10, 1991
Mixer: Andy Wallace

Tracks mixed:	Available on:
Smells Like Teen Spirit [59]	*Nevermind*
In Bloom [48]	*Nevermind*
Come As You Are [60]	*Nevermind*
Breed [46]	*Nevermind*
Lithium [45]	*Nevermind*
Polly [11]	*Nevermind*
Territorial Pissings [64]	*Nevermind*
Drain You [51]	*Nevermind*
Lounge Act [65]	*Nevermind*
Stay Away [66]	*Nevermind*
On A Plain [57]	*Nevermind*
Something In The Way [63]	*Nevermind*
Endless, Nameless [67]	*Nevermind*

Eventually Butch Vig was happy to hand over the mixing to a third party and Geffen drew up a list of names for consideration. Cobain went through the list eliminating candidates until he came to the name of Andy Wallace who had worked with Slayer. "We said, 'Right on' because those Slayer records were so heavy," recalls Krist Novoselic. Geffen's Gary Gersh contacted Wallace and he prepared to start work at Scream Studios on Ventura Boulevard in early June.

The mixes Wallace produced were much sharper sounding (and more radio friendly) than the 'darker' ones that Vig had worked on. This was especially noticeable on the way he mixed the guitar sounds on "Smells Like Teen Spirit" [59], but at the other end of the spectrum he kept songs like "Something In The Way" [63] sounding the way they had been recorded. "A lot of the stuff Andy used was real subtle," says Butch Vig, "He'd add a stereo ambience to the vocals and delays and make sure there was really good separation between the instruments. The record sounds so loud. It worked out great." Wallace ensured there was 'space' between the instruments but he also kept to the brief laid down by the band. "They were mainly concerned with making sure there was plenty of bass," he recalls, "I was told to make the sound more thick and beefy, yet discernible. I tried to isolate moments worth featuring, like a certain powerful guitar or drum entrance or vocal passage."

When Wallace had mixed the whole album it was sent to Howie Weinberg in New York for mastering. However, communications got messed up along the way and he mastered it without "Endless, Nameless" [67] as the secret track. "When we got our first CD, and popped it in, we listened to it, 'Oh, let's check to see if that track is there, '" remembers Dave Grohl, "and it wasn't there. I was talking to a friend who works in a record store, and he said a person came in with the CD, and said, 'You know, this thing's screwed up. After the last song there's like, this 10 minutes of dead space, then this total noise song'. He wanted his money back. And the person at that store said, 'Well, I think maybe, it was like a joke of the bands' and he goes 'Well I don't think it's very funny' and he wanted his money back!"

Later Cobain would express dissatisfaction with the way *Nevermind* sounded and (partly because of its overwhelming success) he would try and distance himself from it. But at the time he was more than happy with the finished product. And so were millions of album buyers.

Smells Like Teen Spirit

1991
7" vinyl
Smells Like Teen Spirit [59] / Even In His Youth [42]
Geffen DGCCS7   US
Smells Like Teen Spirit [59] / Drain You [51]
Geffen DGC5   UK
12" vinyl
Smells Like Teen Spirit [59] / Even In His Youth [42] / Aneurysm [54]
Geffen DGCS 21673   US
Smells Like Teen Spirit [59]

Geffen PRO-A-4314   US   orange vinyl promo
Smells Like Teen Spirit [59] /Even In His Youth [42] / Aneurysm [54]
Geffen PRO-A-4314   US   yellow vinyl
Smells Like Teen Spirit [59] /Even In His Youth [42] / Aneurysm [54]
Geffen GET21712   Germany   picture disc
Smells Like Teen Spirit [59] / Drain You [51] / Even In His Youth [42]
Geffen DGCT5   UK
Smells Like Teen Spirit [59] / Drain You [51] /Aneurysm [54]
Geffen DGCTP5   UK   picture disc
Cassette
Smells Like Teen Spirit [59] / Even In His Youth [42]
Geffen DGCCS19050   US
Smells Like Teen Spirit [59] / Even In His Youth [42] / Aneurysm [54]
Geffen DGCSS21673   US
Smells Like Teen Spirit [59] / Drain You [51]
Geffen DGCS5   UK
CD
Smells Like Teen Spirit [59] / Even In His Youth [42] / Aneurysm [54]
Geffen DGCDS21673   US
Smells Like Teen Spirit [59]
DGC PROCD4308   US   promo with 'edit' and album
                                  versions
Smells Like Teen Spirit [59] / Drain You [51] / Even In His Youth [42] /
Aneurysm [54]
Geffen DGCCD5   UK

1996
CD
Smells Like Teen Spirit [L59]
DGC/MCA F0010   France   promo

For the members of Nirvana, the six months after the release of *Nevermind* were mind-blowing. Every TV show wanted them to drop by, every magazine wanted a cover story and every radio station wanted an interview. In fact, they were suddenly the biggest and most sought-after band in the world. They were also touring, so in between all of these requests for their time there was little time left to make new music.

101

They didn't manage to get back into a studio until almost a year after recording *Nevermind*. "You know, whatever has happened was surely out of our control, and I'm glad it's happened," said Krist Novoselic in 1992. "You know it's nice to sell that many records, it's nice to turn on people to something different."

For Kurt Cobain, as the leader of the band, it was a different case. He found even more pressure being exerted on him and was defensive about ending up in such a position. "It's not my fault. I never wanted the fame involved," he said, "That's a totally different story. I don't want to start my own record label. God, I know I couldn't do that, but I'd like to give some money to some labels who are putting out great music, help in that way. Hopefully we can have a recording studio too, a little 8-track recording studio, so we can make good demos. And that's pretty much the plans. And just get some new shoes."

A US tour of over 30 shows took the band up to Christmas 1991 by which point *Nevermind* was just about double platinum. A first trip to Japan and Australia opened 1992, with a new EP – *Hormoaning* – issued to promote it. The songs on the new EP would be taken from the Music Source session (see session {24}) and a BBC Peel session {R5}.

In February Kurt and Courtney Love were married in Hawaii and their daughter, Frances Bean, was born in August.

Over the summer Cobain started working up more ideas for what was becoming *Nevermind's* eagerly awaited follow-up. "The next album will be completely different," he said. "We've already started working on a completely different sound. Some of the new songs we've been writing or trying to write don't sound anything like *Nevermind*. There'll be a complete change, because what keeps playing music exciting is to change and experiment. It's a lot more psychedelic, and it's very abrasive and weird and stupid. And there won't be much structure to the songs. It's not as if we're going to start playing very technical jazz shit, but it'll be different. I think 'Aneurysm' is a good example of what it will sound like."

Session number

{28}

Venue: The Laundry Room, Seattle, WA.
Date: April 7, 1992
Producer: Barrett Jones
Players: Kurt Cobain (guitar, vocals), Krist Novoselic (bass), Dave
　　　Grohl (drums)

Tracks recorded:	Available on:
Oh, The Guilt [55]	Split single w/ The Jesus Lizard, *With The Lights Out* box set
Curmudgeon [69]	Lithium single, *With The Lights Out* box set
Return of the Rat [70]	*8 Songs For Greg Sage, 14 Songs For Greg Sage, With The Lights Out* box set

With studio time hard to fit into the schedule, Nirvana made a brief stop at Barrett Jones' home studio to record three tracks. "We had all been hanging out together since I had moved to Seattle," says Jones, "So I knew them pretty well." Jones was a friend of Dave Grohl and Grohl had been lodging with him when he was home from tour. "I'd first met Dave when he was 14 or 15 and I was 18. When his first band Freak Baby recorded in the original Laundry Room Studio in my parents' house – the control room was in the laundry room. Dave was the guitar player of the band at the time, but a few months after that recording they kicked out the bass player and Dave started playing drums. The drummer then went to bass and they changed their name to Mission Impossible. The 8-track studio set up was in Jones' basement, when he later moved to larger premises, he kept the name for his new facility. The whole session took less than three days to record and mix. "It was really casual and easy and we were just having a good time doing it," recalls Jones.

Oh, The Guilt [55]
Stop-start riffing and a crunching guitar helped push this split single up the UK charts, taking the Jesus Lizard to commercial heights that they never dreamed of reaching on their own. Barrett Jones remembers that the session was "quick and smooth." The extra sound effects were a recording of Cobain flicking a cigarette lighter. Adam Kasper remixed this track for the *With The Lights Out* box set.
Also see session {24}

Curmudgeon [69]
A real rarity in the Nirvana canon, this song seemed to appear out of nowhere and disappear just as quickly. This is the first session that the track was recorded at, having been played live just once the previous fall. It was polished to be used as a future b-side and opens with a lopsided groove set up between Cobain's unconventional guitar and Novoselic's overpowering bass line. Lyrically it's hard to understand apart from the repeating "She don't need!" Not the most inspiring song in the Nirvana catalog. Also remixed by Adam Kasper for the *With The Lights Out* box set.

Return Of The Rat [70]
Issued on both the vinyl tribute box set (*8 Songs For Greg Sage And The Wipers*) and the CD version (*14 Songs For Greg Sage And The Wipers*), this cover is faithful to the original. A three-minute tear through the track, with a minimalist lyric and a Cobain guitar solo at 1:16. Nirvana were going to contribute another Wipers song, D-7 [100] from a BBC session, but licensing problems scuppered the idea and so this track was recorded in its stead. Again, this was remixed by Adam Kasper for the *With The Lights Out* box set.

104

Come As You Are

1992
7" vinyl
Come As You Are [60] / Drain You [L51]
DGC DGCCS7   US
Come As You Are [60] / Endless, Nameless [67]
DGC DGC7   UK
Come As You Are [60] / Drain You [L51]
DGC GES19120   France
Come As You Are [60] / Endless, Nameless [67]
DGC GES19065   Germany

12" vinyl
Come As You Are [60]
DGC PROA4416   US   promo
Come As You Are [60] / School [L34] / Drain You [L51]
DGC DGCS21707   US
Come As You Are [60] / Endless, Nameless [67] / School [L34]
DGC DGC7   UK
Come As You Are [60] / Endless, Nameless [67] / School [L34]
DCC DGCTP7   UK   picture disc
Come As You Are [60] / Endless, Nameless [67] / Drain You [L51]
DGC GET21699   Germany
Come As You Are [60] / Endless, Nameless [67] / Drain You [L51]
DGC GET21712   Germany   picture disc
Come As You Are [60] / Endless, Nameless [67] / Drain You [L51]
DGC GET21699   Australia
Cassette
Come As You Are [60] / School [L34] / Drain You [L51]
DGC DGCCS21707   US
Come As You Are [60] / Endless, Nameless [67]
DGC DGCCS19065   Australia
CD
Come As You Are [60]
DGC CDPRO4375 1992 US   promo
Come As You Are [60] / School [L34] / Drain You [L51]
DGC DGCDS2l707   US
Come As You Are [60] / Endless, Nameless [67] / School [L34] / Drain
   You [L51]
DGC DGCTD7   UK

Lithium

1992
12" vinyl
Lithium [45] / Been A Son [L40] / Curmudgeon [69]
DGC DGCS21815   US
Lithium [45] / Been A Son [L40] / Curmudgeon [69]
DGC   DGCTP9   UK   picture disc
Lithium [45] / Been A Son [L40] / Curmudgeon [69]
DGC GET21815 Germany
Cassette
Lithium [45] / Been A Son [L40] / Curmudgeon [69]
DGC DGCCS21815   US
Lithium [45] / Been A Son [L40] / Curmudgeon [69]

DGC DGCCS19134   Australia
CD
Lithium [45]
DGC CDPR04429   US   promo
Lithium [45] / Been A Son [L40] / Curmudgeon [69]
DGC DGCDM21815   US
Lithium [45] / Been A Son [L40] / Curmudgeon [69] / D-7 [R100]
DGC DGCTD9   UK

1996
CD
Lithium [L45] Geffen NIR 96010   Holland

In Utero

"I never listen to *Nevermind*. I haven't listened to it since we put it out. That says something. I can't stand that kind of production and I don't listen to bands that do have that kind of production, no matter how good their songs are. It just bothers me." Harsh words indeed. Even more so when you consider that it was Kurt Cobain speaking them. By late 1992 it was clear that the next Nirvana album was going to be very different from its multi-platinum predecessor. Fame hadn't been too kind to Cobain. Both he and Courtney Love were being hounded by the press over their drug use; the constant demands on Cobain's time for touring and press relations was getting him down; tensions were rising within the band and he was publicly saying that he hated the album that was making him rich. He wasn't about to make the same 'mistake' again, and the band wanted to make a definite step back towards their punk roots on the next album, away from the more professionally produced sounds of *Nevermind*.

Many of the songs that would end up on *In Utero* had again been penned over a fairly long time period. "Rape Me" [71] had been written during the *Nevermind* sessions, while a number of songs had been played live over the previous three years: "Dumb" [90] (first played live in September 1990 – see radio session {R41}), "Radio Friendly Unit Shifter" [58] (November 1990), "Pennyroyal Tea" [52] (August 1991), "All Apologies" [56] (November 1991) and "tourette's" [72] (August 1992).

Though the band had been working on new material at rehearsals, the first real session to try and capture any number of these 'new' songs took place with Jack Endino; it would be his last work with the band. He recorded six new tracks (five of them only as instrumentals) at Word Of Mouth Studios (see session {29}), formerly called Reciprocal Studios. Touring commitments then halted any further studio work until a few days were grabbed in Brazil in January 1993 (see session {31}).

In the meantime, a compilation album – *Incesticide* – was released in December 1992. Nirvana's two labels had both been planning a compilation album – Sub Pop had proposed one with the none-too-subtle title of *Cash Cow*, while Geffen's would have collected more recent out-takes and radio sessions together. The final version contained six

109

tracks from radio sessions plus b-sides and various other previously unreleased tracks – it reached number 14 in the UK charts and 39 in America.

The third week of January 1993 had the band working in the Ariola Ltda BMG studio in Rio de Janeiro. Here five future *In Utero* songs were demoed with Craig Montgomery acting as producer. One take from this session ("Gallons Of Rubbing Alcohol Flow Through The Strip" [79]) would be used directly on *In Utero*. Three weeks later in Minnesota *In Utero* was recorded for real with Steve Albini at the low-key Pachyderm Studios (see session {34}).

For *In Utero* the band were adamant that they wanted to work with the well-known renegade 'recordist' (he refused to be labelled as a producer) Steve Albini. It was his 'basic' working techniques that ultimately caused a certain amount of friction between the band, the label and Albini himself. Though the actual sessions went well, after some reflection and quite possibly some record label intervention, the album was sonically reshaped due to concerns over the quality of the mixing. "The mixing we'd done with Steve Albini was so fast it was ridiculous" said Cobain afterwards, "those tapes we took away from the studio sounded very different when we played them at home. For three weeks none of us could work out what was wrong and we didn't know what the fuck we were going to do. Then we realized it was the vocals and bass weren't loud enough." So as Andy Wallace had been on *Nevermind*, Scott Litt was brought in to add some fresh impetus to some key tracks. Albini fired back with an interview for the *Chicago Tribune* saying, "I have no faith this record will be released, it's not a record for wimps." Litt went to work in May 1993 and consequently the band and Albini fell out. A more, dare it be said, radio friendly version was issued the following September.

Over the summer, the band took some time off, did some press and played a single show in New York. This show was a sign of things to come as they employed a second guitarist (John Duncan) to flesh out the sound and played an acoustic set with Lori Goldston on cello. These new additions to the live show would be kept during the *In Utero* tour with Pat Smear taking over as the permanent second guitarist. "Heart-Shaped Box" [73] was released as the pre-album single in Europe and reached number five in the UK. During the autumn, the band made

110

numerous TV appearances during breaks in the US tour and MTV's *Unplugged* (see session {T81}) and *Live And Loud* (see session {T91}) showcased opposite ends of the band's ever widening musical spectrum.

The album itself underwent several name changes before the final title was settled upon. *I Hate Myself And Want To Die* and *Verse Chorus Verse* were being considered as late as April and May 1993. *In Utero*, meaning in the womb, i.e. waiting to be born, was reportedly a line from a Courtney Love poem which Cobain spotted and liked. Thematically introverted, the album focuses on the pressures of success on several songs. "Teenage angst has served me well / Now I'm bored and old," sings Cobain to open "Serve The Servants" [88] in a not-so-subtle reference to the soar away success of "Smells Like Teen Spirit" [59]. He seems to address the same topic on "Rape Me" [71], which also carries a parody of the melody of "Smells Like Teen Spirit" [59], and on "Frances Farmer Will Have Her Revenge On Seattle" [89] he could well be singing of the witch hunt that Courtney Love was undergoing during the battle to get custody of Frances Bean.

In Utero

1993
Cassette

Geffen GEF/C 24607	US**	promo
DGC DGCC24607	US	
Geffen GEFC24536	UK *	
Geffen GEFC24536	Australia*	

LP

DGC D6C24607	US	clear vinyl
Geffen GEF24536	UK	
Geffen GEF24536	Australia	
DCC MVJG 25004	Japan	

CD

DGC DGCD24607	US	
Geffen GEFCD24536	UK*	
Geffen GEFD24536	Australia*	

1994
Cassette

DCC DGCC24705	US***

CD

DCC DGCD24705	US***

1996
LP

Universal Music MVJG-25004	Japan

CD

Ultra Disc UDCD690	US	gold audiophile

1997
CD

Mobile Fidelity Sound Lab UDCD690	US	gold audiophile

1998
LP

Simply Vinyl SVLP0048	UK	180g vinyl

2003
LP

DGC 4245361	US	Albini mix
Geffen 424516-1	UK	Albini mix

2007
LP

Universal Music UICY-93360	Japan

2008
LP

Geffen GEF 24536	Germany	180 gm

2009
LP
Universal Music B00 12765-01 US   180gm

2011
SHM-CD
Universal Music UICY-5127   Japan

* = includes "Gallons of Rubbing Alcohol Flow Through the Strip" [79]
** = includes "I Hate Myself And Want To Die" [92]
*** = includes "Pennyroyal Tea" [52a] remix

Basic track listing:
Serve The Servants [88] / Scentless Apprentice [75] / Heart-Shaped Box [73] / Rape Me [71] / Frances Farmer Will Have Her Revenge On Seattle [89] / Dumb [90] / Very Ape [78] / Milk It [76] / Pennyroyal Tea [52] / Radio Friendly Unit Shifter [58] / tourette's [72] / All Apologies [56]

Note 1: All non-US CDs and cassettes have the extra track Gallons Of Rubbing Alcohol Flow Through The Strip [79]

Note 2: The 1994 US re-issues on CD and cassette had numerous changes – "Rape Me" [71] was re-titled as "Waif Me", the Scott Litt "Pennyroyal Tea" [52a] remix was included and elements of the artwork were amended (a turtle on the back sleeve for example). The changes were implemented mainly because of concerns expressed by US retail giants Wal-Mart and K-Mart.

Packaging notes:
The front cover of the album shows 'Brunnhilde: The Transparent Woman', a model from the Smithsonian Museum Of Science which was used to teach children about anatomy. Cobain added the wings. The inner artwork includes a montage of live and studio photos of the band, a couple of photo session shots, a trio of pictures of a fire-damaged Republican Party office from the 1992 Los Angeles riot and a shot of Cobain in a wheelchair at the 1992 Reading Festival. The lyrics to eleven of the thirteen tracks were reproduced – "tourette's" [72] just says

114

"Culk, Tisk, Sips" and for "Gallons Of Rubbing Alcohol Flow Through The Strip" [79] it simply says "Whatever". The picture on the actual CD is Michael DeWitt who acted as a nanny for Frances Bean.

In Utero reviews:

Melody Maker:	"God knows we still need people who can speak their truth like this."
NME:	"... a love letter written down and screamed out by a man scared of the contentment he's slipped into." 8/10
Q:	"If this is the way Cobain is going to develop the future is lighthouse-bright." 4/5
Rolling Stone:	"... brilliant, corrosive, enraged and thoughtful, most of them all at once." 3½/4
Vox:	"*In Utero* pokes a scalpel blade into Cobain's own messy entrails." 8/10
Seattle Post Intelligencer:	"... a brilliant follow-up to its blockbuster '*Nevermind*.' It is abrasive and uncompromising, yet pop-savvy enough to appeal to the new mainstream audience Nirvana helped create."
San Francisco Chronicle:	"Most of ''In Utero'' ... consists of brutal songs that give no quarter and expect none. Yet the raw potency and painful honesty of the album are what make it a triumph."
Globe and Mail (Canada):	"... a delightful combination of rage and glee."

Session number

{29}

Venue: Word Of Mouth Studios, Seattle, WA
Dates: October 25 and 26, 1992
Producer: Jack Endino
Players: Kurt Cobain (guitar, vocals), Krist Novoselic (bass), Dave
    Grohl (drums)

Tracks recorded:	Available on:
tourette's (instrumental) [72a]	not available
Dumb (instrumental) [90a]	not available
Pennyroyal Tea (instrumental) [52a]	not available
Rape Me [71]	***With The Lights Out*** **box set**
Radio Friendly Unit Shifter (instrumental) [58a]	not available
Frances Farmer Will Have Her Revenge On Seattle (instrumental) [89a]	not available

By 1992, Reciprocal Studios had changed its name to Word Of Mouth
Studios. It had been Reciprocal from 1986 to 1991 before changing
ownership, and to some extent, equipment. The eight-track Otari tape
machine had stayed in use, though these sessions were one of the last
times it was used. Nirvana had decided to try out some new songs with
Jack Endino for the first time in over two years. Two days were booked
from midday to midnight, but the first day was relatively unproductive,
as Cobain didn't show. Novoselic and Grohl spent the time setting up
and, in the words of Jack Endino, "getting drum sounds... and then
waiting." Cobain was in the midst of legal battles to gain full custody
of Frances Bean, which undoubtedly took precedence over a recording
session. On the 26th he arrived at 'dinner time' – about six hours after the
scheduled start. In the final six hours he added vocals to only one song,

"Rape Me" [71], while five more tracks were played as instrumentals. Courtney Love and Frances Bean were present on the second day. These eight-track demos have never leaked out as Jack Endino confirms that not even a cassette copy was run off. Endino also recalls that Cobain's equipment for this session consisted of "A small Fender guitar, perhaps a Mustang, a bottom-of-the-line orange Boss pedal, very basic... and this top-of-the-line Mesa Boogie rack gear that sounded kind of colorless and washed out – but was loud as fuck." All the tracks were recorded live and only "Rape Me" [71] had overdubs added.

Towards the end of the second day the studio had some unexpected visitors in the shape of the Seattle Police Department. People living close to the studio had complained about the noise of Dave Grohl's drumming. "It was only the second time in seven years that it ever happened at the building," says Endino, "I had to go to the door and deal with the cops myself. The walls were pretty thick but not enough for Dave. They just said 'keep the noise down'. The cops had heard of Nirvana, and were not unamused, but remained firm. We waited until they left and cut a couple more tracks."

Most of the information about this session comes from Endino's memory as paper records weren't kept. He says that he "Didn't generate session stuff like this..., it was a pretty casual operation; eight-track analog studio, seventeen bucks an hour. In fact, in fifteen years I've encountered 'session sheets' – which song was recorded what day – about twice in ten countries. The reason being that no one running a studio seems to care about this info anymore as long as the studio bills are paid. The band paid cash as they went."

Also see session {34}

Rape Me [71]

The band demo of this track starts, quite disconcertingly, with the sound of a baby crying (this continues through the song), otherwise it's almost the finished song. An earlier acoustic demo was also included on *With The Lights Out* which has completely different lyrics for the verses.

Also see sessions {34}, {41}

In Bloom

1992
7" vinyl
In Bloom [48] / Polly [L11a] Geffen GEF34   UK
12" vinyl
In Bloom [48] / Sliver [L50] / Polly [11a]
Geffen GFSTP34   UK   picture disc
Cassette
In Bloom [48] / Polly [L11a] Geffen GFSC34   UK
In Bloom [48] / Polly [L11a] Geffen GEFCS19097Australia
CD
In Bloom [48]
DGC PR0CD44632   US   promo
In Bloom [48] / Sliver [L50] / Polly [11a]
Geffen GFSTD34   UK
In Bloom [48] / Sliver [L50] / Polly [11a]
Geffen GEFDM21760   Australia
In Bloom [48] / Sliver [L50] / Polly [11a]
Geffen MVCG13002   Japan

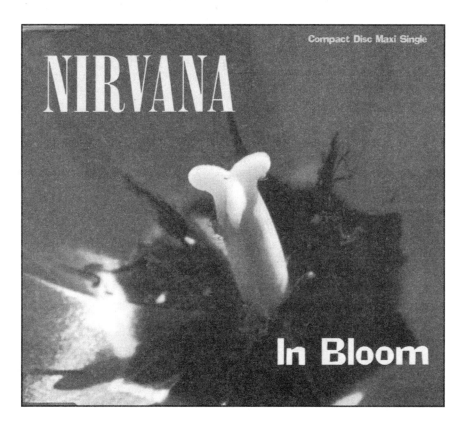

Session number

{30}

Venue: practice space, Seattle, WA,
Date: late 1992
Producer: none
Players: Kurt Cobain (guitar, vocals), Krist Novoselic (bass), Dave
    Grohl (drums)

Tracks recorded:	Available on:
Scentless Apprentice [75]	*With The Lights Out* box set

Sharing a practice space with power-pop quartet the Posies, Nirvana worked on fledgling versions of their new songs during the winter. Only one track has surfaced to date, but it's likely that the bulk of *In Utero* was worked on here.

Scentless Apprentice [75]

A bit of guitar doodling precedes the early take of this track which opens with a three-way jam and eventually twists itself into a vaguely recognizable song after about three minutes. Kurt Cobain only adds a few snatches of unintelligible lyrics here and there. Clearly a work in progress.

    Also see sessions {31}, {34}

Session number

{31}

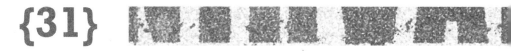

Venue: Ariola Ltda BMG, Rio de Janeiro, Brazil
Date: January 19 to 22, 1993
Producer: Craig Montgomery
Players: Kurt Cobain (guitar, bass, vocals), Krist Novoselic (bass),
    Dave Grohl (drums), Patty Schemel (drums), Courtney
    Love (vocals, guitar)

Tracks recorded:	Available on:
Heart-Shaped Box [73]	*With The Lights Out* box set
Scentless Apprentice [75]	*With The Lights Out* box set
Milk It [76]	*With The Lights Out* box set
Moist Vagina [77]	*With The Lights Out* box set
Perky New Wave Number [aka Very Ape] [78]	not officially released
Gallons Of Rubbing Alcohol Flow Through The Strip [79]	*In Utero* **(Non-US CD** version), *With The Lights Out* box set
Untitled Song #1 [80]	not officially released
Untitled Song #2 [81]	not officially released
Seasons In The Sun [82]	not officially released
Miss World [83]	*My Body The Hand Grenade*
It's Closing Soon [84]	not officially released
I Hate Myself And Want to Die [92]	*With The Lights Out* box set
The Other Improv	*With The Lights Out* box set

Nirvana traveled to South America to play two massive festivals in January 1993. The first of these was in Sao Paulo and brought in a crowd of 110,000 which witnessed one of the stranger shows that Nirvana ever performed. The bizarre set included Duran Duran's 'Rio', Kim Wilde's 'Kids In America', Queen's 'We Will Rock You' and Terry

121

Jacks' 'Seasons In The Sun' [82]. The last of these covers would be recorded within a few days. The band had a week off until the second festival in Rio de Janeiro. They had planned to spend the time working on some demos at a Rio studio, as did Courtney Love, who was present for the trip along with Hole's drummer Patty Schemel.

Soundman Craig Montgomery was available to 'produce' these sessions which were spread over several days and featured a mix of Love and Cobain compositions being played. As usual for demos, Cobain had a lot of work still to do on most of the lyrics and in many cases just sang a live guide vocal with the basic track. They did take time to add overdubs though which gives the impression that they were going to use these tapes for more than just practicing the songs. Later on, Steve Albini told of being sent a 'practice tape' which could have actually been these sessions.

The versions that have been circulated seem to have been recorded at different times and may well be taken from more than one day of recording. Overall the songs are quite close to the finished versions, but sparsely arranged and recorded. Few overdubs are included and Cobain's vocals seem to be live in the studio; occasionally he forgets words and slips into semi-mumbles. This session was the first major Nirvana one to leak onto the internet and it's all the more surprising because this happened nine years after it was recorded. It's also notable that only newer compositions were run through in Brazil, the older ones that made it onto *In Utero* ("Dumb" [90], "Radio Friendly Unit Shifter" [58], "Pennyroyal Tea" [52], "All Apologies" [56] and "tourette's" [72]) weren't attempted.

Heart-Shaped Box [73]

This long (almost 5½ minutes), somewhat rambling take of *In Utero's* first single shows that Cobain had finished a lyric for it (he has full verses in place) but he re-wrote numerous parts before recording it for the album just three weeks later. The first verse was over 50% identical to the final one, the chorus has just minor changes and later Cobain sings, "I've been locked in heart-shaped coffins for too many weeks." A rambling guitar solo snakes its way through thirty seconds from the 3:13 mark.

If one song ever epitomized the effect that Courtney Love had on Kurt Cobain's song writing then "Heart-Shaped Box" [73] is it. While sharing an apartment during 1992 they also shared note books in which they would sometimes take turns to write the first part of a lyrical couplet and leave the book open for the other to later add the second half. It's not known if any of these co-written lyrics were used on *In Utero* – Love isn't officially credited – but in other ways she was directly (if inadvertently) involved. The heart-shaped box in question is the one which Love gave as a present to Cobain in the early stages of their relationship. "Forever in debt to your priceless advice" was taken from a note Cobain had written to Love. Love had first heard the hypnotic opening riff to this track at the apartment towards the end of 1992 when she'd cheekily asked Cobain if she could have it – he said no. When he finally played her this demo it still had the working title of Heart-Shaped Coffin.

Also see sessions {34}, {35}

Scentless Apprentice [75]

"That's a really good example of the direction we're going in," said Kurt Cobain, "We actually collaborated on that song – it came together in practice, and it was just a totally satisfying thing to finally contribute equally to a song, instead of me coming up with the basics of a song."

The same length as the *In Utero* version (to the second), this track is very close to the finished product. Novoselic and Grohl form a very tight rhythm section, Cobain's guitar is crunchy and concise, and enough overdubs are present to give a real feel for the finished song. As usual it is the lyric that is furthest from being the finished article, though most of the screams are well practiced and in place. The guitar solo at 2:18 is just a searing rush of aural adrenaline before Cobain's guide vocals take over again.

Also see sessions {30}, {34}

Milk It [76]

Forty seconds longer than the *In Utero* version, this demo take has the same discordant opening and much of the same instrumental tracking but differs lyrically. The first verse is mainly mumbled and, though the screaming chorus is present, most of the words were re-worked before recording with Steve Albini.

Also see session {34}

123

Moist Vagina [aka MV] [77]
This first take of the future b-side was considerably (around 1½ minutes) shorter than the final version as it fades out before the usual elongated instrumental ending. Cobain's vocals are more straightforward than the Albini version and, again, the lyric is unfinished.

Also see session {34}

Perky New Wave Number [aka Very Ape] [78]
Taking into account this working title, it's not surprising that the song had a definite new wave feel to it. This early demo also had vastly different lyrics to the *In Utero* version with one line claiming, "I'm so tired of being new wave." Musically it is very similar to the final version, but does last 20 seconds longer than the album take and segues into "Gallons Of Rubbing Alcohol Flow Through The Strip" [79]. Whether this was how the two tracks were played live in the studio or whether they were linked during mixing is unclear.

Also see sessions {32}, {34}

Gallons Of Rubbing Alcohol Flow Through The Strip [79]
This track was used directly from this session on non-US CD versions of *In Utero*. It was placed, in a similar fashion to how "Endless, Nameless" [67] was used on *Nevermind*, a good while after "All Apologies" [56] finished – but this time the track was listed on the CD sleeve. As mentioned above, it was a track that followed on directly from "Perky New Wave Number" [78] and the separation of the two songs accounts for the rather abrupt start that "Gallons Of Rubbing Alcohol Flow Through The Strip" [79] has on the album as it was 'disentangled' from the mix. The track itself is a sprawling, musically sparse vehicle for Cobain's alternating spoken word and screamed lyric. The overall effect brings memories of Jim Morrison rambling over Doors' improvisations to mind. Eventually it all falls away leaving a single electric guitar to slowly battle its own feedback into the ground.

Untitled Song #1 [80]
The first of two so far unknown, untitled tracks at this session is a chugging, grinding, mid-tempo number with numerous stops and starts. Dave Grohl keeps a plodding beat that Krist Novoselic furnishes with

some down-home basic bass lines over the 5:42 take. Kurt Cobain talks and growls his way through an impenetrable lyric which is, in many parts, little more than a guide vocal. Parts that can be clearly understood include the spoken word interludes, one of which hauntingly says "If we did not have chemicals / You would not be writing my death certificate." Another repeated line is "My milk is your shit" which Cobain finally chose to use in the *In Utero* version of "Milk It" [76].

Untitled Song #2 [81]

The second unknown track from this session is a hardcore Dave Grohl effort. Known among fans as "Meat" or "Eat Meat", because of the numerous mentions of the subject in the lyric, Grohl intones "Meat" over and over a pre-recorded hardcore thrash metal backing track. The take could be considered a Grohl solo project as he played all the instruments. Craig Montgomery seems to have had some fun with the mix as instruments and childlike, high-pitched voices appear and disappear from each channel, seemingly at random to create an even more surreal feel to a strange track.

Seasons In The Sun [82]

Nirvana were in the mood for cover versions during the Brazil trip and played several of them at the two concerts. This, though, is three and a quarter joyously shambolic minutes of the Terry Jacks' classic, which reached number one in 1974 in both the US and UK; it had been the first single Cobain had ever bought. Sounding like a well-rehearsed bar band, Nirvana plod their way through it and, apart from a couple of lyrical changes, the take is pretty faithful to the original. Whether he forgot the words and substituted his own, or whether he was just being playful is uncertain but Cobain sang his own lines of "I have bought three turds / If I could be God I would kill birds" in the second verse and "All my tears are salty / I think that now I will start to wee."

Miss World [83]

This Hole demo received an official release on the *My Body The Hand Grenade* compilation in 1997 but it's unclear if any members of Nirvana play on it (though Cobain was rumoured to be playing guitar and/or

125

bass) as the liner notes only state that it was recorded at this session and does not list the players.

It's Closing Soon [aka Closing Time] [84]

Courtney Love gave John Peel a tape of this track (and others?) in 1995 and he duly played it on his show. The version in general circulation is pretty rough with some wordless harmony vocals from Courtney changing to the repeated refrain of "I never know why"; the whole thing fades out after 2:36. It could be a fair assumption to make that this line-up of Love-Schemel-Cobain also played on "Miss World" [83].

Session number

{32}

Venue: home recording, Seattle, WA.
Date: early 1993
Producer: none
Players: Kurt Cobain (guitar, vocals)

Tracks recorded:	Available on:
Pennyroyal Tea [52]	*With The Lights Out* box set
Serve The Servants [88]	*With The Lights Out* box set
Very Ape [78]	*With The Lights Out* box set

As Kurt Cobain continued to work at home on the songs that would form *In Utero,* he made piles of cassettes of his work. The *With The Lights Out* box set let a small fraction of these into the public domain. This trio of vocal and acoustic guitar takes show how fragile the original versions sounded, though on "Very Ape" [78] Cobain manages to get the sense of urgency across with just an acoustic guitar. "Pennyroyal Tea" [52] is a complete take, while "Serve The Servants" [88] is a 90-second clip.

Session number

{33}

Venue: unknown venue, Seattle, WA
Date: early 1993
Producer: none
Players: Kurt Cobain (guitar, vocals), Courtney Love (guitar,
vocals), Patty Schemel (drums)

Tracks recorded:	Available on:
Hello Kitty [85]	unconfirmed
Lemonade Nation [86]	unconfirmed
Twister [87]	unconfirmed

Never in general circulation, this session took place at an undisclosed
Seattle location under the spoof band name 'Nighty Nite'. Courtney Love
explained to writer Poppy Z Brite that, "We pretended we were two sisters
from Marysville, 17 and 16, Dottie and Clara. We put the pitch way up on
the four-track and we made up these really stupid songs like 'Lemonade
Nation", 'Twister' and 'Hello Kitty', just crap like that. Sent the tapes out
to all the appropriate people: Maximumrocknroll [sic], Kim and Thurston,
Bikini Kill, Fugazi, Calvin, Slim Moon. Huge Buzz." No more has ever
been disclosed about this tape and none of the supposed recipients have
ever come forward to confirm that they actually received a copy.

Session number

{34}

Venue: Pachyderm Studios, Cannon Falls
Dates: February 14 to 26, 1993
Producer: Steve Albini
Players: Kurt Cobain (guitar, vocals), Krist Novoselic (bass), Dave
   Grohl (drums), Kera Schaley (cello)

Tracks recorded:	Available on:
Rape Me [71]	*In Utero*, All Apologies single, *Nirvana*
Scentless Apprentice [75]	*In Utero*
Heart-Shaped Box [73]	*In Utero*, Heart-Shaped Box single, *Nirvana*
Milk It [76]	*In Utero*
Dumb [90]	*In Utero*, *Nirvana*
Radio Friendly Unit Shifter [58]	*In Utero*
Very Ape [78]	*In Utero*
Pennyroyal Tea [52]	*In Utero*, *Nirvana*
Frances Farmer Will Have Her Revenge On Seattle [89]	*In Utero*
tourette's [72]	*In Utero*
Serve The Servants [88]	*In Utero*
All Apologies [56]	*In Utero*
Moist Vagina [aka MV] [77]	All Apologies single
Marigold [91]	Heart-Shaped Box single, *With The Lights Out* box set
Sappy [12]	*No Alternative*, *With The Lights Out* box set
I Hate Myself And Want To Die [92]	*The Beavis & Butt-Head Experience*

Many things about *In Utero* were a direct reaction to *Nevermind* and the success it enjoyed. The choice of studio (a low-key one, well away from the major media centers), the choice of material (edgier, punk and new wave songs) and the choice of producer (Steve Albini) were all engineered to put some distance between Nirvana and their breakthrough album. "I don't listen to records like that at home," said Kurt Cobain about *Nevermind* in 1993, "I can't listen to that record. I like a lot of the songs. I really like playing some of them live. In a commercial sense I think it's a really good record, I have to admit that, but that's in a Cheap Trick sort of a way. But for my listening pleasure, you know, it's too slick."

"I know Kurt liked the way *Nevermind* sounded," replied Krist Novoselic "That was just a reaction to a lot of things. It was kind of a reaction to get Albini. We didn't want to be sell-outs and Albini is known for having integrity. It just seemed like it made sense, going back to our roots instead of just making another really slick album. The material on the record, too, was dark. It's intensely beautiful but at the same time it's very dark and abrasive. Whereas *Nevermind* was kind of like a bubblegum record."

It wasn't just the production of the album that was a result of the previous eighteen months, the lyrics were pretty hard-hitting too. "Listening to some of the lyrics," Dave Grohl told Michael Azerrad, "and knowing what they're pertaining to is kind of strange because there's a lot of spite, a lot of 'Fuck you' or 'I've been fucked over' and a lot of lines that refer to money or legalities or babies. It's intense but at the same time it just seems like Kurt feels like he's backed up against a wall and he's just going to scream his way out."

The band arrived in Minnesota on Valentine's Day 1993. They were met at the airport by Brent Sigmeth, the Pachyderm Studios engineer who was starting his first day in a new job. "I was supposed to hold up a sign that said 'The Simon Ritchie Bluegrass Ensemble'," Sigmeth recalled, "which I didn't! I just waved at them. Kurt and Krist were coming through and I said, 'I'm your ride'." 'Simon Ritchie' was the real name of the Sex Pistols bassist Sid Vicious and Nirvana had booked Pachyderm under the moniker of 'The Simon Ritchie Bluegrass Ensemble.' Cobain had previously used the pseudonym 'Simon Ritchie' when checking into hotels (he had also used Axl Rose's real name,

Bill Bailey, for this purpose). Like their last recording trip to the mid-west in 1990 (see session {19}) it was a cold and snowy environment. Pachyderm had its own on-site residential buildings and the band soon settled in.

It was the first time they had actually met Steve Albini in person and they wasted no time in setting up their equipment. Albini had insisted on a flat rate fee of $100,000 for his services. It may sound like a lot but he refused a royalty agreement that was pretty much guaranteed to make him five times that sum – a figure that Albini described as an "absurd amount of money". When you add Albini's fee to the studio rental costs, $24,000 in one report (though Cobain was quoted as saying it was $17,000 – either way it was peanuts), and you get a miniscule cost for the follow-up to a multi-million selling album.

As well as the three band members, Albini and Sigmeth, there were two others present as the session began. Robert Weston was the 'studio maintenance technician' and his girlfriend, Carter Nicole Launt, was the chef. Albini had even more experience at Pachyderm than the house engineer Sigmeth, as Albini had worked there before on PJ Harvey's *Rid Of Me* and The Wedding Present's *Seamonsters*. True to his punk ethics, Albini refused to be listed as a 'producer', insisting that he simply recorded the bands he worked with, not 'produce' them in any shape or form. As he sees himself as a 'recordist' he takes this part of the process very seriously using a myriad of specially positioned microphones – five for the snare drum alone. Once he had been asked to work on *In Utero,* Albini had to go back and listen to Nirvana's previous work. "As absurd as it sounds, at the time I wasn't that familiar with Nirvana's music," admits Albini, "I had heard it at other people's houses. I couldn't count myself a fan at that point and I didn't think particularly that they were the best of the bands of that generation and of that geographic/temporal nexus. I picked up their other records and listened to them. It didn't really change my impression. Their weakest album is obviously *Nevermind*. It's also the least representative of the band as I knew them. As their friends described them, that record was the least like they were. There was a strange intensity to all their records, and there was a sort of subtle perversion to almost everything that came out of Kurt's mouth that I liked. And Dave Grohl is an absolute monster of a drummer, so it's hard to imagine a record with him drumming on that wouldn't at least be fun to listen to."

Albini had also been critical of the band's previous production. Talking about *Nevermind* he commented that "To my ears, it is sort of a standard hack recording that has then been turned into a very, very controlled, compressed radio-friendly mix. That is not, in my opinion, very flattering to a rock band. There was a lot of double-tracked vocals and stuff, which is a hack production technique to make vocals sound special. It sounds like that not because that's the way the band sounds but because that's the way the producer and the remix guy and the record company wanted it to sound." Perhaps he was unaware that at the time it was the way Cobain and co. had wanted *Nevermind* to sound.

Work started in earnest on Monday 15 February and continued for twelve days, concluding on Friday 26. The band would rise around 10 a.m., eat and then start work at midday until midnight with a break for lunch in the afternoon and dinner in the evening. The basic tracking went very well and was completed by the Friday of the first week as most songs were first takes recorded live. Sixteen songs were recorded in this time – twelve for the album ("Gallons Of Rubbing Alcohol Flow Through The Strip" [79] came from the Rio sessions {31}), a couple of b-sides and a couple that were subsequently given away to compilations, "I Hate Myself And Want To Die" [92] and "Sappy" [12]. Cobain had initially been working from a list of eighteen possible songs, so either two were dropped or were recorded but have never surfaced. Steve Albini said that "I'm sure some of that stuff exists as master tapes, but I really don't know." Overdubs were added over the middle weekend in between a trip to see the Cows play in Minneapolis, and mixing was completed from Monday 22 to Friday 26.

One of the reasons for working so swiftly was that the band was very well-rehearsed with these songs. "We just focused intensely on rehearsing," said Novoselic. "We had the songs down tight. So we showed up in Cannon Falls, we set up our gear and we started playing. We tracked almost all the songs in the first two days. Some of the songs, I think over half of the songs, we did first take. We knew that Albini didn't want to deal with some big-time rock band or have to coddle some half-assed musicians. So, we knew how to rock! We'd been rockin' for years, we had our licks down. I remember Albini standing there by the tape machine with his arms folded, bobbing his head and we would just pop 'em out one after the other. 'Well, that sounded good. Let's do this

132

song.'" Cobain's lyrics were also closer to being finished than at many previous sessions. Despite reports that he was again finishing them in the studio, most had been sung live sometime over the previous three years. "They were as prepared as any band I've ever worked with," commented Steve Albini. "On every record there are a few little things that somebody asks you to do that you have to figure out. At the end of "Rape Me" [71], there was meant to be this really extreme vocal. I can't remember which song it was, I think it was the Milkmaid ("Milk It" [76]) song, or whatever it's called, the vocal had to sound more crazy than it had up to that point. So I had to find a way to make the vocal leap forward at the end. Those are things you solve at the moment. But there were no magic tricks. Making records is a very straightforward process, it's not black magic." Albini used the studio's vintage 24-track Neve board for recording, a favorite of the band's, and Cobain played a battered old guitar through a Fender Quad Reverb amp. As things were going so well there was time for a few prank telephone calls – to the likes of Eddie Vedder, Gene Simmons and Evan Dando – and some hi-jinx and practical jokes around the studio.

Courtney Love visited Pachyderm during the second week of recording; however, she and Albini did not get along. "I think it was stressful for Kurt," recalled Carter Nicole Launt. "I think she put a lot of pressure on him and wasn't always as approving of the way the songs were. She was very critical of his work, and actually was kind of confrontational with people there." Though the band was initially happy with the recordings, Love's scepticism proved to be founded and later things had to change. As the session drew to a close Albini recalls, "Everybody was really happy. There was this really serious, really congratulatory sense of accomplishment. I thought they did a great job. I've been asked repeatedly if Kurt was on drugs while I was there. And I've been around people who use dope a lot, and on the one hand I know how they behave and on the other hand I know how deceptive they can be. And my best estimate was that no, he wasn't, he was being very productive. That was a period of his life where he was very focused."

The initial track listing taken from Pachyderm ran as follows – Rape Me [71] / Scentless Apprentice [75] / Heart-Shaped Box [73] / Milk It [76] / Dumb [90] / Radio Friendly Unit Shifter [58] / Very Ape [78] / Pennyroyal Tea [52] / Francis Farmer Will Have Her Revenge on Seattle

[89] / tourette's [72] / Serve the Servants [88] / All Apologies [56] / Moist Vagina [77] / Marigold [91] / Sappy [12] / I Hate Myself And Want To Die [92]. It's likely that the final four tracks on the tape were for demo purposes only.

"It was the easiest recording we've ever done, hands down," said Kurt Cobain. It had been very easy, too easy, and it had been done fast, in hindsight perhaps too fast. When they left Minnesota things seemed fine, but that was all about to change.

Rape Me [71]

The second full studio recording of this track, it having been played with Jack Endino the previous October (see session {29}) but not in Brazil. Then it had been the only completed song, which wasn't surprising as Cobain had actually written it back in 1991 at the end of the *Nevermind* sessions. Some analysts viewed it as a response to "Polly" [11], only this time from the victim's, not the rapist's, perspective. More likely though it is a response to "Smells Like Teen Spirit" [59] and the domino-like media effect it had on Cobain's life – even the opening riff is a parody of his most famous song and it follows the trademark quiet verse/loud chorus dynamic. The line "My favorite inside source" refers to anonymous comments quoted in major media outlets about Courtney Love's drug use while pregnant, supposedly from someone close to the band.

The initial session tapes from Pachyderm had this as the lead-off track, which indicates that maybe the band had pencilled it in as the album opener, though by the time it had been re-sequenced it was in the middle of the pack. Obviously the title of this song caused some controversy and US retail giants Wal-Mart and K-Mart threatened to ban the album from their stores. Geffen got around the problem by persuading the band to change the title of this song on the sleeve to "Waif Me". The album was re-issued in America with this alteration in 1994.

Also see sessions {29}, {34}

Scentless Apprentice [75]

This track was possibly a sign of where the band would have been heading in future years. Unlike the previous routine of Cobain sketching

134

out a song and then showing it to the others, this one was worked up as a trio in the practice room and all three take co-credits for writing the music. It was also much more of a noise fest than most of the tracks on *Nevermind* had been and fits in well with typical Steve Albini inspired songs. Cobain closely based the lyric on one of his favorite books – Patrick Suskind's novel *Perfume: The Story Of A Murderer* (which had originally been published in Suskind's native German as *Das Parfum* in 1985).

Suskind's book tells the story of a child that has no smell of his own but has an amazing sense of smell which leads him to become an apprentice to a perfumer – hence the title of this song. Many of Cobain's lyrics are direct references to the book – "Like most babies smell like butter", "Every wet nurse refused to feed him" and "I promise not to sell your perfumed secrets" are examples of this. In interviews Cobain discussed how the book's central character had been someone that he had related to in earlier life. "I felt like that guy a lot," he explained, "I just wanted to be as far away from people as I could, their smells disgust me. The scent of human."

Other songs on the album have references to babies and parenthood: "Heart-Shaped Box" [73] "Throw down your umbilical noose", "Radio Friendly Unit Shifter" [58] "All of a sudden my water broke" to name but two. Musically, Dave Grohl's hypnotic drumming leads the track into Cobain's spiralling guitar blasts. The vocals are delivered in a rough growl and are punctuated with impassioned howls of "Go away!"
Also see sessions {30}, {31}

Heart-Shaped Box [73]

As was usual in these Albini sessions, work started in earnest during the early afternoon. Albini was aware of this track, having been sent a rough tape of the Rio sessions in advance of traveling to Minnesota, but by the time Cobain was ready to put down his vocals he'd re-jigged both the lyric and title of this track. As previously referenced, the heart-shaped box in question was a present he'd been sent by Courtney and the line "Forever in debt to your priceless advice" came from a note Cobain had sent to Love sometime earlier.

The song opens with a twice-repeated descending guitar riff before Dave Grohl's drums kick in just before Cobain's almost spoken first verse at 0:11. It begins with a reference to his own star sign (Pisces)

135

while the sonic outline of the song again follows the Pixies' quiet verse/ screamed chorus (with twisted guitar) formula as "Smells Like Teen Spirit" [59] and "Lithium" [45] had done on *Nevermind*. The major departure this time though was the clear effect that becoming a father had had on Cobain as his lyrics touch on such gynaecological topics as a 'broken hymen', 'umbilical noose' and 'baby's breath' – also in keeping with the album cover artwork of body parts and babies. Cobain told Michael Azerrad that the song was about children suffering with cancer: "Every time I see these documentaries or infomercials about the little kids with cancer I just freak out," he said. "It affects me on the highest emotional level, more than anything else on television."

The heart-shaped box could be a metaphor for either Cobain's growing claustrophobia as a high-profile star or a sly comment on his growing drug addictions – or both. When the guitars take off at 0:47 and the suddenly tortured vocals move the song along in a different direction it can catch one off-guard the first time you hear it, but by the second time you are both anticipating and looking forward to it. The sloppy guitar solo that starts at 2:44 was one of the things that was later amended during re-mixing.

After the sessions were done and the band had returned to the west coast it became clear that, although Dave Grohl's relatively restrained drumming and Krist Novoselic's melodic bass line had taken the song to new heights, they weren't happy with the end product. Steve Albini's sparse multi-microphoned recording had not done the song justice and well-respected R.E.M. producer Scott Litt was given the task of remixing this and several other tracks (see session {29}) before the album could be mastered.

In a 2001 *NME* [*New Musical Express*] poll, readers were asked to cast their vote for the best ever Nirvana song and "Heart-Shaped Box" was chosen as a clear winner.

Also see sessions {31}, {35}

Milk It [76]

Another track that concerns itself with bodily fluids and disease. Starting with a discordant arrangement, it becomes a schizophrenic number alternating between gentle noodling and full blown blasts of guitar and screaming with little warning that the changes are about to happen. Cobain reprises some of the lyric from Untitled Song #1 [80] from the Rio sessions (see session {31}) singing "her milk is my shit / My shit is her milk".

Also see session {31}

Dumb [90]
This delicate song had been around for quite a while (three years in fact), but had only previously been worked on in the studio as an instrumental (see session {29}) with Jack Endino. The addition of Kera Schaley's cello adds a sentimental air to the song, but a close listen to the lyrics reveals a dark undercurrent. Cobain seems to be caught between thinking he's actually happy or just stupid before explaining that he has some glue which he is about to inhale and then he'll "float around and hang out on clouds."

Also see session {29}

Radio Friendly Unit Shifter [58]
This track's title was changed at the last moment – advance cassettes had it listed as "What Is Wrong With Me?" – to be used as a sly dig at money-driven label executives. Cobain's *Journals* also have this song titled "4 Month Media Blackout" and "9 Month Media Blackout" and both have slightly differing lyrics. Little of the final lyric alludes to the subject matter of the new title though. Cobain is heard to say, "What's your name, do you like me?" under the opening 23 seconds of squealing guitar work. When the song does burst to life it's clearly not a radio-friendly track at all. Almost five minutes in length it twists and turns but all the time with a pounding beat being kept by Dave Grohl while Krist Novoselic keeps pace with some nifty bass work. Cobain's enunciation is mumbled through most of the verses, only coming to the fore of the mix during the "what is wrong with me" choruses.

Also see sessions {24}, {29}

Very Ape [78]
The working title of "Perky New Wave Number" perfectly sums up this sub-two minute romp. Cobain's driving guitar riff opens proceedings before another eastern-sounding guitar motif is woven across the

137

chugging mix. It's been noted that the line "out of the ground / into the sky" is similar to the line "out of the blue / in to the black" from Neil Young's "My My Hey Hey". The aforementioned Young song also included the lyric "It's better to burn out than fade away" – a line that Cobain would later use in his suicide note.

Despite the promptness of this track, Cobain managed to fit in a short guitar solo (when *In Utero* was re-issued on 180g vinyl this track featured, for some unknown reason, a longer guitar solo) with two verses and an outro section.

Also see sessions {31}, {32}

Pennyroyal Tea [52]

Another song pulled from the depths of Cobain's song writing catalog, this track had first been played live back in April 1991 and was possibly several months old at that point. Despite the fact that Cobain had written some words for the song initially, the band recording with Jack Endino (see session {29}) had only been attempted as an instrumental. The early live versions had two major differences to this released take. The opening line was changed from "I'm on... and Demerol" to "I'm on my time with everyone" and the overall tempo of the song was much slower.

Kurt Cobain used this song to reference another pregnancy issue – this time the question of abortion. Pennyroyal tea was historically used as a herbal remedy for a number of purposes, one of which was to cause a woman to abort her foetus. The drawback was that a near-lethal dose was required to induce the required result. Cobain was fascinated by this rather ironic situation that was a kind of herbal Russian Roulette.

The formulaic quiet verse/loud chorus was again in evidence and no doubt played a part in it being selected for release as a single and for remixing by Scott Litt (see session {35}). Litt removed the sound of Cobain clearing his throat, which was on most versions of *In Utero* and generally 'cleaned' up the mix.

Also see sessions {23}, {29}, {32}, {35}

Frances Farmer Will Have Her Revenge On Seattle [89]

Long before the grunge movement put Seattle in the media spotlight, the city had another tragedy on its hands with actress Frances Farmer. She had started a successful Hollywood movie career in the late 1930s

138

but the pressure of fame led her to a series of drunken scenes which culminated with her own mother having her committed to a Washington State mental institution. After 'treatments' of electric shock therapy she never regained her former self and spent years in and out of hospital. In her autobiography she explained that she'd been raped on an almost nightly basis whilst in the 'care' of the authorities. She died aged fifty-six and hers was a story that Cobain empathized with.

Through the lyric a gravelly-voiced Cobain explains that Farmer will have her revenge on the city that ruined her by causing a volcano to erupt (presumably Mount St Helens, which is under 100 miles from Seattle) – "She'll come back as fire / to burn all the liars / and leave a blanket of ash on the ground." He also made a reference to witch hunts ("In her false witness / We hope you're still with us / To see if they float or drown") which he also did in "Serve The Servants" [88]. This was presumably in connection to how he felt Courtney Love was being treated by the press. They had previously cemented their connections with Farmer when Love had worn one of the actress's dresses at their wedding.

Also see session {29}

tourette's [72]

Tourette's Syndrome is an affliction in which the sufferer cannot control his or her movement and speech and can be prone to involuntarily shouting out obscenities and abuse. The title is very apt as Cobain's vocal delivery could well have been that of a Tourette's sufferer when the song was debuted at the 1992 Reading Festival in England. The tune itself is a ninety-second thrash with Cobain screaming over the top. Not surprisingly the *In Utero* liner notes didn't list the lyrics for this track.

Also see session {29}

Serve The Servants [88]

The eventual choice as the album opener, this track is a relatively straightforward rocker. The caveat is that Cobain sings a blatantly autobiographical lyric addressing his own mythmaking ("That legendary divorce is such a bore") his family ("I tried hard to have a father / But instead I had a dad / I just want you to know that / I don't hate you anymore"), the treatment of Courtney Love ("If she floats than she is

139

not / A witch like we had thought"), and his elevation to a superstar ("Teenage angst has paid off well / Now I'm bored and old"). Quite heavy going for an opening song, but nobody said this was going to be an easy album; quite the reverse.

This is the first known studio attempt at this track which contains a melodic guitar line and tight rhythm work from Novoselic and Grohl. Cobain's lyric is well up in the mix and unlike on some other songs on *In Utero*, his enunciation is quite clear emphasizing that, as opposed to the comparatively sparse lyrics on *Nevermind*, *In Utero* was going to showcase the fact that Cobain had lots to say.

Also see session {32}

All Apologies [56]
This track had been kept locked up for over two years since recording it with Craig Montgomery in 1991 (see session {24}). The *In Utero* version kept the same basic structure but removed the earlier version's tambourine and made the guitars a lot heavier. Scott Litt later remixed it for release as a double A-sided single with "Rape Me" [71]. Some reviewers compared this track to an R.E.M. song, with whom Scott Litt had produced five albums, and who Cobain was increasingly mentioning in his interviews.

Also see sessions {24}, {35}

MV [aka Moist Vagina] [77]
Recorded for use as a b-side, this was the second controversially titled song from these sessions. Not surprisingly it soon became known as MV. The track is a slow to mid-paced vehicle for Cobain to shout some explicit lyrics over.

Also see session {31}

Marigold [91]
The only Dave Grohl composition to see the light of day as a Nirvana track, this was released as a b-side to "Heart-Shaped Box" [73]. Grohl had written the song (and recorded it as a solo project) back in 1990. On this version he plays drums, sings and probably plays guitar, as it's thought that Kurt Cobain didn't take part on this track at all. It is a slow semi-ballad, the type of which would appear on several Foo Fighters' albums in later years.

140

Sappy [12]

This was far from the first time that Nirvana tried to record this track. The only difference here is that the recording was a little bit tighter, the vocal was spot on and the guitar solo was well planned out.

Also see sessions {5}, {16}, {26}

I Hate Myself And Want To Die [92]

Initially written as "Two Bass Kid", because the final title was going to be used to name the album. Eventually the track was given to a Beavis and Butt-head compilation. This could actually have been a pretty good single, but the band obviously didn't rate it that highly and never played it live. The grinding melody picks up after a short shot of feedback and some studio chuckling. When the track breaks down at 1:30 Cobain can just about be heard reading out one of Jack Handy's Deep Thoughts from the *Saturday Night Live* TV show.

Also see session {31}

Heart-Shaped Box

1993
7" vinyl
Heart-Shaped Box [73] / Marigold [91]
Geffen GFS54 UK
Heart-Shaped Box [73] / Marigold [91]
Geffen GES19191   Germany   red vinyl
12" vinyl
Heart-Shaped Box [73] / Gallons Of Rubbing Alcohol Flow
Through The Strip [79]
DGC PROA4558   US   promo
Heart-Shaped Box [73] / Milk It [76] / Marigold [91]
Geffen GFST54   UK

Cassette
Heart-Shaped Box [73] / Milk It [76] / Marigold [91]
Geffen GFSC54   UK
Heart-Shaped Box [73] / Milk It [76] / Marigold [91]
Geffen GEFD218449   Australia
CD
Heart-Shaped Box [73]
DGC PROCD4545   US   promo
Heart-Shaped Box [73]
DGC GED21849   UK   promo
Heart-Shaped Box [73] / Milk It [76] / Marigold [91]
Geffen GFSTD54   UK
Heart-Shaped Box [73] / Milk It [76] / Marigold [91]
Geffen GEFCS19191   Australia
Heart-Shaped Box [73] / Milk It [76] / Marigold [91]
Geffen GED21856   France   card sleeve
Heart-Shaped Box [73] / Milk It [76] / Marigold [91]
Geffen MVCG13008   Japan

Session number

{35}

Venue: Bad Animals Studio, Seattle
Date: May 1993
Producer: Scott Litt
Players: Kurt Cobain (guitar, vocals), Krist Novoselic (bass), Dave
    Grohl (drums)

Tracks recorded:	Available on:
All Apologies [56a]	*In Utero*, All Apologies single
Heart-Shaped Box [73a]	*In Utero*, Heart-Shaped Box single, *Nirvana*
Pennyroyal Tea [52a]	Pennyroyal Tea (recalled) single, *In Utero* (post-1994 Wal-Mart and K-Mart versions), *Nirvana*

This, possibly the most controversial Nirvana session, was in fact not even a
'real' session. The lead up to, and fall-out from, this brief liaison with R.E.M.
producer Scott Litt produced more column inches than any other single
Nirvana session. Though things had been fine when everyone departed
Minnesota, Nirvana claimed that the songs sounded different once they got
back home. By April, reports were leaking out that Geffen and the band's
management were unhappy with the way *In Utero* sounded. Chicago writer
Greg Kot found himself in the middle of the storm after the publication of
his article in the *Chicago Tribune* headed "Record Label Finds Little Bliss
in Nirvana's Latest." The general slant of the article was that members of
the Geffen hierarchy wanted the album re-mixed. There then followed a
series of phone calls between Cobain, Albini and Novoselic. Each time the
band members said they thought it should be re-worked, each time Albini
said it was as good as it was going to get. Albini had earlier insisted that
any post-production should only be carried out by himself. By saying he
couldn't improve it, he left an opening to bring in someone fresh.

    "I got a call from a journalist in Chicago," says Albini "saying that
Geffen's publicity department had gotten in touch with him and had

144

told him off the record that the next Nirvana record was awful and that it was all my fault. That it was unreleasable and what did I have to say about that? What I said was that Nirvana made the record they wanted to make and the record company could stick it up their ass... ." Krist Novoselic also called him and said: "'Y'know, it just doesn't sound as good as it did in Minnesota.' And I reiterated that I felt like we'd gotten the full monty, I felt like we'd gotten everything we could out of the master that we could when we were in Minnesota. And that I was still of the opinion that we shouldn't tamper with it."

Initially the band had also rejected any suggestions that they should 'tamper' with it. "I know for a while there was a reactionary element to our mindset," says Novoselic. "I know for a while I felt like we shouldn't touch it as a point of principle. But that's not very rational." As the plot started to thicken, rumours of Nirvana buckling under label pressure were circulating. This led to the highly unusual step of Geffen putting out a press release and taking out full-page advertisements in the likes of *Billboard* that listed Cobain as saying, "There has been no pressure from our record label to change the tracks we did with Albini. We have 100% control of our music!"

"The simple truth is, as I have assured the members of Nirvana and their management all along, we will release whatever record the band delivers to us," said Ed Rosenblatt (Geffen's president). "When the band has finished their album, to their satisfaction, they will turn it in and we'll give it a release date. It's that boring and straightforward."

Whatever their reasons, the band went ahead with the remixing of three of the songs (though initially only two of them went on the album ("All Apologies" [56a] and "Heart-Shaped Box" [73a]) and putting the whole album through a rigorous mastering stage with seasoned veteran Bob Ludwig. Speaking about Albini, Cobain said, "If he would have had his way, the record would have turned out way raunchier than it did. He wanted to mix the vocals at an unnecessarily low level. That's not the way we sound good."

Of course, Albini disagreed with this and was unhappy with the extra work that was carried out on his recordings: "For my own personal satisfaction, because I worked on that record and felt close to it, I felt like it sounded better before any tinkering was done. When they sent me a copy I put it on and instantly I was disappointed in the mastering." He goes

145

on to explain: "The dynamic range was narrowed, the stereo width was narrowed, there was a lot of mid-range boost EQ added, and the overall sound quality was softened. And the bass response was compromised to make it sound more consistent on radio and home speaker. But the way I would describe it in non-technical terms is that they fucked it up."

All Apologies [56a]
Krist Novoselic explained that, "I just didn't think the bass was loud enough. I'm trying to watch our idiosyncrasies, but I really didn't think the bass was loud enough." Apart from a couple of minor changes and a general 'cleaning up' of the sound, this track didn't undergo that drastic a transformation. Like the other two remixed tracks, below, this was later issued as a single.
Also see sessions {24}, {34}

Heart-Shaped Box [73a]
This track underwent the most radical changes. First up, Litt added backing vocals, then he removed the original guitar solo effects that Albini had added. "In the old versions, Kurt and Steve put this effect on the guitar solo which I absolutely hated," said Novoselic. "I was arguing with the guys about it. So when we reached the end of the recording people were talking about remixing a couple of bits, and I was like, 'Well yeah, can we remix that guitar solo and take that effect out of it!' The more you listen to things over and over again you can get more and more critical and you start to think 'Yeah, we can do a little better on these couple of songs.'" Cobain also added a new acoustic guitar part giving a final effect that was masterful and the track became a classic of the genre. When taken alongside the noise-fests on the album such as "Scentless Apprentice" [88] and "Radio Friendly Unit Shifter" [58] it becomes clearer that "Heart-Shaped Box" [73] is both the high point of Nirvana's short career and also the beginning of the end, the last of the trademark pop-tinged hard rock classics that they would release.
Also see sessions {31}, {34}

Pennyroyal Tea [52a]
Again, the remixing on this track was relatively straightforward. Scott Litt erased the sound of Cobain clearing his throat before he starts

singing, then he adjusted the bass levels, brought the backing vocals forward and made the whole thing sound a little more polished, which certainly wasn't the intention of the band when they first started recording the album – they had wanted an abrasive punk sound.

Also see sessions {23}, {29}, {32}, {34}

All Apologies

1993
7" vinyl
All Apologies [56] / Rape Me [71] / MV [77]
Geffen GFS66   UK
12" vinyl
All Apologies [56] / Rape Me [71] / MV [77]
Geffen GFST66   UK   with 2 art prints
Cassette
All Apologies [56] / Rape Me [71] / MV [77]
Geffen GFSC66   UK
All Apologies [56] / Rape Me [71] / MV [77]
Geffen GEFCS 21880   Australia

148

CD

All Apologies [56] / Rape Me [71] / MV [77]
Geffen GFSTD66   UK
All Apologies [56] / Rape Me [71] / MV [77]
Geffen GED21880   Germany
All Apologies [56] / Rape Me [71] / MV [77]
Geffen GED21897   France
All Apologies [56] / Rape Me [71] / MV [77]
Geffen GEFDM 21880   Australia
All Apologies [56] / Rape Me [71] / MV [77]
Geffen MVCG13011   Australia

1994
CD

All Apologies [U56] / All Apologies [56]
DGC PROCD4618   US   promo
All Apologies [56]
DCC PROCD4581   US   promo
All Apologies [56] / Rape Me [71]
DCC PROCCD4582   US   promo
All Apologies [56] / Rape Me [71] / MV [77]
MCA MVCG13011   Japan
All Apologies [U56]
Geffen GED21858   Spain   promo

Pennyroyal Tea [52]

1994
7" vinyl
Pennyroyal Tea [52a] / Where Did You Sleep Last Night [U101]
Geffen no cat. number　　UK　　test pressing limited
to 10 copies
Cassette
Pennyroyal Tea [52a] / I Hate Myself And Want To Die [92] /
Where Did You Sleep Last Night [U101]
Geffen DGCC24705　　Germany
CD
Pennyroyal Tea [52a] / I Hate Myself And Want To Die [92] /
Where Did You Sleep Last Night [U101]
Geffen DGCD24705　　Germany
Pennyroyal Tea [52a]
Geffen NIRPRO UK promo

Nirvana opened 1994 with their final US gigs near to home in the Northwest. Shows in Oregon, over the Canadian border in British Columbia, in Spokane, WA and finally a two-night stand in Seattle completed this leg of the tour. At the end of the month they booked in for three days at Robert Lang's Studio with Adam Kasper who'd assisted Scott Litt on the *In Utero* remixing (see session {37}). Two days later they set off for the European leg of the *In Utero* tour. Portugal, Spain, France, Switzerland, Italy, Slovenia and Germany were all visited in a four-week span. At the end of this stint, the gig planned for March 2 in Munich was cancelled when doctors told Cobain to take several weeks off because he had bronchitis and laryngitis. There had been a planned break penciled in the tour for soon afterwards anyway, so no one was too worried and everyone expected the tour to pick up again on March 11.

During this break Kurt Cobain went to Rome to meet Courtney Love and Frances Bean. It was here that on March 4 he was rushed to hospital after overdosing on Rohypnol and champagne and slipping into a coma. He managed to survive but was hospitalized for the next four days before flying back to Seattle a further four days later. What happened over the next month has been open to much conjecture

150

and will probably never be fully known. It is generally accepted that Cobain spent his time recording in the basement of his house on Lake Washington Boulevard with Eric Erlandson from Hole and Pat Smear. He pulled out of a planned session that Michael Stipe had arranged in Atlanta and spent the rest of the month occasionally working on songs at home while taking as many drugs as he could. On April 5, 1994, Kurt Cobain shot himself at his home: he was discovered by an electrician three days later.

In the aftermath of Cobain's suicide, the Scott Litt remix of "Pennyroyal Tea" [52a] single that had been planned for a European release in May 1994 was withdrawn, though some copies filtered out and are now highly collectable. One of the bonus tracks was to have been "I Hate Myself And Want To Die" [92]. Soon afterwards *In Utero* went triple platinum.

Session number

{36}

Venue: home recording, Seattle, WA
Date: early 1994
Producer: none
Players: Kurt Cobain (guitar, vocals)

Tracks recorded:	Available on:
You Know You're Right [93]	*With The Lights Out* box set

Few singer-songwriters have been able to convey the sense of menace and foreboding that Kurt Cobain could with just an acoustic guitar. Perhaps it is because we know what happened soon afterwards, but this acoustic demo of the last Nirvana song to be released has a haunting quality. Because the lyrics vary from the band version issued on the *Nirvana* compilation, it's thought that this take might be much earlier than officially dated.

Also see sessions {37}, {38}, {41}

Session number

{37}

Venue: Robert Lang Studios, Seattle, WA
Date: January 28 and 29, 1994
Producer: Adam Kasper
Players: Krist Novoselic (bass), Dave Grohl (drums), Earnie
    Bailey (theremin)

Tracks recorded:	Available on:
Exhausted [103]	not officially released
Gas Chamber [107]	not officially released
Big Me [116]	not officially released
You Know You're Right [93]	*Nirvana*
Butterfly [94]	unconfirmed
Skid Marks [95]	unconfirmed

For the first two days of this session Kurt Cobain was absent, so Krist
Novoselic and Dave Grohl spent the time working on some of Grohl's
compositions and cover versions. On the first day they tried calling
Cobain at home on several occasions but got no answer. They carried on
regardless and tracked a few songs. Nirvana's guitar technician, Earnie
Bailey, was also present at the session and recalled his involvement
to Rasmus Holmen in 2002: "It [the studio] was built into the ground
below a house in a residential neighborhood. Much more than a
basement studio, this place went down very deep below the ground. He
[Grohl] played drums while I played an old theremin device through an
Echoplex tape echo machine."

The second day was a similar scenario as Cobain again failed to
appear. This time though they didn't try calling, they just worked on a
few things and then went home. Pat Smear, who was in Los Angeles
at the time, waiting for the touring to resume, has a recording of these
takes. "I've got a tape with a few other songs from the same session,"
he says, "I haven't listened to it for years and I don't remember the
songs, but I believe they were Krist and Dave songs without Kurt."

Session number

{38}

Venue: Robert Lang Studios, Seattle, WA
Date: January 30, 1994
Producer: Adam Kasper
Players: Kurt Cobain (guitar, vocals), Krist Novoselic (bass), Dave
        Grohl (drums)

Tracks recorded:	Available on:
You Know You're Right [93]	*Nirvana*
Butterfly [94]	**unconfirmed**
Skid Marks [95]	**unconfirmed**

The existence of up to 8 other tracks from this session remain
unconfirmed.

Surprisingly on the third day, Kurt Cobain arrived at the sessions. Over
a ten hour span the trio tried as many as eleven songs either side of
going out together for pizza. Most of the tracks they worked on were
fragments and jams; Adam Kasper recalls that, "I think they were trying
to open up to more band writing." Only one song was completed – "You
Know You're Right" [93]. The songs that did get an airing during this
final day in the studio seem to be split between Grohl and Cobain's
songs. Cobain played drums on the Grohl efforts which were most likely
the three from the previous two days: "Gas Chamber", which was a
cover of an Angry Samoans' song, "Exhausted" and "Big Me".

"Kurt was very quiet and reserved during much of the recording,"
says Earnie Bailey, "We all took a break and went out for pizza several
blocks away, and Kurt's mood changed to upbeat for a while, then it
was back down soon after we returned to the studio."

Three other songs have since been mentioned by Courtney Love and
it's possible that one or more of them were attempted at this session.
They have been named as "The Son" [96] (Love: "Magical."), "Ivy
League" [97] (Love: "Sick.") and the Cobain/Love co-composition
"Stinking Of You" [98] (Love: "Really cute and Breeder-y."). Whatever

was recorded, it ended up in Krist Novoselic's basement, because he took the master tapes and left them there for some years. "I kept it safe," says Novoselic, "I kept it like a secret."

You Know You're Right [93]

How appropriate that the 'great lost Nirvana song' should have a slow, quiet verse and a fast, loud chorus. Along with other Cobain classics ("Smells Like Teen Spirit" [59] and "Heart-Shaped Box" [73] to name but two) Kurt let the tension build through the verse, only to explode in the chorus – this time with the elongated enunciation of "pain".

As the only song that was completed in this last session, it was another case of Cobain finishing lyrics at the last moment and even the title hadn't been set. "We bombed it together fast," recalls Krist Novoselic, "Kurt had the riff and brought it in, and we put it down. We Nirvanaized it." Dave Grohl remembers that they had worked on it at sound-checks through the last tour and that it was "Something to take our mind off playing 'Smells Like Teen Spirit' every night." Touring guitarist Pat Smear revealed that, "I got a cassette afterwards and Kurt said that I could put my part on later. But we were back on tour and then things got wacky, well, you know the rest. Who knows, maybe he was just being nice so I wouldn't feel left out."

At the session they needed just two practice runs to tighten it up and then they cut the master take in a single run-through. Cobain then agreed to do a rare thing – four vocal takes – before finishing it off with a final guitar overdub. Then it was time to go out for pizza.

For a long time no one discussed, or was even aware of the existence of this song, outside of a few people close to the band. Hole did perform a version of it called "You've Got No Right" for their 1995 *MTV Unplugged* performance and then a live version started doing the rounds under the title of "Autopilot". This erroneous title came from a show in Chicago on October 23, 1993. During the encore Dave Grohl announced, "This is our last song it's called 'All Apologies'" as he thought that was what they were going to play. However they played an embryonic version of "You Know You're Right" [93] but the bootleggers mis-heard him and thought he'd said "Autopilot" not "All Apologies". The live version had many different lyrics, though most of them are semi-mumbled and very difficult to figure out.

In the late 1990s, as stories of the long-awaited box set began to circulate, it emerged that "You Know You're Right" [93] was the last completed studio track and it started to take on mythical proportions. It finally leaked onto the internet a few weeks before the Nirvana compilation hit the shops and then everyone knew that it was an emotionally powerful song. It opens with a gentle guitar knell until, at 0:12, an ominous bass and drum combination kicks in. Cobain's lyric for the first verse sounds like it could take off at any moment as he starts every line with "I". He does break out briefly before the band regain their composure for a second verse which he ends with a sarcastic "Things have never been so swell / I have never felt this well" and then the screamed chorus takes off. Adam Kasper had double-tracked Cobain's voice, and a combination of this effect, the posthumous release and the style of the song makes for some haunting listening. The song ends with each instrument falling away in the mix, first the voice, then the bass and guitar leaving just the drums and cymbals to slowly come to a stop like a clock winding down.

"That was strange," says Dave Grohl, "driving through Los Angeles and seeing all these posters saying 'The new Nirvana single' – I had a chuckle. I almost imagined that being another band.

Also see sessions {36}, {37}, {41}

Butterfly [94]
The second known song from this final studio session has been revealed as this mainly instrumental number. "That's a beautiful song," says Krist Novoselic. It's also known that two demos have been recorded – one is a Cobain solo recording, another is a four-track demo with Cobain on drums and vocals, Pat Smear on guitar and Eric Erlandson on bass which was recorded at Cobain's house. Whether this was played at the session is unconfirmed.

Also see session {37}

Skid Marks [95]
This is a downbeat, mostly instrumental, track with only the title repeatedly shouted out for the chorus. Like much of the unreleased Cobain catalog, the lyrics were far from complete and, as often happened, he would probably only have completed them shortly before recording the song for real.

Also see session {37}

156

Session number

{39}

Venue: Pavilhao Dramatico, Cascais, Portugal
Date: February 5, 1994
Producer: none
Players: Kurt Cobain (guitar, vocals), Krist Novoselic (bass),
      Dave Grohl (drums), Pat Smear (guitar), Melora Creager
      (cello)

Tracks recorded:	Available on:
Jesus Doesn't Want Me For A Sunbeam [108]	*With The Lights Out* box set

This Vaselines cover was recorded live during a soundcheck the day before their show in Lisbon. The strings really add to the delicate guitar parts and subtle percussion, while Kurt Cobain gives a wonderful vocal performance.

157

Session number

{40}

Venue: Kurt Cobain's house, 171 Lake Washington
   Boulevard, Seattle, WA
Date: probably between March 12 and 25, 1994
Producer: none
Players: Kurt Cobain (guitar, vocals, drums), Pat Smear
   (guitar), Eric Erlandson (bass)

Tracks recorded:	Available on:
Do, Re, Mi [99]	*With The Lights Out* box set
Clean Up Before She Comes [10]	not officially released

The existence of other songs from this session remain unconfirmed.

Pat Smear has spoken of some of the impromptu sessions that took place at the Cobain residence in 1994. He explained that, "There was some jamming and some 4-tracks made. Kurt played drums and sang, Eric played bass and I played guitar." Not exactly an in-depth breakdown of what happened but it does confirm that Cobain had been drumming on at least some of these last sessions. How many times this trio played together or if any other players participated is unknown.

Cobain was still making solo home demos throughout this period and had plans to work with Michael Stipe of R.E.M. at some point in the future, though this got no further than the tentative stage. As well as a band version of "Dough, Ray And Me" [99] he also recorded a solo acoustic demo that Jim Barber has played to at least one journalist. It's also been discussed that "Clean Up Before She Comes" [10] (see session {5}) had been resurrected in 1994 and of course any number of the later named, unreleased tracks could have been worked on – including "Butterfly" [94], "Skid Marks" [95], "The Son" [96], "Ivy League" [97], "Stinking Of You" [98] and "Opinion" [102].

Do, Re, Mi [aka Dough, Ray And Me, aka Me And My IV] [99]
"The perfect Alice In Chains song." That's how Kurt Cobain described this song to Courtney Love, but others that have heard the track differ in their opinion of it. Chicago writer Jim DeRogatis was allowed to listen to the track by Love and he wrote about it in both *Spin* magazine and the *Chicago Sun Times*. He compared it to "About A Girl" [14] and claimed it was another Beatles-like tune.

"The sound quality is sketchy, to say the least," wrote DeRogatis, "but as soon as that famously gruff voice kicks in, it's vital, entrancing, and impossible to ignore. In addition to an endearingly rough guitar solo, its other outstanding feature is the moaned/whined/chanted repetition of 'Dough/Ray/Me, Do/Re/Mi' over and over during a long and climactic finale. Deciphering Cobain's cryptic lyrics during a first listen is difficult at best, but I manage to scribble several lines in my notebook: 'If I may/ If I might/Wake me up/See me... If I may/Cold as ice/I only have/Sue me.' Sue me? Sue me? I swear I heard him sing, 'Sue me." It's also been reported that Courtney Love found a napkin with some lyrics and the title "Me and My IV", hence the alternate title for this track. The world at large was allowed to make up their own opinion when it was included on the *With The Lights Out* box set in 2004, but DeRogatis had summed up things pretty well.

Session number

{41}

Venue: Los Angeles, CA
Date: July 2001
Executive Producer: James Barber
Engineer: Adam Kasper
Also present: Krist Novoselic, Dave Grohl

Tracks remastered:	Available on:
You Know You're Right [93]	*Nirvana*
About A Girl [14]	*Nirvana*
Been A Son [40]	*Nirvana*
Sliver [50]	*Nirvana*
Smells Like Teen Spirit [59]	*Nirvana*
Come As You Are [60]	*Nirvana*
Lithium [45]	*Nirvana*
In Bloom [48]	*Nirvana*
Heart-Shaped Box [73]	*Nirvana*
Pennyroyal Tea [52]	*Nirvana*
Rape Me [71]	*Nirvana*
Dumb [90]	*Nirvana*
All Apologies [U56]	*Nirvana*
The Man Who Sold The World [U109]	*Nirvana*
Where Did You Sleep Last Night [U101]	*Nirvana*
Something In The Way [U63]	*Nirvana*

While much legal wrangling surrounded the Nirvana catalog, it slowly reached the point where fans could hear most of the unreleased material that had been the center of so much speculation since Kurt Cobain's death. The first signs that this was starting to happen were noticed in the summer of 2001 when "You Know You're Right" [93] was finally mixed in Los Angeles. "When we first started mixing that song," says Dave Grohl. "It was definitely strange for Krist and me to be in the

160

studio hearing that song again." The song didn't need much work doing to it as Krist Novoselic said: "Just a little bit of compression, maybe a little bit of reverb. We knew what Nirvana should sound like."

"That song has an air of darkness to it," states Grohl, "and it was difficult for Krist and I to sit in and mix. It kind of brings you back to that place in the spring of 1994 when everything didn't seem all right." What else there is to follow has been widely reported and discussed. Sources close to the band claim that Cobain left between 100 and 120 tapes containing demos and fragments of around 200 songs, though only a dozen or less can be considered finished articles. Therefore it was something of a disappointment that the 2004 box set, *With The Lights Out*, contained only a minimal amount of completely new songs, the highlights being a handful of home demos. There was a lot of unheard music though as around 30 takes had eluded the bootleggers until then.

The first release to include 'previously' unheard recordings was the autumn 2002 release of the *Nirvana* compilation. Opening with the long awaited "You Know You're Right" [93] it included a further fourteen tracks (fifteen if you bought the double LP or Japanese CD versions) drawn from the three studio albums, the *Unplugged* session (see session {T8}) and beyond. All of the previously released songs had undergone remastering to allow listeners new sonic insights into familiar songs.

"About A Girl" [14] is the sole track taken from *Bleach*, "Been A Son" [40] is the *Blew* EP version produced by Steve Fisk in 1989 (see session {15}) and "Sliver" [50] is the single/*Incesticide* version. Both *Nevermind* and *In Utero* have four tracks included – the former has each of its singles included and the latter's Scott Litt remix of "Pennyroyal Tea" [52a] is chosen. The selection is rounded out with tracks from the *MTV Unplugged* album.

161

Nirvana

1992
Double LP

Universal 493523-1	UK*
Geffen 493523-1	Europe
CD	
DGC 0694935072	US
Geffen 493523-2	UK
Geffen UICY-1140	Japan*
Geffen 493 523-2	Australia
Polydor Nirvana1#1	Spain	promo**

Track listing:

You Know You're Right [93] / About A Girl [14] / Been A Son [40] / Sliver [50] / Smells Like Teen Spirit [59] / Come As You Are [60] / Lithium [45] / In Bloom [48] / Heart-Shaped Box [73] / Pennyroyal Tea [52] / Rape Me [71] / Dumb [90] / All Apologies [U56] / The Man Who Sold The World [U109] / Where Did You Sleep Last Night [U101]

* includes an extra track, Something In The Way [U63], before The Man Who Sold The World [U109]

** = six track sampler containing: You Know You're Right [93] / Come As You Are [60] / Pennyroyal Tea [52] / About A Girl [14] / Smells Like Teen Spirit [59] / Where Did You Sleep Last Night [U101]

Packaging notes:

A simple black sleeve with silver writing, by long-time Nirvana designer Robert Fisher, sets the tone for this stylish package. Black and white photography throughout nicely complements the reverential liner notes by *Rolling Stone's* David Fricke.

Nirvana reviews:

Q: "Nirvana were smart and literate in a way that did anything but preclude mass appeal." 5/5

Rolling Stone: "Boiling down three albums to one feels beside the point." 4/4

NME: "A touching affirmation that something that's been sold and sold again can endure." 9/10

You Know You're Right

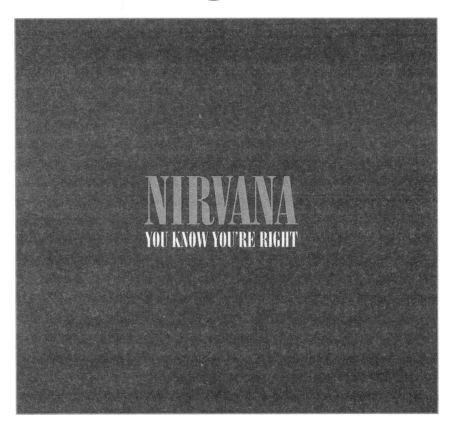

2002
CD
You Know You're Right [93]
DGC   INTR-10853-2   US
You Know You're Right [93]
Universal   CD-R Acetate   Japan
You Know You're Right [93]
Geffen PRO-CD-4835   France
You Know You're Right [93]
Geffen 01141-2   Mexico
All above are single track promo CDs

With The Lights Out

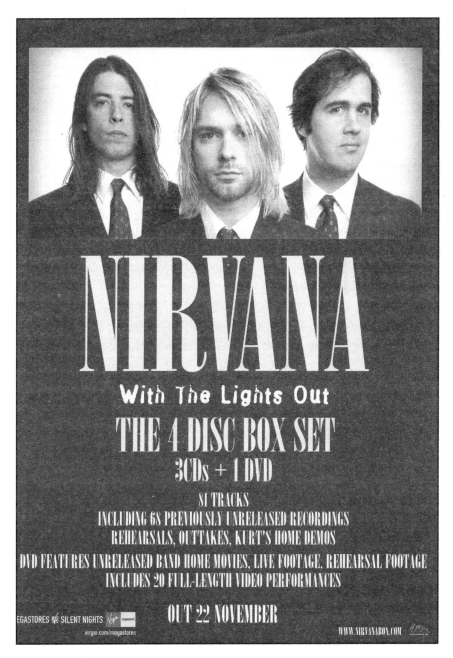

2004
3CD + DVD box set

Geffen B000372700	UK	PAL format
Geffen 602498648384	UK	PAL format
Geffen B0003727-00	US	NTSC format

Disc 1

Heartbreaker / Anorexorcist / White Lace And Strange / Help Me, I'm Hungry / Mrs. Butterworth / If You Must / Pen Cap Chew / Downer / Floyd The Barber / Raunchola / Beans / Don't Want It All / Clean Up Before She Comes / Polly / About A Girl / Blandest / Dive / They Hung Him On A Cross / Grey Goose / Ain't It A Shame / Token Eastern Song / Even in His Youth / Polly

Disc 2

Opinion / Lithium / Been A Son / Sliver / Where Did You Sleep Last Night / Pay To Play / Here She Comes Now / Drain You / Aneurysm / Smells Like Teen Spirit / Breed / Verse Chorus Verse / Old Age / Endless, Nameless / Dumb / D-7 / Oh, The Guilt / Curmudgeon / Return of the Rat / Smells Like Teen Spirit

Disc 3

Rape Me / Rape Me / Scentless Apprentice / Heart-Shaped Box / I Hate Myself And Want To Die / Milk It / MV / Gallons Of Rubbing Alcohol Flow Through The Strip / The Other Improv / Serve The Servants / Very Ape / Pennyroyal Tea / Marigold / Sappy / Jesus Doesn't Want Me For A Sunbeam / Do Re Mi / You Know You're Right / All Apologies

DVD

Love Buzz / Scoff / About A Girl / Big Long Now / Immigrant Song / Spank Thru / Hairspray Queen / School / Mr Moustache / Big Cheese / Sappy / In Bloom / School / Love Buzz / Pennyroyal Tea / Smells Like Teen Spirit / Territorial Pissings / Jesus Doesn't Want Me For A Sunbeam / Talk To Me / Seasons In The Sun

Sliver
(Best Of The Box)

2005
CD
Geffen B0005617-02   US
Geffen 602498867181   UK
Spank Thru / Heartbreaker / Mrs. Butterworth / Floyd The Barber /
Clean Up Before She Comes / About A Girl / Blandest / Ain't It A Shame
/ Sappy / Opinion / Lithium / Sliver / Smells Like Teen Spirit / Come As
You Are / Old Age / Oh, The Guilt / Rape Me / Rape Me (demo) / Heart-
Shaped Box / Do Re Mi / You Know You're Right / All Apologies

Radio and TV Sessions 1987–1994

Right from the very beginning, Nirvana played radio sessions. In fact the first one came just weeks after the first show that Kurt Cobain and Krist Novoselic played together and they soon became semi-regulars on the European session circuit. When the *Incesticide* album was assembled the band chose six tracks from two radio sessions to complete the set. As their career took off the band chose to play more TV shows than radio sessions and on several occasions played whole shows for the cameras. The most famous of these, for MTV's *Unplugged* series, would later be issued as a Nirvana album in its own right.

Session number

{R1}

Venue: KAOS FM, Evergreen State College, Olympia, WA.
Date: May 6, 1987
Show: Free Things Are Cool
Broadcast: live
Presenter: Diana Arens
Players: Kurt Cobain (guitar, vocals), Krist Novoselic (bass),
   Aaron Burckhard (drums)

Tracks recorded:	Available on:
Love Buzz [R27]	not officially released
Floyd The Barber [R17]	not officially released
Downer [R7]	not officially released
Mexican Seafood [R22]	not officially released
White Lace And Strange [R113]	*With The Lights Out* box set
Spank Thru [R5]	not officially released
Anorexorcist [R24]	*With The Lights Out* box set
Hairspray Queen [R19]	not officially released
Pen Cap Chew [R23]	not officially released

Only the second ever recording of any line up of the band in general circulation, this radio session was recorded just six weeks after the band's first show at a house party in Raymond, WA. They wanted to be able to use the session for the purposes of issuing a demo tape and the station wanted to fill some late night air time. A live radio broadcast, even to a limited amount of listeners, must have been a daunting task so early into the band's lifetime and not surprisingly this comes through in the performance.

Love Buzz [R27]
A rather plodding version of what would later be a stand-out live favorite. Cobain has problems with the lyrics, though his guitar playing is pretty good for the most part. Krist Novoselic provides a steady bass line (and

169

a bass solo at 2:20 while Cobain messes with his effects pedal). Aaron Burckhard's drumming is consistent if not spectacular.

Floyd The Barber [R17]

A really heavy, grinding effort which lacks any of the subtleties of the later recorded versions, as the guitars drowned out the vocal through most of the song.

Downer [R7]

After a brief break, Burckhard introduces "Downer" [R7] by playing what sounds like a series of cardboard boxes. He isn't, of course, it's just the lo-fi nature of the equipment and the studio set-up. Cobain's guitar tends to veer towards sounding like a lawnmower at some points (which isn't necessarily a bad thing).

Mexican Seafood [R22]

This is one of the highlights of the short set; the band give a pretty good performance even if Cobain's vocal is a little buried, a little strained and a little eccentric.

White Lace And Strange [R113]

A bizarre choice of cover maybe, but the band had previously played this Thunder And Roses track during their early live shows and they gave it a good thrashing here. In fact, musically it was possibly their best performance of the session.

Spank Thru [R5]

Not the greatest performance of this song by a long way. The vocals are virtually absent from the verse and musically it sounds as though it might all come crashing down at any moment. Sometimes these on-the-edge takes are invigorating, but not this time.

Anorexorcist [R24]

The only known 'studio' recording of this track. A buzz-saw sounding guitar opens the proceedings, before Krist Novoselic's pounding bass pulls the song along into a typical 'grunge' sounding track. It has a couple of pace changes and features a slow section with a painfully howled vocal over the top.

Hairspray Queen [R19]

An indifferent start to this track doesn't bode well for a successful take and this proves to be the case. The band struggles to keep the track going and despite Cobain's acrobatic vocals, the whole thing obviously needed a lot more work before being thrust out on to an unsuspecting population.

Pen Cap Chew [R23]

This was the band's first radio session, and as they had only just started playing as an actual band, it could be said that this session came by a little too early for them. Another poor take closed the session, and it would be hard to spot the band's immense potential at this early stage.

Session number

{R2}

Venue: BBC, Maida Vale Studios, London, England.
Date: October 26, 1989
Show: The John Peel Show
Broadcast: November 22, 1989 and January 22, 1990
Presenter: John Peel
Players: Kurt Cobain (guitar, vocals), Krist Novoselic (bass),
       Chad Channing (drums)

Tracks recorded:	Available on:
Love Buzz [R27a]	not officially released
About A Girl [R14]	not officially released
Polly [R11]	not officially released
Spank Thru [R5a]	not officially released

During the band's first trip to the UK they were immediately invited onto the long running and prestigious *John Peel Show* to record a session. The sessions were usually recorded a week or two before any actual broadcast and then often the songs would be spread out over a week's worth of programs.

Love Buzz [R27]
The difference between this and the take on the KAOS show (session {R1}) is breathtaking. Cobain's vocal is near note perfect, the song moves along at a brisk pace (no doubt helped by the addition of Chad Channing on drums) and musically it is well-honed, as you would expect after two years of touring.

About A Girl [R14]
A clean take which is very close to the *Bleach* version, with just a little more of the drums coming through, making it sound more 'poppy' than the album version.

Polly [R11]
An electric take, but a relatively subdued one, keeping strong melodic line throughout. The song doesn't burst out at all, unlike other electric versions that take off on the later choruses.

Spank Thru [R5]
Again the percussion comes through loud and Cobain's vocals are buried at some points. The overall mix is a little tinny, though the actual performance is fairly strong.

Session number

{R3}

Venue: VPRO Studios, Hilversum, Holland.
Date: November 1, 1989
Players: Kurt Cobain (guitar, vocals), Krist Novoselic (bass),
          Chad Channing (drums)

Tracks recorded:	Available on:
About A Girl [R14a]	**not officially released**
Dive [R39]	**not officially released**
Love Buzz [R27b]	**not officially released**

The second radio session of the trip saw Nirvana make their Dutch debut in front of a studio audience. The tape of this session has subsequently been removed from the VPRO archive and no one is claiming responsibility for its current whereabouts. All three tracks have turned up on various bootleg recordings which seem to have been taken from recordings made by fans of the original radio broadcast.

Dive [R39]

Kurt Cobain asks: "What are we going to play? Have we decided?" Someone calls out "Dive" and Cobain agrees, "let's play 'Dive' then 'About A Girl'." "Dive" [R39] comes across as a typical reading of the track, without too much passion or energy, though Cobain does give his usual 101% on the chorus.

About A Girl [R14a]

"About A Girl" [R14a] is a slightly beefed-up take with a strong drum and bass combo to carry along Cobain's rough vocal performance.

Love Buzz [R27b]

Another radio session, another take of "Love Buzz" [R27b]. Again, a competent session with some nice guitar work and a clean vocal performance.

Session number

{R4}

Venue: KAOS FM, Evergreen State College, Olympia, WA.
Date: September 25, 1990
Show: Boy Meets Girl
Broadcast: live
Presenter: Calvin Johnson
Players: Kurt Cobain (guitar, vocals), Calvin Johnson (vocals)

Tracks recorded:	Available on:
Opinion [R102]	*With The Lights Out* box set

| Lithium [R45] | *With The Lights Out* box set |
| Been A Son [R40] | *With The Lights Out* box set |

This was the day that Dave Grohl passed his audition for Nirvana. That evening Kurt Cobain headed over to Olympia where he dropped in on Calvin Johnson's show with some of his new compositions. During the show Cobain would play versions of the then-unreleased "Lithium" [R45], "Polly" [R11a], "Dumb" [R90], a cover of The Wipers' "D-7" [R100] and "Opinion" [R102]. "I just wrote most of the lyrics this evening," Cobain told the host, "While I was driving with one foot. I wanted it to be as spontaneous as possible, you know? I just thought I'd just come here and say 'Hi'."

Opinion [R102]

While most unreleased Nirvana songs have titles that have been, at best, guessed at or, at worst, completely made up, this one is known because Cobain introduced it as such on this radio broadcast. "Congratulations you have won / It's a year's subscription of bad puns" is the opening line of this acoustic take. The song is a fairly fast melodic tune containing two four-line verses (the first verse is repeated later to give a third verse) and a chorus that is simply "My opinions" repeated four times. At the end of the song Cobain asks, "Don't you think that song sounds like [the Beatles'] Taxman?" It doesn't.

Session number

{R5}

Venue: BBC, Maida Vale Studios, London, England.
Date: October 21, 1990
Show: The John Peel Show
Broadcast: November 3, 1990
Presenter: John Peel
Players: Kurt Cobain (guitar, vocals), Krist Novoselic (bass), Dave
       Grohl (drums)

Tracks recorded:	Available on:
D-7 [R100a]	not officially released
D-7 [R100]	**Lithium single, *With The Lights Out* box set**
Molly's Lips [R104]	*Incesticide*
Son Of A Gun [R105]	*Incesticide*
Turnaround [R106]	*Incesticide*

For their second Peel show, the band decided to run through a set of covers. The Wipers' "D-7" [R100], Devo's "Turnaround" [R106] and a pair of tracks by the Vaselines, "Molly's Lip" [R104] and "Son Of A Gun" [R105]. The final three of these songs were considered good enough to be later issued on the *Incesticide* compilation.

D-7 [R100]
Two slightly different takes of this track have leaked out into collector's circles. In each case the band follows something well-used in its own repertoire – the quiet/loud dynamic – to good effect.

Molly's Lips [R104]
When put up against this version, the Vaselines' original sounds quite twee. Nirvana manage to put their stamp so thoroughly all over this song it sounds as if it's one of their own and sits very well next to the likes of "Sliver" [50] and "Stain" [41].

Son Of A Gun [R105]
Again, a pop-punk take of a Vaselines' song that sounds like a Nirvana composition. The driving guitars and Dave Grohl's pounding drums set it apart from the original version.

Turnaround [R106]
As Nirvana had dabbled with a few new wave sounding songs it wasn't too surprising that they would cover a track by a leader of the new wave movement – Devo. This take sounds well practiced, right down to Cobain's spoken word interludes.

175

Session number

{R6}

Venue: BBC, Maida Vale Studios, London, England.
Date: September 3, 1991
Show: The John Peel Show
Broadcast: November 3, 1991
Presenter: John Peel
Players: Kurt Cobain (guitar, vocals), Krist Novoselic (bass), Dave
    Grohl (drums)

Tracks recorded:	Available on:
Drain You [R51]	*With The Lights Out* box set
Dumb [R90]	*With The Lights Out* box set
Endless, Nameless [R67]	*With The Lights Out* box set

By the time Nirvana arrived in London to record their third Peel session in three years, they were completely worn out from being on the road across Europe during the previous month. On arrival, Kurt Cobain instantly fell asleep on the couch in the control room. Novoselic and Grohl went for some food and on their return a decision had to be made about whether the session would be able to go ahead. Cobain was finally roused and the band managed to get through three songs (not the usual four) before having to throw in the towel on grounds of fatigue.

Drain You [R51]
Kurt Cobain's tiredness shows through here as the song lacks its usual vitality. There are no obvious mistakes or problems with the take, it just doesn't have the spark that set it off as a stand-out track on *Nevermind*.

Dumb [R90]
Under the circumstances, this was a pretty good, if slow, take on the unreleased "Dumb" [R90]. Cobain does sound a little tired, but overall his vocal delivery is fairly good. The drum/bass combo is tight as always and the song was showing great promise.

176

Endless, Nameless [R67]
Perhaps because they knew this was the last song and perhaps because they had a lot of weary anger to get out, they jammed away for an eight and a half minute version of *Nevermind's* hidden final track.

Session number

{R7}

Venue: BBC, Maida Vale Studios, London, England.
Date: November 9, 1991
Show: The Mark Goodier Show
Broadcast: November 18, 1991
Presenter: Mark Goodier
Players: Kurt Cobain (guitar, vocals), Krist Novoselic (bass), Dave
       Grohl (drums)

Tracks recorded:	Available on:
Aneurysm [R54]	*Incesticide*
Been A Son [R40]	*Incesticide*
(New Wave) Polly [R11a]	*Incesticide*
Something In The Way [R63]	**not officially released**

Just two months after the last Peel session, Nirvana were back at the BBC for a session for the *Mark Goodier Show*. Three of the four tracks were used on the *Incesticide* compilation.

Aneurysm [R54]
A masterful take of one of Nirvana's best and most complicated songs. Starting off with a solo guitar it then shifts up a few gears into a fast, new-wave type phase before abruptly switching tempo again to a slower, more melodic swagger before Kurt Cobain even starts singing, 80 seconds into the track.

Been A Son [R40]
A perfectly constructed pop song that does its job and gets the heck out

before it overstays its welcome. Typical of many of the songs that the band chose to record for radio sessions.

(New Wave) Polly [R11a]
Had been attempted less successfully at the first Peel session (see session {R2}) two years earlier. Here it is given another electric treatment which flies away right off the bat. The speed of this version gave rise to it being christened the 'new wave version' as opposed to just another electric run through.

Something In The Way [R63]
An atmospheric reading of this haunting track. The only song not released from this session, possibly because of the overly husky sounding vocals. Musically, it starts off acoustically before switching to an all-out electric band version during the choruses, before switching back again for the subsequent verses.

Session number

{R8}

Venue: VPRO Studios, Hilversum, Holland.
Date: November 25, 1991
Show: Twee Meter De Lucht In
Broadcast: November 26, 1991
Players: Kurt Cobain (guitar, vocals), Krist Novoselic (bass),
         Dave Grohl (drums)

Tracks recorded:	Available on:
Grohl Jam [R114]	not officially released
Where Did You Sleep Last Night? [R101]	**not officially released**
Here She Comes Now [R47]	**not officially released**
Here She Comes Now (alternate take) [R47a]	not officially released
Unknown Song [R115]	not officially released

Much mystery surrounds this Dutch session as it's known that an hour of material was recorded, but very little of it has leaked out or been broadcast.

Here She Comes Now [R47]
A relatively straightforward version of the Velvet Underground song that the band had earlier recorded for a tribute album (see session {19}).

Where Did You Sleep Last Night? [R101]
Not as emotional as the beautifully stark *Unplugged* version (see session {T8}), this take is a little too fussy with too much percussion and too many things going on.

Session number

{T1}

Venue: Channel Four Studios, London, England.
Date: November 8, 1991
Show: The Word
Broadcast: live
Presenters: Terry Christian and Katie Puckrik
Players: Kurt Cobain (guitar, vocals), Krist Novoselic (bass), Dave
       Grohl (drums)

Tracks recorded:	Available on:
Smells Like Teen Spirit [T59]	not officially released

For Nirvana's first ever live TV performance they certainly knew how to create a stir. *The Word* had long been known for its slightly out of control youth TV slot but Kurt Cobain still managed to spice things up by announcing, "I just want all the people in this room to know that Courtney Love, the lead singer of the sensational pop group Hole, is the best fuck in the world."

Smells Like Teen Spirit [T59]
With the crowd roaring its approval for Cobain's Courtney Love announcement, the band burst into its breakthrough single and gave a competent if unspectacular performance.

Session number

{T2}

Venue: BBC Television Studios, London, England.
Date: November 26, 1991
Show: Top Of The Pops
Broadcast: November 27, 1991
Players: Kurt Cobain (guitar, vocals), Krist Novoselic (bass), Dave
Grohl (drums)

Tracks recorded:	Available on:
Smells Like Teen Spirit [T59a]	not officially released

After the Courtney Love comment on their first TV appearance, Nirvana weren't about to start taking things seriously on this, their second. In the early 1990s, *Top Of The Pops* was going through a phase of only allowing the vocals to be live in the studio – the musical track was played from a tape and the band had to mime along which obviously would not endear Nirvana to the show. However, they were convinced to appear and so they did, providing one of the show's more surreal moments.

Smells Like Teen Spirit [T59a]
As the backing track opened, Krist Novoselic started swinging his bass above his head, and Kurt Cobain stepped forward with an inane grin on his face, doing some fake strumming. Only Dave Grohl pretended to do anything like play. The biggest spoof occurred when Cobain began to sing. Instead of his usual singing voice he employed a kind of gothic lounge singers croon and even performed mock-fellatio on the microphone. The censors obviously weren't paying too close attention either as he sang an opening line of "load up on drugs, kill your friends".

180

Session number

{T3}

Venue: Channel Four Studios, London, England.
Date: December 6, 1991
Show: Tonight With Jonathan Ross
Broadcast: December 6, 1991
Presenter: Jonathan Ross
Players: Kurt Cobain (guitar, vocals), Krist Novoselic (bass), Dave
      Grohl (drums)

Tracks recorded:	Available on:
Territorial Pissings [T64]	*Live! Tonight! Sold Out!* video

Nirvana's live TV appearances weren't going too well so far. By this, only their third appearance, they were already falling out with the show's producers about what songs to play. They wanted "Smells Like Teen Spirit" [59], the band offered "Lithium" [45] as a compromise.

Territorial Pissings [T64]
"Let music be the food of love," smirked the host, Jonathan Ross. "Now with the song 'Lithium', probably the biggest band in the world right now – Nirvana." At this point Krist Novoselic stepped forward, towering over the mic stand, but his intro was not picked up: this would have been the first sign that something was amiss. A vicious guitar line then started up and the band launched into a blistering take of "Territorial Pissings" [T64]! At the song's conclusion, Cobain knocked over his amps and the drum-kit was semi-destroyed before the band swiftly disappeared behind a curtain leaving a squeal of feedback. The camera switched to a clearly bemused Ross who quipped, "Hope we didn't wake the neighbours up. Nirvana, there doing the song we didn't actually expect, but they asked me to tell you that they're available for children's parties ..."

Session number

{T4}

Venue: MTV Studios, New York, NY.
Date: January 10, 1992
Show: MTV's 120 Minutes
Broadcast: January 26, 1992
Players: Kurt Cobain (guitar, vocals), Krist Novoselic (bass), Dave
    Grohl (drums)

Tracks recorded:	Available on:
On A Plain [57] (Soundcheck)	not officially released
Stain [41] (Soundcheck)	not officially released
Drain You [T51]	not officially released
School [T34]	not officially released
Molly's Lips [T104]	not officially released
Polly [T11]	not officially released
Aneurysm [T54]	not officially released
Smells Like Teen Spirit [T59b]	not officially released
Territorial Pissings [T64a]	not officially released

The first of three relatively long sets that the band would perform specifically for the MTV cameras. The whole show has never been broadcast but each song has now been leaked out including the two-song soundcheck. Kurt Cobain had dyed his hair purple for the occasion as the band sped through a varied collection of songs – three from the current *Nevermind* album, a cover and three older songs.

Session number

{T5}

Venue: NBC Studios, New York, NY.
Date: January 11, 1992
Show: Saturday Night Live
Broadcast: live
Players: Kurt Cobain (guitar, vocals), Krist Novoselic (bass), Dave
        Grohl (drums)

Tracks recorded:	Available on:
Smells Like Teen Spirit [T59c]	not officially released
Territorial Pissings [T64b]	not officially released

Invited on as the musical diversion on this long running comedy show,
Nirvana rose to the occasion with two superlative performances. Krist
Novoselic wore his hair tied back in a ponytail.

Session number

{T6}

Venue: Los Angeles, CA.
Date: September 9, 1992
Show: MTV Video Music Awards
Players: Kurt Cobain (guitar, vocals), Krist Novoselic (bass), Dave
        Grohl (drums)

Tracks recorded:	Available on:
Lithium [T45]	not officially released

Again the band had some 'discussion' about which song they would play
during this awards show. When their moment finally came they must have
given the producers a heart attack as they played eight seconds of the

183

intro to "Rape Me" [71] before switching tack and putting in a storming rendition of "Lithium" [T45]. Cobain couldn't resist his mischievous side though and he changed the last verse to: "I am a turd / I'm so excited / I can't wait to meet you there / I don't care / I'm so retarded."

Incesticide

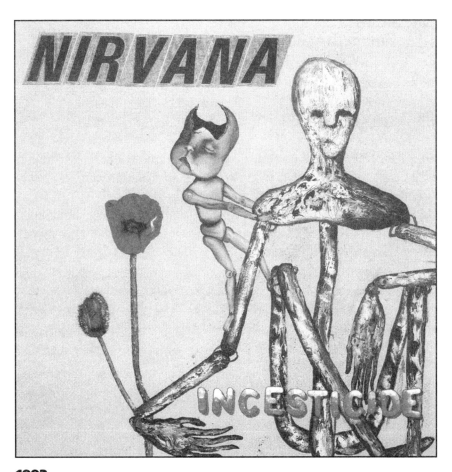

1992
Cassette
DGC DGCC24504   US
DGC DGCC1D24504   US   promo

MCA GEFC24504	Canada	promo
Geffen GEC24504	Germany	

LP

DGC DGC24504	US	blue vinyl
Geffen GEF24504	Holland	
DGC MVJG25003	Japan	

CD

DGC DGCD24504DJ	US	promo
DGC DGCD24504	US	
Geffen CGEFD24504	Canada	
Geffen GEFD24504	Australia	
Geffen GED24504	Germany	promo limited to 500 copies
MCA MVCG100	Japan	

1996
LP

Geffen MVJG-25003	Japan

2004
CD

Geffen UICY-9719	Japan

2007
CD

Geffen UICY-93359	Japan	limited edition

2011
LP

Original Recordings	US	180gm
Group ORGM-1005		

SHM-CD

Universal Music UICY-75126

Track listing:
Dive [39] / Sliver [50] / Stain [41] / Been A Son [R40] / Turnaround [R106] / Molly's Lips [R104] / Son Of A Gun [R105] / (New Wave) Polly [R11a] / Beeswax [21] / Downer [7] / Mexican Seafood [22] / Hairspray Queen [19] / Aero Zeppelin [20] / Big Long Now [30] / Aneurysm [R54]

185

Packaging Notes:
Pretty basic overall. A Cobain painting for the front cover and minimal liner notes (though some US versions did come with extra Cobain notes – but one has to ask why didn't all copies get this bonus?). The inside of the CD booklet showcased collage photographs of the band – including an array of ex-drummers.

Incesticide reviews:

Q:	"Hardly a classic compilation, but a must for fans nevertheless." 3/5
Rolling Stone:	"...will remind Nirvana's audience that freedom to fail is the only useful definition of artistic freedom." 3/4
NME:	"... the inevitability of patchy quality." 7/10 for side one, 3/10 for side 2
Select :	"The 15 tracks take you back to when the insanity was an outrageous fantasy." 3/5

Session number

{T7a}

Venue: NBC Studios, New York, NY.
Date: September 23, 1993
Show: rehearsals for Saturday Night Live
Broadcast: never broadcast
Presenter: n/a
Players: Kurt Cobain (guitar, vocals), Krist Novoselic (bass),
Dave Grohl (drums), Pat Smear (guitar)

Tracks recorded:	Available on:
Heart-Shaped Box [T73]	not officially released
Heart-Shaped Box (alternate take) [T73a]	not officially released
Rape Me [T71]	not officially released

Pat Smear was due to make his Nirvana TV debut on Saturday Night Live and the band stopped by for a rehearsal two days earlier.

Session number

{T7}

Venue: NBC Studios, New York, NY.
Date: September 25, 1993
Show: Saturday Night Live
Broadcast: live
Presenter: Charles Barkley
Players: Kurt Cobain (guitar, vocals), Krist Novoselic (bass), Dave
Grohl (drums), Pat Smear (guitar)

Tracks recorded:	Available on:
Heart-Shaped Box [T73b]	not officially released
Rape Me [T71a]	*SNL25 - The Musical Performances Volume 2*

Taking the chance to showcase both their new guitarist and the new
album, the band ran through two tracks from *In Utero*, the second of
which, "Rape Me" [T71a] would later show up on an NBC compilation.
The back of this album would omit the song title though, just leaving a
blank space where it should be.

Session number

{T8a}

Venue: Sony Studios, New York, NY.
Date: November 18, 1993
Show: rehearsals for MTV Unplugged
Broadcast: never broadcast
Presenter: n/a
Players: Kurt Cobain (guitar, vocals), Krist Novoselic (bass,
accordion), Dave Grohl (drums, vocals), Pat Smear
(guitar), Lori Goldston (cello)

Tracks recorded:	Available on:
About A Girl [U14a]	not officially released
Come As You Are [U60a]	not officially released
Jesus Doesn't Want Me For A Sunbeam [U108a]	not officially released
The Man Who Sold The World [U109a]	not officially released
Pennyroyal Tea [U52a]	not officially released
Dumb [U90a]	not officially released
Polly [U11a]	not officially released
Plateau [U110a]	not officially released
Oh, Me [U111a]	not officially released
Lake Of Fire [U112a]	not officially released
All Apologies [U56a]	not officially released

Initial rehearsals had been taking place for two days in New Jersey before the band moved into New York for a three-hour practice on the morning of the show. The set list had undergone a few changes in the last week, with "Molly's Lips" [104], "Been A Son" [40] and Dave Grohl's "Marigold" [91] all being considered until late on. The songs listed above were filmed during the practice on the morning of the show, some of which were attempted several times. Pat Smear has talked about the preparations for *Unplugged* and said, "We'd rehearsed acoustically a few times before the tour started because we had an acoustic part in the set and we worked on several other songs because we knew *Unplugged* was coming up. We tried to learn the Meat Puppets' songs ourselves but Curt Kirkwood's playing style is so unique that we could never make them sound quite right. Krist or Kurt suggested that we just have them come up and do it themselves. Kurt obviously got a kick out of promoting the bands and musicians he liked and was totally unselfish that way."

Session number

{T8}

Venue: Sony Studios, New York, NY.
Date: November 18, 1993
Show: MTV Unplugged
Presenter: n/a
Players: Kurt Cobain (guitar, vocals), Krist Novoselic (bass,
accordion, guitar), Dave Grohl (drums, vocals, bass),
Pat Smear (guitar), Lori Goldston (cello), Curt Kirkwood
(guitar), Cris Kirkwood (guitar)

Tracks recorded:	Available on:
About A Girl [U14]	*MTV Unplugged In New York*
Come As You Are [U60]	*MTV Unplugged In New York*
Jesus Doesn't Want Me	*MTV Unplugged In New York*
For A Sunbeam [U108]	
The Man Who Sold The	*MTV Unplugged In New York*
World [U109]	
Pennyroyal Tea [U52]	*MTV Unplugged In New York*
Dumb [U90]	*MTV Unplugged In New York*
Polly [U11]	*MTV Unplugged In New York*
On A Plain [U57]	*MTV Unplugged In New York*
Something In The Way	*MTV Unplugged In New York*
[U63]	
Plateau [U110]	*MTV Unplugged In New York*
Oh, Me [U111]	*MTV Unplugged In New York*
Lake Of Fire [U112]	*MTV Unplugged In New York*
All Apologies [U56]	*MTV Unplugged In New York*
Where Did You Sleep Last	*MTV Unplugged In New York*
Night? [U101]	

For many people, Nirvana's *Unplugged* appearance became their lasting
memory of the band. While they had spent the previous six years

189

spreading their noisy word, it was the intimate, acoustic setting for these songs that hit home the most. The set gained added poignancy because of Cobain's suicide just five months later and the stage flanked with flowers and candles, with hindsight, resembled a funeral setting. It was almost as if Cobain was singing his goodbyes. Producer Alex Coletti added insights for the Nirvana Fan Club website about the performance: "After the show, I brought the band into the control room to watch back some tape with the director and myself. There was a wonderful feeling in the room – everyone was really happy with what they were seeing and hearing. It's a really rewarding experience. I'll never forget Kurt asking Beth [McCarthy, the director] to try to put a shot of him smiling in the show. He said he'd been accused of not smiling and wanted us to help him out." Videos exists of the full show, lasting about twenty minutes longer, with all the between song discussions and banter with the audience. When the official CD of the show was issued it had undergone mixing by Scott Litt.

About A Girl [U14]

"This is off our first record, most people don't own it," quipped Kurt Cobain to open this memorable show. Like many of the Nirvana songs that Cobain had originally written on a battered old acoustic guitar, this track fitted the *Unplugged* format perfectly.

Come As You Are [U60]

This is one of the tracks that might have been expected to struggle with the transition from an electric to acoustic setting, but the band actually pulled it off pretty well, thanks in a large part to Krist Novoselic's dominant bass playing.

Jesus Doesn't Want Me For A Sunbeam [U108]

The first cover of the night was this track by the Vaselines. Like most of the other covers performed during the show (see below) it contained references to death, which in hindsight, along with the funereal set dressing made it seem like Cobain was playing at his own wake. The blackness of the song was almost too depressing to bear. Krist Novoselic donned an accordion for the song and, like much of the show, Dave Grohl's backing vocals played an important part in making the song sound as good as it did.

190

The Man Who Sold The World [U109]

This cover of the David Bowie song sounds like it could have been written specifically for Cobain and his own self-doubts about being a corporate 'sell-out'. More than any other track, this also shows that Nirvana weren't really unplugged for the show (they were using amplifiers). Krist Novoselic's ascending bass line was one of its highlights.

Pennyroyal Tea [U52]

"Am I going to do this by myself?" Cobain asked before putting in a haunting solo rendition. Gone was the polish of the Scott Litt remix, and all that was left were Cobain's guitar and his plaintive cries for some medicative help. The pain and resignation were never as blatant.

Dumb [U90]

Using a similar arrangement to other shows featuring Lori Goldston's cello, Nirvana provided another downbeat, introspective track to the session. The show was quickly descending into a very poignant record of a tragic career.

Polly [U11]

Played as the original demos had been, but with Goldston's cello adding to the tension, this stripped-down reading of the rape song was another in a fast growing list of haunting tracks that the band were performing.

On A Plain [U57]

A surprise inclusion to the set, "On A Plain" [57] had been a whirlwind of electric guitars when recorded for *Nevermind* and the transition here is remarkable.

Something In The Way [U63]

A close rendition of the *Nevermind* version, though the cello was a little higher in the mix, this song fitted perfectly to both the acoustic setting and the subdued nature of the set list.

Plateau [U110]

For the first of a trio of Meat Puppets songs, Cobain introduced the Kirkwood brothers as the 'Brothers Meat'. This version is almost note-for-note an exact copy of the album version (until the original's electric guitar solo at the end) from Meat Puppets II, with Cobain doing his best vocal impression of a Kirkwood.

Oh, Me [U111]
Another faithful reproduction, though this time the vocal delivery is quite distinct from the original. The guitar playing here is a little more polished too.

Lake Of Fire [U112]
Another song mentioning death, and ruminating on either a trip to heaven, or to the lake of fire for the 'bad folks' to fry. Novoselic and Grohl combine to set up a nice little groove which the various guitar embellishments are picked over.

All Apologies [U56]
A similar arrangement to the original version just with the guitars switched from electric to acoustic models. Otherwise it's a pretty straightforward take which ambles along before ending with an impressive Grohl/Cobain vocal coda.

Where Did You Sleep Last Night? [U101]
Introduced as being written by Cobain's favorite performer, the blues guitar legend Lead Belly. Cobain had already recorded a studio version of this with Mark Lanegan (see session {M11), but this take blew all others away. Without doubt a highlight of the show, the song builds with steadily mounting menace as Cobain's increasingly frantic vocals carry the track to new heights of anguish and paranoia. A fitting way to end a landmark performance.

MTV Unplugged In New York

1994
Cassette
DGC DGCC24727   US
Geffen 090716   UK   promo
LP
DGC DGC24727   US
DGC DGC24727   US   white vinyl

Geffen GEF24727	France	
Geffen GEF24727	Germany	
Geffen GEF24727	Germany	white vinyl
MCA MVJG25005	Japan	

CD

DGC DGCD24727	US	
DGC DGCD24727DJ	US	promo
Geffen GED24727	UK	
MCA MVCG163	Japan	
DGC CDGCD24727	Canada	

1998
LP

| Simply Vinyl SVLP0053 | UK | 180g vinyl |

2000
CD

| Geffen GED24727 | Brazil | |

2007
CD

| Universal MusicUICY-93361 | Japan | limited edition |

DVD

| Geffen B0010263-09 | US | NTSC format |
| Geffen 1750630 | Australia | PAL format |

2008
LP

| DGC 720642442517 | UK | |
| Geffen 0720642472712 | UK | Back To Black series |

SHM-CD

| Universal Music UICY-91062 | Japan | |

2009
LP

| Geffen SVLP 053 | UK | |
| Universal Music BOO 12764-01 | US | 180gm |

SHM-CD

| Universal Music UICY - 94347 | Japan | |

2011
SHM-CD
Universal Music   UICY-75128 2011   Japan

Track listing:

About A Girl [U14] / Come As You Are [U60] / Jesus Doesn't Want Me For A Sunbeam [U108] / The Man Who Sold The World [U109] / Pennyroyal Tea [U52] / Dumb [U90] / Polly [U11] / On A Plain [U57] / Something In The Way [U63] / Plateau [U110] / Oh, Me [U111] / Lake Of Fire [U112] / All Apologies [U56] / Where Did You Sleep Last Night? [U101]

Note: The show was first issued on DVD in 2008

Packaging notes: A basic, but effective collection of photos from the show with a list of credits but little else.

MTV Unplugged In New York reviews:

NME:	"... makes its makers sound legendary. Your hankies should be at the ready." 9/10
Q:	"*Unplugged* shows that the boy still had much to offer. 'It's better to burn out ...?' Is it really?" 4/5
Rolling Stone:	"It represents some of Nirvana's best as well as suggesting, in its acoustic nature, ways the band could have developed and grown." 4/4
Seattle Post-Intelligencer:	"The new album captures the spare, simple brilliance of the MTV telecast, which showed a different side of the band that epitomized grunge."
Houston Chronicle:	"... the performance is strong, consistent and rendered with a delicacy that Nirvana's rock albums can't touch."

Session number

{T9}

Venue: Pier 48, Seattle, WA.
Date: December 13, 1993
Show: Live And Loud
Broadcast: December 31, 1993
Presenter: n/a
Players: Kurt Cobain (guitar, vocals), Krist Novoselic, (bass),
    Dave Grohl (drums), Pat Smear (guitar)

Tracks recorded:	Available on:
Radio Friendly Unit Shifter [T58]	not officially released
Drain You [T51]	not officially released
Breed [T46]	not officially released
Serve The Servants [T88]	not officially released
Rape Me [T71a]	not officially released
Sliver [T50]	not officially released
Pennyroyal Tea [T52]	not officially released
Scentless Apprentice [T75]	*From The Muddy Banks Of The Wishkah*
All Apologies [T56]	not officially released
Heart-Shaped Box [T73a]	not officially released
Blew [T31]	not officially released
The Man Who Sold the World [T109]	not officially released
School [T34]	not officially released
Come As You Are [T60]	not officially released
Lithium [T45a]	not officially released
About A Girl [T14]	not officially released
Endless, Nameless [T67]	not officially released

This was the third MTV special that the band recorded and one that was a direct contrast to the *MTV Unplugged* show (see session {T8}).

196

This time it was an all-out sonic attack with Cobain's and Smear's twin guitars blasting away at every opportunity. Grohl's drumming was back to its vicious best and Novoselic's bass drove vibrations deep into the chests of all those present. Despite the whole performance being of a very high standard, MTV chose to include only a small number of the songs recorded. "Scentless Apprentice" [T75] was mixed by Andy Wallace and included on the *From The Muddy Banks Of The Wishkah* live album.

Session number

{T10}

Venue: Canal Plus Studios, Paris, France
Date: February 4, 1994
Show: Nulle Part Ailleurs
Players: Kurt Cobain (guitar, vocals), Krist Novoselic (bass), Dave
Grohl (drums), Pat Smear (guitar)

Tracks recorded:	Available on:
Rape Me [T71b]	**not officially released**
Pennyroyal Tea [T52a]	**not officially released**
Drain You [T51a]	**not officially released**
Sliver [T50]	not officially released
Polly [T11a]	not officially released

An excellent performance that found the band in high spirits before a very enthusiastic Parisian studio audience. The band made an extra effort for this show when they all wore matching outfits of black trousers, white shirts, black waistcoats and thin black ties. The whole effect was reminiscent of an early Beatles performance and the band bowed after each track. The band's good mood also gave the fans in the studio an extra treat as they waited behind after the TV recording had finished to play more songs, including "Sliver" [T50] and "Polly" [T11a] which were never used in the broadcast.

197

Rape Me [T71b]
The band are obviously enjoying playing this after some US stations had blocked it and they give a tight performance, the transition from verse to rowdy chorus is excellently executed.

Pennyroyal Tea [T52a]
A very poignant electric reading of this track. Cobain's vocals on the chorus are strained but clear and he later cheekily changes the Leonard Cohen line to "give me a Leonard Nimoy afterworld." The song builds to a shattering climax leaving a joyous, chanting, studio crowd to scream for more.

Drain You [T51a]
A blistering run-through, with Cobain again switching the odd word here and there – at one point he sings "slay you" in place of "drain you". When Cobain's guitar picks up a fault he tosses it aside and continues singing with both hands around the top of his microphone stand.

Session number

{T11}

Venue: RAI Studios, Rome, Italy.
Date: February 23, 1994
Show: Tunnel
Players: Kurt Cobain (guitar, vocals), Krist Novoselic (bass), Dave
        Grohl (drums), Pat Smear (guitar), Melora Craeger (cello)

Tracks recorded:	Available on:
Serve The Servants [T88]	**not officially released**
Dumb [T90]	**not officially released**

A rather subdued outing for Nirvana's last TV appearance; within the week they would also play their last concert. The show gets the name *Tunnel* because bands are required to play in the entrance of a stage prop tunnel. Krist Novoselic takes center stage between the two guitarists, Kurt Cobain wears a gold coloured coat.

Serve The Servants [T88]

A strong take of *In Utero's* lead-off track with a fine vocal (Cobain takes time to clearly pronounce the line "That legendary divorce is such a bore") and band performance. The solo at 2:07 is a highlight.

Dumb [T90]

Melora Craeger's cello is never more prominent than on this take of Dumb [T90], especially during the bridge, giving a baroque feel to the song and Cobain's gravelly voice comes to the fore.

Live Tracks On Official Releases

For many bands the live album is used only as a contract-filling exercise and adds nothing to their catalog. Many bands also use live recordings as extras on CD and 12" singles when they've run out of songs to use as b-sides. In Nirvana's case there is little filler in their catalog and their use of live recordings as b-sides was minimal. They issued a slew of impressive b-sides like "Dive" [39], "Even In His Youth" [42], "Aneurysm" [54], "Curmudgeon" [69] and "Marigold" [91] and while they were undoubtedly a very powerful live attraction, there was only a single live album (*From The Muddy Banks Of The Wishkah*) issued (if you count the *MTV Unplugged* set as a TV session) in the time since Kurt Cobain's death.

As it stands Nirvana released live versions of eight tracks on various singles: "Spank Thru" [5], "Polly" [11], "About A Girl" [14], "School" [34], "Been A Son" [40], "Sliver" [50], "Drain You" [51] and "Molly's Lips" [104].

More recently the amount of live material has increased dramatically with the *Live at Reading* DVD, the Paramount live show included on the *Nevermind* re-issues and various live takes included on the *With The Lights Out* box set.

Nirvana's tours provided crucial snapshots of the band's evolution, beginning with drudgy grunge-fests in the early days, through the power pop era of the *Nevermind* shows and then expanding to a four piece, with the addition of Pat Smear, for the *In Utero* tour. This final tour also allowed glimpses to be peeked of what the future might have held. Segments of the shows were played out as a five-piece with a cello being used to recreate some of the more poignant songs from the albums. Who would have predicted that when listening to *Bleach* a couple of years earlier?

Below is a chronological listing of all the shows that have had tracks taken for use on official Nirvana recordings.

Venue: Astoria Theatre, London, England
Dates: December 3, 1989

Players: Kurt Cobain (guitar, vocals), Krist Novoselic (bass),
   Chad Channing (drums)

Tracks recorded:	Available on:
Polly [L11]	*From The Muddy Banks Of The Wishkah*
Breed [L46]	*From The Muddy Banks Of The Wishkah*

By the time of this gig at the tail end of the European tour with Tad, the band were worn out. Like many shows which they opened, there was no time for a soundcheck, hence the awkward 50 second tuning up intro which was also used to open the *From The Muddy Banks Of The Wishkah* album. The version of "Polly" [L11] played here, like in the other shows on this tour, was a full-on electric version featuring a stiff drum beat and crystal-clear Cobain vocals placed bang in the center of the mix. "Breed" [L46], still known as "Imodium" at this stage, is played at a slightly slower tempo with lyrics similar to those recorded with Butch Vig five months later (see session [15]). Mudhoney also played at this show (which was not on December 5 as noted in the album liner notes) to complete the line-up for what was billed as the Sub Pop 'Lame Fest'.

Venue: Pine Street Theater, Portland, OR.
Dates: February 9, 1990
Players: Kurt Cobain (guitar, vocals), Krist Novoselic (bass),
Chad Channing (drums)

Tracks recorded:	Available on:
About a Girl [L14]	Sliver [50] single
Spank Thru [L5]	Sliver [50] single
Molly's Lips [L104]	Molly's Lips [104] single

This opening show on the short (ten day) West Coast tour was recorded in its entirety, though only these three tracks have so far been used on official releases. All are pretty representative of the band in a live setting with Chad Channing behind the drum kit. "About A Girl" [L14] is especially fast, and the percussion sounds like it's being played on a biscuit tin at times.

Venue: Paramount Theater, Seattle, WA
Dates: October 31, 1991
Players: Kurt Cobain (guitar, vocals), Krist Novoselic (bass), Dave
Grohl (drums)

Tracks recorded:	Available on:
School [L34]	Come As You Are [60] single
Drain You [L51]	Come As You Are [60] single
Been A Son [L40]	Lithium [45] single
Negative Creep [L33]	*From The Muddy Banks Of The Wishkah*

By the first Halloween after the release of *Nevermind*, the Nirvana bandwagon was really starting to gather pace. This gig in their adopted hometown showcased them at their blistering best as they played almost all of their new album. Cobain's elliptical guitar work leads into a heavy take of "School" [L34] which follows on nicely from "Endless, Nameless" [67] on the "Come As You Are" CD single. The quiet "you're in high school again" mini-break explodes gloriously at 2:03 with a truly blood-curdling howl. "Drain You" [L51] on the other hand is relatively restrained with respect to its studio incarnation. The riotous side of the band makes another appearance, as a pounding version of "Negative Creep" [L33] rounds out the quartet of songs taken from this show.

201

Venue: Vi De Porta, Rome, Italy
Dates: November 19, 1991
Players: Kurt Cobain (guitar, vocals), Krist Novoselic (bass), Dave
Grohl (drums, backing vocals)

Tracks recorded:	Available on:
Spank Thru [L5a]	*From The Muddy Banks Of The Wishkah*

The second time that one of Nirvana's oldest songs, "Spank Thru" [5],
had a live version issued and by 1991 it was a rare addition to the
live show. This fairly brisk take has extra impact with the addition of
Dave Grohl's masterful drumming which speeds up the whole song
considerably. Kurt Cobain's vocal is at times reminiscent of his 'gothic
lounge singing voice' – like the one he used on *Top Of The Pops* (see
session {T2}). The guitar solo is markedly different from the studio one
but beautifully executed.

Venue: Paradiso, Amsterdam, Holland
Dates: November 25, 1991
Players: Kurt Cobain (guitar, vocals), Krist Novoselic (bass), Dave
Grohl (drums, backing vocals)

Tracks recorded:	Available on:
School [L34a]	*From The Muddy Banks Of The Wishkah*
Been A Son [L40a]	*From The Muddy Banks Of The Wishkah*
Lithium [L45]	*From The Muddy Banks Of The Wishkah*
Blew [L31]	*From The Muddy Banks Of The Wishkah*

Luckily Nirvana had the tape machines (and cameras) rolling for what
would be one of their best gigs during the autumn of 1991, recorded in
Holland. At least a half dozen clips are included in the *Live! Tonight!
Sold Out!* video and these four live tracks were also used from the same
show. A typically abrasive "School" [L34a] opens the *From The Muddy
Banks Of The Wishkah* album (a different live version of this song was
also used on the "Come As You Are" [60] single, see above). "Been A
Son" [L40a] was issued from this show and an alternate live version was
also issued (see the "Lithium" [45] single, above). "Lithium" [L45a]
itself was used from this show, this time with a slightly different guitar

strum at the start and "Blew" [L31] ends the album with a suitably tight and commanding performance.

Venue: O'Brien Pavilion, Del Mar, CA, USA
Dates: December 28, 1991
Players: Kurt Cobain (guitar, vocals), Krist Novoselic (bass), Dave
　　　　Grohl (drums, backing vocals)

Tracks recorded:	Available on:
Sliver [L50]	In Bloom [48] single
Polly [L11a]	In Bloom [48] single
Drain You [L51a]	*From The Muddy Banks Of The Wishkah*
Aneurysm [L54]	*From The Muddy Banks Of The Wishkah*
Smells Like Teen Spirit [L59]	*From The Muddy Banks Of The Wishkah*

Another popular show, which supplied five tracks for live releases, saw Nirvana sandwiched on a high profile roster between Pearl Jam and the headlining Red Hot Chili Peppers. "Sliver" [L50] was a decent, if workmanlike, take. "Polly" [L11a] wasn't the usual live electric band version but a stripped-down take with some nice backing vocals from Dave Grohl and a standout bass line from Krist Novoselic. The three other songs from this show are all popular live favorites and found places on the *From The Muddy Banks Of The Wishkah* album and play in order on that compilation. "Drain You" [51] had already been issued as a live track so, for the album, this slightly alternative take was picked out with Cobain playing with a modified guitar effects pedal. "Aneurysm" [L54] is a typically dramatic take of one of the band's best songs and "Smells Like Teen Spirit" [L59] has the full speed treatment which, like other live versions (see "Spank Thru" [L5a] as another example), thrusts the song along at a breakneck pace. It's almost as if the band are so sick of playing their most famous song that they want to get it over with as quickly as possible. By now Dave Grohl was coming to the end of his first full year in the band, as he commented: "Ever since I've been in this band we've been touring. Five nights of playing. Two days of doing press. When we're not on stage, we're eating, or sleeping, or shitting, and that's about it. It's enough to drive anybody insane."

Venue: Reading Festival, Reading, England
Dates: August 30, 1992
Players: Kurt Cobain (guitar, vocals), Krist Novoselic (bass), Dave
   Grohl (drums, backing vocals)

Tracks recorded:	Available on:
Breed [L46]	*Live at Reading*
Drain You [L51]	*Live at Reading*
Aneurysm [L54]	*Live at Reading*
School [L34]	*Live at Reading*
Sliver [L50]	*Live at Reading*
In Bloom [L48]	*Live at Reading*
Come As You Are [L60]	*Live at Reading*
Lithium [L45]	*Live at Reading*
About a Girl [L14]	*Live at Reading*
tourette's [L72]	*Live at Reading, From The Muddy Banks Of The Wishkah*
Polly [L11]	*Live at Reading*
Lounge Act [L65]	*Live at Reading*
Smells Like Teen Spirit [L59]	*Live at Reading*
On a Plain [L37]	*Live at Reading*
Negative Creep [L33]	*Live at Reading*
Been a Son [L40]	*Live at Reading*
All Apologies [L56]	*Live at Reading*
Blew [L31]	*Live at Reading*
Dumb [L90]	*Live at Reading*
Stay Away [L66]	*Live at Reading*
Spank Thru [L5]	*Live at Reading*
Love Buzz [L27]	*Live at Reading* DVD version only
The Money Will Roll Right In [L123]	*Live at Reading*
D-7 [L100]	*Live at Reading*
Territorial Pissings [L64]	*Live at Reading*

Amid rumours questioning Kurt Cobain's health and the future of
Nirvana, the band managed to pull out what is widely recognized as

one of their finest shows. UK rock magazine *Kerrang!* puts it firmly at #1 in their list of "100 Gigs That Shook The World".

Cobain was pushed on stage in a wheelchair (this can be seen in the *Live! Tonight! Sold Out!* video) for a show that was filmed and recorded by the BBC. Subsequent radio broadcasts haven't included some of the more interesting moments (they concentrated on the 'hits') from this show including one of the very few times that (the yet-to-be-released) tourette's [72] was played live.

After a false start, Dave Grohl announces the track saying, "This is a new song that we don't really feel like actually going through the trouble of putting out ourselves."

"This song is called 'The Eagle Has Landed'," interjects Cobain.

"It's for all of you bootleggers to go ahead, and go!" concludes Grohl. This would be the last ever Nirvana show in the UK.

Venue: Civic Center, Springfield, MA.
Dates: November 10, 1993
Players: Kurt Cobain (guitar, vocals), Krist Novoselic (bass), Dave
    Grohl (drums, backing vocals), Pat Smear (guitar, backing
    vocals)

Tracks recorded:	Available on:
Sliver [L50a]	*From The Muddy Banks Of The Wishkah*

A sloppy delivery of what was usually a very powerful song. Cobain's vocal seems incredibly laid back and detached compared to the studio version. Again this song had already been issued as a live b-side so another take was required for *From The Muddy Banks Of The Wishkah*. The extra guitar power provided by Pat Smear is in full effect here especially on the chorus which is in danger of being drowned out.

Venue: Pier 48, Seattle, WA
Dates: December 13, 1993
Players: Kurt Cobain (guitar, vocals), Krist Novoselic (bass), Dave
Grohl (drums), Pat Smear (guitar)

Tracks recorded:	Available on:
Scentless Apprentice [L75]	*From The Muddy Banks Of The Wishkah*

One of the four *In Utero* songs used on *From The Muddy Banks Of The Wishkah*. For full details of this show see session {T9}.

Venue: Great Western Forum, Inglewood, CA.
Dates: December 30, 1993
Players: Kurt Cobain (guitar, vocals), Krist Novoselic (bass), Dave
Grohl (drums, backing vocals), Pat Smear (guitar,
backing vocals)

Tracks recorded:	Available on:
Heart-Shaped Box [L73]	*From The Muddy Banks Of The Wishkah*

As 1993 drew to a close, Kurt Cobain was at the end of his tether as far as touring was concerned. "We might not go on any more long tours," he said, "The only way we could tour is if I could find some way to keep my stomach from acting up. We could record and play shows every once in a while, but to put myself through the physical strain of seven months of touring is too much for me." The strain is noticeable on this version of the band's most popular song which is also one of the most disappointing on the *From The Muddy Banks Of The Wishkah* album. The crispness of many live takes is lost, though one of the few highpoints is the added backing vocals from Pat Smear especially during the first and second verses.

Venue: Seattle Center Arena, Seattle, WA.
Dates: January 7, 1994
Players: Kurt Cobain (guitar, vocals), Krist Novoselic (bass), Dave
      Grohl (drums, backing vocals), Pat Smear (guitar)

Tracks recorded:	Available on:
Milk It [L76]	*From The Muddy Banks Of The Wishkah*

"Now that we're playing larger stages we have an amazing PA system which allows me to hear everything. That's how I judge a good show – by the monitors." Taking this Kurt Cobain statement as a measuring stick, then this was probably one of the better shows at the end of Nirvana's touring lifetime. Despite this being something of a thrashing monster of a song, he manages to combine the full frontal sonic assault with some crisp playing and sharp vocals, even if a large portion of them are screamed. The discordant guitar picking comes through loud and clear before descending back into chaos. The liner notes for *From The Muddy Banks Of The Wishkah* contain another error here with this show being played on January 7, not the 5th as noted.

From The Muddy Banks Of The Wishkah

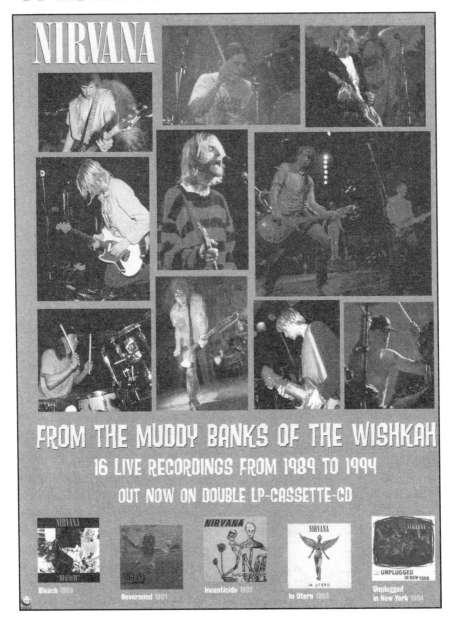

1996
Cassette

DGC DGCC-A-25105	US	promo
DGC DGCC-25105	US	
Geffen GEC 25105	UK	

Double LP

DGC DGC2-25105	US
Geffen GEF 25105(2)	UK

CD

DGC DGCD-25105	US	
DGC DGCD-25105	US	promo
DGC CD ACETATE	US	promo
Geffen GED 25105	UK	
Geffen GED 25105	Australia	
Geffen GEFD-25105	Australia	
DGC DGCSD-25105	Canada	

2003
Double LP

Geffen 425105-1	UK	remastered

2007

Universal Music UICY-93362	Japan	limited edition

2011
SHM-CD

Universal Music UICY-7512	Japan

Basic track listing:
intro / School [L34a] / Drain You [L51a] / Aneurysm [L54] / Smells Like Teen Spirit [L59] / Been A Son [L40a] / Lithium [L45] / Sliver [L50a] / Spank Thru [L5a] / Scentless Apprentice [L75] / Heart-Shaped Box [L73] / Milk It [L76] / Negative Creep [L33] / Polly [L11] / Breed [L46] / tourette's [L72] / Blew [L31]

The double vinyl version of the album featured sixteen bonus clips of between-song conversations, some of which are quite humorous, to fill up some time (the CD version was only fifty-four minutes long), in fact they fill the whole fourth side of the album. These clips were mainly taken from the US shows at the Springfield Civic Center, Springfield, MA (six clips), the Great Western Forum, Inglewood, CA (four clips) and the Seattle Center Arena, Seattle, WA and the Paramount Theater, Seattle, WA (three clips each). All of these shows are noted above.

Packaging notes:

The liner notes provided by Krist Novoselic are pretty perfunctory and do little more than list the shows that are referenced (sometimes incorrectly) elsewhere in the booklet. The photos are a fairly predictable collage of live shots with a couple of venue billboards thrown in for good measure.

From The Muddy Banks Of The Wishkah reviews:

Melody Maker:	"... a self conscious attempt not to glorify the band as a live act, but to portray highs and lows."
NME:	"... a gloriously electrifying aural photo-book of a truly legendary rock'n'roll band." 9/10
Q:	"Cobain burnt out, but it's unlikely Nirvana will ever fade away." 4/5
Rolling Stone:	"... you have to wonder how a band this noisy ever got so fucking famous." 4½/5
Toronto Star:	"That's punk spirit for you, and *Wishkah* captures it."
New York Times:	"Think of it as Nirvana Unpolished, an album that will separate the punks from the posers."

Live, single track promos taken from *From The Muddy Banks of the Wishkah* album as follows:

1996

DGC PROCD 1033	CD	US	Aneurysm [L54]
DGC PROCD 1033	CD	UK	Aneurysm [L54]
DGC PROCD 1070	CD	US	Drain You [L51a]
Geffen NIR 96010	CD	Holland	Lithium [L45]
DGC MCA F0010	CD	France	Smells Like Teen Spirit [L59]

Videos & DVDs

Track: In Bloom [V48]
Filmed on: April 1990
Filmed at: New York, NY.
Director: Steve Brown

This uses the version of "In Bloom" [48] recorded with Butch Vig at Smart Studios in 1990 (see session {15}). Filmed during a stop in New York during the tour immediately following the Vig sessions, this is the only professional promotional video clip featuring Chad Channing. During a show in New York, Krist Novoselic was so disappointed by the band's performance he shaved his head as a penance and he's seen in this clip both with and without hair.

Track: Smells Like Teen Spirit [V59]
Filmed on: August 17, 1991
Filmed at: GMT Studios, Culver City, CA.
Director: Sam Bayer
Awards: MTV Music Video Award: Best Alternative Video 1992

Starting just before lunch, the entire shoot was wrapped up in a single day. The director, Sam Bayer, had arrived in Los Angeles never having directed a music video, but he did have a contact at Geffen and that led to his getting the call for Nirvana's first professional video. Despite the fact they were signed to a major label, the band was only given a budget of $25,000 for the shoot. Problems began when Cobain and Bayer didn't like each other from the off. Cobain had certain ideas for the video that didn't match with Bayer's and vice versa. "Kurt was so pissed off with me," recalls Bayer, "That look in his eye, the way he pushed his face into the camera at the end of the take – which was very antagonistic, and kind of directed at me – it created something quite wonderful."

The set was supposed to be Kurt Cobain's take of a twisted high school rally. The audience, which was recruited by putting out announcements on a local college radio station, gradually gets more animated during the

211

song before invading the basketball court which the band are playing on. The clips of a janitor mopping the floor are a cheeky reference to Cobain's own short stint as a school cleaner years before.

The video went a long way to breaking Nirvana into the mainstream after it was put into heavy rotation on MTV. It was recently announced as the most played video during MTV Europe's first fifteen years.

Track: Come As You Are [V60]
Filmed on: January 21, 1992
Filmed at: unknown Los Angeles sound stage, CA.
Director: Kevin Kerslake

Kevin Kerslake would work on four Nirvana videos (before falling out with Cobain and being dropped from the "Heart-Shaped Box" [V73] shoot) and for this initial one he put in a very MTV-friendly treatment. The video is basically a studio performance shot with a few effects thrown in for good measure. To disguise the band member's faces he films them from behind a pane of glass that has water flooding down it. Kurt Cobain is seen swinging from (and in) a chandelier and film of the band members is projected onto large screens behind them as they play in the studio. Other shots show a baby swimming after a dollar bill in a swimming pool and a revolver swirling around in the same pool as Cobain sings, "I don't have a gun."

Track: Lithium [V45]
Filmed on: various dates
Filmed at: various locations
Director: Kevin Kerslake

Having liked the "Come As You Are" [V60] film, the band hired Kerslake again for this clip. Cobain's initial preference for having an animated video was scrapped when it was estimated it would take several months to prepare, so Kerslake used footage from a series of *Nevermind* shows for this live film. Kerslake uses some nice slo-mo edits and frequent picture-into-picture fades that work quite well to make the standard live footage a little more interesting.

212

Track: In Bloom [V48a]
Director: Kevin Kerslake
Awards: MTV Music Video Award – Best Alternative Video 1993

For this second attempt at "In Bloom" [V48a] (this time using the musical track from *Nevermind*) the band and Kerslake attempted to spoof 1960s TV shows like the *Ed Sullivan Show*. Filmed in black and white, the band are introduced by a Sullivan-like actor, cut with footage of screaming girls from what could be a Beatles' show. When the curtain is drawn back the band are shown wearing matching striped suits; Cobain has his hair slicked into a side parting and he's wearing black-rimmed glasses. The band mime their way through the song in a Herman's Hermits manner. As the song progresses the clips of the band in suits are interspersed with the 1960s audience and then subliminal shots of the band wearing dresses are slipped in. Slowly these snippets become more frequent and last longer. Eventually the band is shown back in suits as the song ends and the host returns to thank the "nice, decent, clean-cut young men."

A second version of the film shows only the band wearing dresses. They give up miming to the backing track early on and destroy the whole set, knocking the stage props over. A third version shows just the footage of the band in suits.

Track: Sliver [V50]
Filmed on: March 1993
Filmed at: Kurt Cobain's house, 171 Lake Washington Boulevard,
        Seattle, WA.
Director: Kevin Kerslake

To promote the *Incesticide* compilation (though filmed months after it had been issued) Kerslake and Cobain combined to make this low budget film. Recorded on grainy Super 8 film stock, the band is filmed playing in Cobain's garage. Frances Bean, then just seven months old, was also present and appears in the video (after all Cobain is singing the song from the point of view of a young child). The garage appears to be a typical teenage band practice space with posters on the wall and various junkyard props lying around – a mannequin, some toys and an old lamp stand.

213

Track: Heart-Shaped Box [V73]
Filmed on: summer 1993
Filmed at: unknown
Director: Anton Corbijn
Awards: MTV Music Video Award – Best Alternative Video 1994

While the previous Nirvana promotional videos had basically been live montages or variations on studio performance clips, the band really came into their own with this ambitious film. Like much of *In Utero*, the film has numerous anatomical references. The band are first seen sitting in a hospital room while an elderly man lies on a bed with a drip connected to his arm (later a snapshot of the drip bag shows it to contain a foetus). The dishevelled old man is then shown wearing a loin cloth and Santa Claus hat as he climbs a crucifix and is then seen hanging from it. A young girl (actually Cobain's half-sister Brianne O'Connor) skips by in a Ku Klux Klan outfit before spying more foetuses hanging from weird shaped trees. The whole film brilliantly brings the underlying themes and atmospheres of *In Utero* to visual life, a stunning achievement. It doesn't hurt that the actual song is so good either.

Track: Sappy [V12]
Filmed on: various dates
Filmed at: various locations
Director: unknown

Little is known about this video that has occasionally surfaced on MTV. Despite it being played on commercial TV and having a title bar written in the style of official Nirvana releases, it seems to have been compiled by an unofficial source. The film is a montage of TV and live performances and predicts the style later used on the "You Know You're Right" [V93] clip which would follow eight years later.

Track: You Know You're Right
Filmed on: various dates
Filmed at: various locations
Director: Chris Hafner

The problem of how to come up with a video for a new Nirvana track eight years after Kurt Cobain's death was an interesting one. The way that Hafner got around it was to use a myriad of TV and live clips from the band's career to create a high-speed retrospective. He also manages to cleverly use some Cobain close-ups that make it seem that he is actually singing the song.

Video: Live! Tonight! Sold Out!
Director: Kevin Kerslake
Players: Kurt Cobain (guitar, vocals), Krist Novoselic (bass), Dave
        Grohl (drums)

Tracks recorded:	Location:
Love Buzz [V27]	Oct 19, 1991 (Dallas, TX, USA)
About A Girl [V14]	Oct 31, 1991 (Seattle, WA, USA)
Breed [V46a]	Oct 31, 1991 (Seattle, WA, USA)
Polly [V11]	Oct 31, 1991 (Seattle, WA, USA)
Endless, Nameless [V67]	Oct 31, 1991 (Seattle, WA, USA)
Aneurysm [V54]	Nov 25, 1991 (Amsterdam, Holland)
Love Buzz [V27a]	Nov 25, 1991 (Amsterdam, Holland)
Come As You Are [V60a]	Nov 25, 1991 (Amsterdam, Holland)
Territorial Pissings [V64]	Nov 25, 1991 (Amsterdam, Holland)
Drain You [V51]	Nov 25, 1991 (Amsterdam, Holland)
Sliver [V50a]	Nov 25, 1991 (Amsterdam, Holland)
Smells Like Teen Spirit [V59a]	Nov 27, 1991 (London, England)
Territorial Pissings [V64a]	Dec 7, 1991 (London, England)
Negative Creep [V33]	Feb 22, 1992 (Honolulu, HI, USA)
Aneurysm [V54a]	January 23, 1993 (Rio de Janeiro, Brazil)
Dive [V39]	January 23, 1993 (Rio de Janeiro, Brazil)

215

Something In The Way [V63]	February 14, 1992 (Osaka, Japan)
On A Plain [V57]	June 26, 1992 (Roskilde, Denmark)
Lithium [V45a]	August 30, 1992 (Reading Festival, England)

This, the first Nirvana long-form video, is almost the visual version of *The Montage Of Heck* [15] (see session {5}) as it brings together samples of everything the band was involved in. And I mean everything. Bits of TV shows and infomercials, spoofs, skits and jokes, interviews, candid backstage shots, live performances, various sound and visual collages, footage shot on a trans-Atlantic flight, at award shows and with the tour van, it's all here in a beautifully skewed mix of dizzying editing. Musically the film features live takes of around sixteen complete(ish) songs filmed during the band's *Nevermind* tours of 1991-92. Kurt Cobain had been heavily involved in the production of this film, but it was continually pushed back until his death, after which Novoselic and Grohl decided to try and complete the film as Cobain had wished. It was finally released in November 1994.

Some of the most interesting footage includes the fight between Cobain and a bouncer at the Trees Club in Dallas (Cobain splits the bouncers head open with his guitar, the bouncer starts attacking the Nirvana front man and the show is soon over). A strange live performance of "Come As You Are" [60] is showcased with Cobain deciding to screech his way through the vocal rather than sing it. All the famous TV slots are here, at least in part. An amazing film of an amazing time in 1990s music.

Video: 1991: The Year Punk Broke
Director: David Markey

Players: Kurt Cobain (guitar, vocals), Krist Novoselic (bass), Dave Grohl (drums)

Tracks recorded:	Location:
Negative Creep [V33]	August 20, 1991 (Cork, Ireland)
Smells Like Teen Spirit [V59]	August 20, 1991 (Cork, Ireland)
Endless, Nameless [V67]	August 23, 1991 (Reading Festival, England)
School [V34]	Sept 1, 1991 (Rotterdam, Holland)
Polly [V11]	Sept 1, 1991 (Rotterdam, Holland)

The Year Punk Broke was primarily a vehicle to record Sonic Youth's late summer tour in 1991. As things turned out though, it was Nirvana that really broke through and soon had almost twin billing with the art rock giants. The 95-minute film features live performances by Sonic Youth (eight tracks), Nirvana (five tracks), Dinosaur Jr. (two tracks) and single appearances by Babes In Toyland, Gumball and old skool punks the Ramones. Some of Nirvana's live performances are interspersed with clips from other shows. As well as the live performances, the bands are seen back stage and out and about around Europe.

Live At Reading

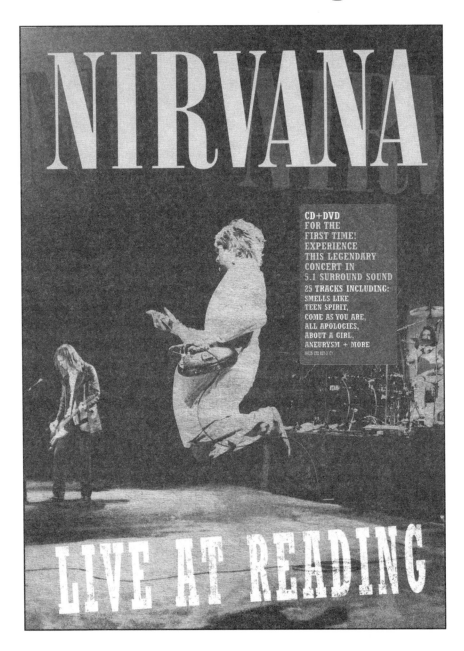

2009

Double LP

DGC BOO13538-01	US	

CD

DGC 0625272036-7(6)	UK	

CD + DVD

DGC B0013501-00	US	digipak
DGC 06025272037	UK	
DGC 06252720347-3(7)	UK	PAL format
DGC 2720373	Australia	PAL format

SHM-CD/DVD

Geffen UICY-94346	Japan	NTSC format

2010

Double LP

Universal Music B1353801	UK	24 tracks

Breed [L46] / Drain You [L51] / Aneurysm [L54] / School [L34] / Sliver [L50] / In Bloom [L48] / Come As You Are [L60] / Lithium [L45] / About A Girl [L14] / tourette's [L72] / Polly [L11] / Lounge Act [L65] / Smells Like Teen Spirit [L59] / On A Plain [L37] / Negative Creep [L33] / Been A Son [L40] / All Apologies [L56] / Blew [L31] / Dumb [L90] / Stay Away [L66] / Spank Thru [L5] / The Money Will Roll Right In [L123] / D-7 [L100] / Territorial Pissings [L64] + Love Buzz [L47], only on the DVD version

Live At Reading Reviews

Time Out:	"… a crucial recording of one of the greatest rock bands of the twentieth century."
Salt Lake Tribune:	"On the night of *Live at Reading*, Nirvana's singing and scorching musicianship proved they were the best band in the world."
San Antonio Express-News:	"A gift for fans of a band that was gone way too soon."

Miscellaneous Non-Nirvana Sessions

Session number

{M1}

Venue: Reciprocal Studio, Seattle, WA, USA
Date: August 1989
Producer: Jack Endino
Players: Mark Lanegan, Kurt Cobain (guitar), Krist Novoselic (bass)

Tracks recorded:	Available on:
Where Did You Sleep Last Night?	*The Winding Sheet* (Mark Lanegan solo album)
They Hung Him On A Cross	*With The Lights Out* box set
Grey Goose	*With The Lights Out* box set
Ain't It A Shame	*With The Lights Out* box set

Session number

{M2}

Venue: Razor's Edge Studio, San Francisco, CA.
Date: December 1989
Producer: Jack Endino
Players: Mark Lanegan, Kurt Cobain (backing vocals)

Tracks recorded:	Available on:
Down In The Dark	*The Winding Sheet* (Mark Lanegan solo album)

Session number

{M3}

Venue: The Laundry Room, Seattle, WA.
Date: November 1992
Producer: Barrett Jones
Players: Kurt Cobain (guitar, vocals)

Tracks recorded:	Available on:
The 'Priest' They Called Him [M74]	The 'Priest' They Called Him single

Kurt Cobain was a big fan of William Burroughs' writing and jumped at the chance of working with him. The two didn't actually meet in a studio but Cobain recorded his guitar part and sent the tapes on for the addition of Burroughs' spoken word part. "It was just me and Kurt," recalls Barrett Jones, "The whole thing took less than an hour. I put a mic in front of his guitar amp and recorded straight to DAT, and he just made noise and feedback for forty minutes or so. They sent the DAT off and mixed it in with Burroughs talking."

The guitar noise that Cobain recorded was edited down to just twelve minutes to fit in with the time it took for Burroughs to read his piece. When Cobain sent the tapes to the label he also posted the following note: "Hi Thor, This here noise is just well, plain olde noise. Start it as soon as William begins to speak and let it go for as long as you like. I would prefer it to go until the noise is over but I assume you have some kind of time frame you need to work within. Love Kurdt."

Session number

{M4}

Venue: Razor's Edge Studio, San Francisco, CA.
Date: August - September 1992
Producer: Kurt Cobain
Players: the Melvins, Kurt Cobain (guitar)

Tracks recorded:	Available on:
Hooch	*Houdini* – Cobain produces
Joan Of Arc	*Houdini* – Cobain produces
Set Me Straight	*Houdini* – Cobain produces
Spread Eagle Beagle	*Houdini* – Cobain produces and plays guitar
Sky Pup	*Houdini* – Cobain produces and plays guitar
Pearl Bomb	*Houdini* – Cobain produces

222

Biographies

Steve Albini
Producer (recordist), 1993

While Albini is very well known as a producer of sorts, he first gained notoriety as a musician. As guitarist and lead singer with his first band Big Black he made waves through the indie landscape after signing to the influential Touch & Go label in the early 1980s. After four Big Black albums the band split in 1987 and Albini formed the short lived band Rapeman. He built up an impressive resumé as a 'recordist' – he says he doesn't produce bands, he only records them – working with the Pixies and the Wedding Present amongst others. He was a slightly controversial choice of producer for Nirvana's third album and his basic recording and mixing caused problems with Geffen when they heard the initial tapes. Scott Litt was brought in to remix some tracks after Albini refused to do any post-production on them. Albini's latest band is Shellac.

Also see session {34}

Aaron Burckhard
Drums, 1987 and 1988

Not the first drummer to play with Kurt Cobain (Greg Hokanson gets that honor) but he was the first to play any kind of session with Cobain and Krist Novoselic, on the KAOS radio show in 1987. Burckhard was a neighbor of Cobain in Aberdeen and started jamming with him and Novoselic before the band had any name. Burckhard needed a lot of persuasion to rehearse, which went against the grain as far as Cobain was concerned as the guitarist wanted to practice almost every day. Later the three musicians played under the name Skid Row but Burckhard left the band before it had been named Nirvana. Skid Row played a handful of shows during 1987 but by October, Burckhard had obtained a job as a Burger King assistant manager and found it impossible to get the time to rehearse; he saw the band as nothing more than an amusing hobby, so his time with the future Nirvana seemed over. He briefly filled in

223

again during a drummer shortage in 1988 but never played at an actual recording session. He later played with Attica.

Also see session {R1}

Greg Babior
Producer, 1989

Worked with the band on their trip to record at Evergreen State College in Olympia, WA, where the college's video room was used. This was also Jason Everman's only session with the band.

Also see session {14}

Kurt Cobain
Vocals, guitar, 1982-1994

With his early death, Kurt Cobain has become an icon of the late 20th century, going far beyond the singer, guitarist, songwriter of a rock band. Born in Hoquiam, Washington in 1967, Cobain was traumatized by the divorce of his parents when he was 7 years old. He started to write his own songs in the early 1980s, and he began putting bands together by the middle of the decade after meeting Krist Novoselic. As Nirvana started getting more and more attention, Cobain became more withdrawn due to a combination of uncertainty about how to handle his rapidly found fame and a long-running stomach ailment, which both took their toll on him. Drug use escalated despite his marriage to Courtney Love and the birth of a daughter, Frances Bean Cobain, in August 1992. As the *In Utero* tour hit Europe in the late winter of 1994 Cobain was at his lowest ebb. A suicide attempt in Rome left him in a coma and just weeks after cancelling the European tour and returning to Seattle he took his own life at the age of just 27.

Also see session – all except {37}

Chad Channing
Drums, 1988-1990

Born in California in 1967, Channing's family moved around during his formative years before settling in Washington State. He was drumming for Tick Dolly Row when he saw his first Nirvana show (they were playing under the name Bliss at the time) in 1988 and soon found himself in the band. His debut session was to record the "Love Buzz" [27] single and he remained with the band for two years, playing on *Bleach* and demos for what would later become *Nevermind*. It was during these latter sessions with Butch Vig that tensions between Channing and the other band members started to become more pronounced and after the short tour following these sessions he left the band. Post-Nirvana he played with the Methodists and Fire Ants. In 2008 he provided vocals for the band Before Cars.

Also see sessions {9} to {19} inclusive, {R2}, {R3}

Melora Craeger
Cello, 1994

With Kera Schaley (who played on *In Utero*) not available and Lori Goldston not traveling for the European dates of the *In Utero* tour, Craeger was drafted in to play cello during the acoustic parts of each set. She usually played with the band on "Dumb" [90], "All Apologies" [56] and "Polly" [11]. She also appeared on an Italian TV show with the band in February 1994.

Also see session {T11}

Dale Crover
Drums, 1987-88 and 1990

As drummer with the Melvins (1985-1996), Crover met Kurt Cobain in Olympia, WA and played with him in early bands such as Fecal Matter, Brown Cow/Brown Towel and Stiff Woodies. He had two stints drumming with Nirvana in 1987/88 and 1990 before concentrating on the Melvins.

Also see sessions {3}, {6}, {7}

John Duncan
Guitar, 1993

John Duncan, or Big John as he is more commonly known, had been in numerous bands through the 1980s. Starting out in Zeitgeist he then played guitar for the Exploited and Blood Uncles before joining Goodbye Mr McKenzie with future Garbage singer Shirley Manson. Duncan played second guitar for Nirvana for just one show in New York on July 23, 1993 before Pat Smear joined in that capacity.

Jack Endino
Producer, 1988-1992

Endino started out in the music business playing guitar in Skin Yard, a Seattle band that he formed with bassist Daniel House in 1985. Future Soundgarden drummer Matt Cameron was added for a while and vocals were handled by Ben McMillan. The band recorded five albums and toured extensively between 1986 and 1992, going through a number of different drummers in the process. A compilation CD was issued in 2002. Endino co-founded Reciprocal Recording with Chris Hanzsek in 1986 and worked there until 1993 (the studio changed its name to Word Of Mouth in 1991). During the late 1980s/early 1990s Endino worked with most of the grunge elite – Soundgarden, Green River, Mudhoney and Tad. He recorded Nirvana's first session in January 1988 and worked on the *Bleach* album, several sessions here and there over the next three years (including the "Sliver" [50] single) and finally did some early *In Utero* demos with the band. *Bleach* really helped Endino make a name for himself and he's been busy ever since. Subsequently he's worked with the likes of Bruce Dickinson (1996), Mudhoney (2000), Therapy? (2001) and Hot Hot Heat (2002).

Also see sessions {7} to {13}, {16}, {20}, {21}, {29}, {M1}, {M2}

Jason Everman
Guitar, 1989

Jason Everman's claim to fame is that he funded the recording of *Bleach* for the band and in return he was credited as playing on the album (even though he didn't). He joined them for the subsequent tour but left after encountering 'musical differences' with the rest of the band, although whether he quit or was fired depends on who you ask. "We kicked him out 'cos he didn't like to do the songs that we like. He wants to play slow, heavy grunge and we want to write pop songs," said Kurt Cobain in 1990. Everman next showed up as a member of Soundgarden, but his stint with them was equally brief, he played bass for the band for just six months. Later he played in Mind Funk and after quitting music he joined the Army Ranger School and then went into the military full time with the Navy.

Also see session {11}

Steve Fisk
Producer, 1989

Fisk has recorded a lot of bands in his time including the likes of Soundgarden, Soul Coughing, the Geraldine Fibbers, the Posies, the Wedding Present, Beat Happening and the Screaming Trees.

Also see session {15}

Dave Foster
Drums, 1988

Though Dave Foster never played a Nirvana session, he was a member of the band for a short time in the early part of 1988, including their first ever show as Nirvana on April 24. The outgoing Dale Crover suggested him to the band and though he lived in Aberdeen (Cobain was living in Olympia, WA and Novoselic was in Tacoma) he got the job. On practice nights Cobain would drive his battered old Datsun from Olympia to Aberdeen to collect Foster and to Tacoma where the band had a practice space. After the practice he would then have to do the same trek in reverse. Foster dressed differently to Novoselic and Cobain and had short hair and despite Cobain's protestations he didn't change. After Foster was briefly jailed for an altercation with a local Mayor's son, Cobain fired him in April 1989. It was time for another change of drummer.

Also see sessions – none

Lori Goldston
Cello, 1993-94

Goldston is a classically trained cellist who can also play jazz and folk guitar and percussion. She received her music training in New York before moving to Seattle in the mid-1980s. She formed the Black Cat Orchestra in 1991 and has played with various bands and jazz groups in the Pacific Northwest. She played with Nirvana on the US legs of the *In Utero* tour bringing a new dimension to their live shows as the band slowed things down for an acoustic set in mid-show. Her most memorable performance was probably on the *MTV Unplugged* show in November 1993.

Also see session {T8}

Dave Grohl
Drums, backing vocals, 1990-1994

Before joining Nirvana, Dave Grohl had a reputation as one of rock's hardest hitting drummers. During his tenure on the Nirvana drum stool he cemented this reputation beyond all question. Two years younger than Kurt Cobain, he was born in Ohio and grew up in Virginia. His early bands included Freak Baby and the hardcore Mission Impossible – with the former he played guitar and recorded at the local 4-track basement studio of Barrett Jones. Grohl then played drums in Dain Bramage and finally Scream from 1987 to 1990 when he auditioned for Nirvana. Buzz Osbourne told Grohl that Nirvana were looking for a drummer and the rest is history. After Nirvana, Grohl formed the Foo Fighters and started another chapter of his musical career as a lead singer/guitarist. He has also played occasional side projects as a drummer including a stint with the Queens Of The Stone Age and a collaboration with Killing Joke in 2003.

Also see sessions {24} to {41} inclusive

Greg Hokanson
Drums, 1985

Hokanson played drums in the Fecal Matter trio (with Cobain on guitar and Dale Crover on bass) which practiced during 1985. When Cobain wanted to go and record some tracks on his Aunt Mari's four-track recorder in December 1985 only Crover could be convinced to go and so Hokanson drifted out of the fold.

Also see sessions – none

Barrett Jones
Producer, 1992

Jones had been a long-time friend of Dave Grohl and had originally recorded his early bands back in Virginia. After moving to Seattle he met the rest of Nirvana and worked on the April 1992 session that gave rise to three separate releases – the "Oh, The Guilt" [55] single, "Curmudgeon" [69] which was the b-side for "Lithium" [45] and "Return Of The Rat" [70] for the Greg Sage compilation. He also produced Kurt Cobain's lengthy guitar recordings for the William Burroughs single "The 'Priest' They Called Him" [M74] in November 1992.

Also see sessions {28}, {M3}

Adam Kasper
Producer, 1994
Kasper oversaw the final Nirvana recordings at the Robert Lang Studio in January 1994. He has also worked with the likes of Pearl Jam and the Foo Fighters

Also see sessions {37}, {38}

Curt Kirkwood and Cris Kirkwood
Guitars, 1993
The Arizona brothers Kirkwood had their first release as the Meat Puppets with the *In A Car* EP way back in 1982. After signing with SST they were part of an exciting rush of new American bands that also included the Replacements, Husker Du and R.E.M. in the first half of the 1980s. Their landmark Meat Puppets II album from 1994 was one of Kurt Cobain's favorites. When he wanted to cover not one, not two, but three of the songs from it for Nirvana's *Unplugged* session in 1993 it made sense for him to invite the brothers to actually come and play the songs with Nirvana. The covers of "Lake Of Fire" [112], "Oh, Me" [111] and "Plateau" [110] proved to be the first time that many people had heard Meat Puppets songs, but this surely gave them an appetite to hear more.

Also see session {T8}

Scott Litt
Remixer, 1993
Litt is perhaps best known for producing a handful of R.E.M.'s albums through the mid-1980s to mid-1990s. He was brought in after the controversial Steve Albini sessions to remix a few tracks. He also mixed the *MTV Unplugged* recording for its official release.

Also see session {35}

Craig Montgomery
Producer, 1992-1993
Montgomery had worked as the band's sound man for a while and finally got the chance to produce a session when a friend of his allowed them to use the up-market Music Source Studio on New Year's Day 1991. He also worked on the Nirvana/Hole session during the trip to Brazil in January 1993.

Also see sessions {24}, {31}

Krist Novoselic
Bass, 1987-1994

Of Croatian descent, Novoselic changed the spelling of his name from Chris to Krist after the Croat war of independence in 1992. The gangly bassist met Kurt Cobain in Aberdeen after spending his early years in California. The two hit it off immediately and were soon playing in bands together. After the demise of Nirvana, Novoselic put out an album with his new band Sweet 75 in 1997 but it was a commercial disappointment and they broke up soon afterwards. He returned as a member of Eyes Adrift but that band also split up after one album. Novoselic announced in 2003 that he was quitting the music business to concentrate on a political career.

Also see sessions {6} to {41} inclusive

Doug Olsen
Engineer, 1990

Worked as an engineer at Smart Studios and assisted Butch Vig recording the *Nevermind* demos in March 1990. "Smart was very informal then, I was not called an assistant engineer, although technically that's probably what I was doing" he says. "It seemed like every band that came into Smart had a copy [of the *Nevermind* demos tape], every band that would come in was really in to it."

Also see session {19}

Dan Peters
Drums, 1990

Of Nirvana's myriad drummers, Dan Peters probably made the biggest impact in the shortest time. In just two months he managed to play one show, record a classic single and be photographed with the band for a cover shoot without ever really being a permanent member. Peters had played with Mudhoney as they debuted with their superlative *Superfuzz Bigmuff* album in 1988 but by 1990 was thinking of jumping ship. He played drums on Nirvana's lightning-fast session for "Sliver" [50] but after a single show with Nirvana in September 1990 he was replaced by Dave Grohl.

Also see session {20}

230

Kera Schaley
Cello, 1993

Chicago cellist Schaley had played with rock bands since she had been in high school. "I was playing my cello a lot because I was a depressed teenager and it was my outlet," she says. After moving to Athens, GA, she played with Low and Vic Chestnutt before contributing to "Dumb" [90] and "All Apologies" [56] on *In Utero*. She formed Martyr & Pistol, a trio that put out an album entitled *Reconstructive Surgery* in 2000.

Also see session {34}

Pat Smear
Guitar, 1993-1994

By the time Pat Smear (real name George Ruthenburg) joined Nirvana in 1993 as second guitarist the 34-year-old had already had a lifetime of punk rock experience behind him. The Los Angeles native had formed the hometown Germs with Darby Crash in 1977 and led the West Coast punk movement. Smear had to endure the loss of Crash to an overdose in December 1980 and the Germs were over. He put out two solo albums (*Ruthensmear*, 1987 and *So You Fell In Love With A Musician*, 1992) and turned down a chance to join the Red Hot Chili Peppers before Kurt Cobain asked him to come on board in the summer of 1993. Smear played on the *In Utero* tour and appeared on all the band's TV appearances during that period. Later he re-united with Dave Grohl in the Foo Fighters for a while and has also played with Mike Watt.

Also see sessions {T7} to {T11} inclusive

Butch Vig
Producer, 1990-91

Butch Vig began his musical career as the drummer for Fire Town, a band that released two albums on the Atlantic label in the 1980s. From 1983 he was producing the likes of Killdozer in his own Smart Studios which he'd opened in 1980. He initially worked on *Nevermind* demos with the band in 1990 before traveling to Los Angeles to record the album a year later. After the explosive success of *Nevermind* he was seen as the hot producer of the 1990s but he turned his attention back to drumming when he formed Garbage with Smart Studio co-owner

Steve Marker, Duke Erikson and vocalist Shirley Manson. The group went on to have a number of hit albums and singles during the late 1990s.

Also see sessions {19} and {26}

Andy Wallace
Engineer, 1991
By the time Nirvana was looking for a mixing engineer for *Nevermind*, Andy Wallace had already gathered a varied and impressive number of credits to his name. Madonna, the Doors and Slayer were just three of his successes. He was responsible for bringing out the radio-friendly sound of *Nevermind* and must take credit for helping to make it as readily accessible as it turned out, by using a selection of techniques, some of which he'd used on dance records in the 1980s.

Also see session {27}

The Studios

Nirvana worked in many different studios around the Pacific Northwest. The only excursions from home territory were the *In Utero* sessions with Steve Albini in Minneapolis and the impromptu session while in Brazil for a festival in early 1993. Despite mainly working close to home the band changed producers and engineers frequently, usually on a studio-by-studio basis. Starting with the then cheapest in Seattle (Reciprocal) they worked at eleven different venues before their final recordings at the relatively luxurious Robert Lang Studios in January 1994. While there are countless home and practice venues that were also used, here is a full list of the professional facilities that the band utilized between 1988 and 1994.

Ariola Ltda BMG
Address: Rio de Janeiro, Brazil
History: unknown
Technical specification: not available
Clients include: not available
Nirvana sessions: January 19 to 22, 1993 {31} with Craig
  Montgomery

Bad Animals
Address: 2212 4th Avenue, Seattle, WA.
History: Originally called Steve Lawson Productions when it opened on Seattle's 6th Avenue in 1979, it soon grew to a three studio outfit and moved into the former Kaye Smith Studio premises at its current location in 1990. Lawson opened Studio X within the complex with Heart's Ann and Nancy Wilson, renaming it Bad Animals in 1992. In 1999 the studio was bought by employees Dave Howe, Mike McAuliffe, Tom McGurk and Charlie Nordstrom. Now does much film and TV work and has recorded the voices of Demi Moore and Tom Skerrit among others.

233

Technical specification: no longer used for rock recordings
Clients include: R.E.M., Soundgarden, Alice In Chains, Neil
Young, Heart, Johnny Cash, Pearl Jam
Nirvana sessions: May 1993 {35} remixing with Scott Litt
Staff: Dave Howe, Mike McAuliffe, Tom McGurk, Charlie
Nordstrom and Wendy Wills.

Evergreen State College
Address: Library 1324, 2700 Evergreen Parkway, Olympia, WA,
98505.
History: Evergreen State College was created by Washington State
Legislature in 1967, officially opening its doors to students in 1971.
KAOS (Kicking Ass Olympia Style) Radio began broadcasting
on January 1, 1973.
Technical Specification: Three studio cameras, sound mixing board,
availability to project 16mm, Super 8 and 35mm footage.
Clients include: not applicable
Nirvana sessions: June 1989 {14} with Greg Babior and March 20,
1990 {18} unproduced

Music Source Studios
Address: Seattle, WA, USA
History: unknown
Technical specification: n/a
Clients include: radio advertisers
Nirvana sessions: August 1989 {15} with Steve Fisk and January 1,
1991 {24} with Craig Montgomery

Pachyderm Studio
Address: 7840 Co. 17 Blvd., Cannon Falls, MN.
History: Built into a hillside next to a 40-acre wildlife park 40 miles
from Minneapolis, has its own four bedroom lodging with sauna
and indoor pool.
Technical specification: Vintage tube microphones, a classic Neve
8068 console and Studer tape machines

234

Clients include: P.J. Harvey (Rid Of Me), Live (Throwing Copper), Soul Asylum (Grave Dancer's Union), The Jayhawks (Hollywood Town Hall), Babes In Toyland (Fontanelle)
Nirvana sessions: February to March 1993 {34} with Steve Albini
Staff: House engineer Brent Sigmeth

Reciprocal Studio
Address: no longer operational
History: 1986 to 1991.
Co-founded by Jack Endino with Chris Hanzsek. Ownership and some equipment changed in summer 1991 and the facility was re-named Word Of Mouth Recording, until that closed in 1993.
Technical specification: n/a
Clients include: Tad
Nirvana sessions: January 23 1988 {7}, June 11, 1988 {9}, June 30, 1988 {10}, July 16, 1988 ({11}, September 27, 1988 {12}, December 1988–January 1989 {13}, 2 and 3, January 1990 {16}, July 11, 1990 {20}, July 24, 1990 {21} and October 25 and 26, 1992 {29} all with Jack Endino
Staff: Jack Endino

Robert Lang Studios
Address: 19351 23rd Avenue N.W, Shoreline, WA
History: Founded above Puget Sound, north of Seattle, in the early 1970s
Technical specification: Main room 34x28 feet (24 foot ceiling), 48 input SSL EIG+ console, 28 different microphones, a Mark IV Mellotron, numerous drums and percussion
Clients include: Afghan Whigs, Candlebox, Heart, Ken Stringfellow, Silkworm, Sir Mix-A-Lot, Sunny Day Real Estate, Tad, Therapy
Nirvana sessions: January 28 and 29, 1994 {37}, January 30, 1994 {38} all with Adam Kasper
Staff: Engineers – Justin Armstrong, Geoff Ott, Brian Valentino, Dave Taylor.
Assistant Engineers – Mark Branch, Ryan May, Austin Poole

Scream Studios

Address: 11616 Ventura Boulevard, Studio City, CA 91604.

History: founded in 1989

Technical specification: 25'x 22' control room, 24'x 28' triangular recording room. Sony 3348 Digital 48 Track Recorder, Mitsubishi X-850 Digital 32 Track, Studer A-820 1/2" 2 Track Recorders, 24 Bit Digital Paqrat Recording System

Clients include: Macy Gray, Bob Dylan, Faith Hill, Ozzy Osbourne, Paul McCartney, J-Lo

Nirvana sessions: June 1 to 10, 1991 {27} mixing with Andy Wallace

Smart Studios

Address: 1254 East Washington Avenue, Madison, WI.

History: Formed in 1980 by Butch Vig and Steve Marker on a 4-track machine in a basement. Moved into a warehouse and added an 8-track machine in 1983 and then again, 4 years later, into its present location.

Clients include: Beck, Butthole Surfers, Cheap Trick, Depeche Mode, Everclear, Garbage, Killdozer, Marie Osmond, Nine Inch Nails, Sonic Youth, Young Fresh Fellows

Nirvana sessions: April 2 to 6, 1990 {19} with Butch Vig

Staff: Butch Vig and Steve Marker (owners), Mike Zirkel, Doug Olsen, Mark Haines, Lonya Nenashev

Sound City Studios

Address: 15456 Cabrito Road, Van Nuys, CA.

Technical specification: 30 different microphones. Studio A: 40x50 feet (25 foot ceiling), isolation booths, Custom Neve 8028 24 track console. Studio B: 26x18 feet (14 foot ceiling), booth

Clients include: Tom Petty, Michael Jackson, Perfect Circle, Elton John, Smashing Pumpkins, Weezer, the Melvins, Johnny Cash, Nick Cave, Cheap Trick, 1-7, Bob Dylan, Neil Young, Red Hot Chili Peppers, Fleetwood Mac, Rage Against The Machine

Nirvana sessions: May 2 to 31, 1991 {26} with Butch Vig

The Laundry Room

Address: Greenwood, Seattle, WA.

History: Initially started literally in Barrett Jones' laundry room in Arlington, VA, before he moved to the West Coast

Technical specification: 28x14 feet (14 foot ceiling), 8, 16 and 24 track tape machines, Sony JH-600 28x24 input board, 25 different microphones

Clients include: Bush, Jimmy Eat World, the Melvins, Pussy Galore, Velocity Girl

Nirvana sessions: April 1992 {28}

Staff: Barrett Jones (owner), Greg Williamson, Alex Kostelnik

Discography

Collectors should be wary of counterfeit items, especially for the more expensive and withdrawn promotional items. Various eastern European and Asian releases have also flooded the market claiming to be official releases but these are invariably fakes.

1988
Singles
7" vinyl
Love Buzz [27] / Big Cheese [28]

Sub Pop SP23	US	limited to 1,000 numbered copies

1989
Albums
Bleach
Cassette

Sub Pop SP34a	US
Tupelo TUPMC6	UK

LP

Sub Pop SP34	US	initial 1000 on white vinyl with free poster
Sub Pop SP34	US	pressing of 1001-2000 with free poster
Sub Pop SP34	US	various color vinyl
Tupelo TUPLP6	UK	initial 300 on white vinyl
Tupelo TUPLP6	UK	nos. 301-2300 on green vinyl
Tupelo TUPLP6	UK	
Waterfront DAMP114	Australia	on red, yellow or blue vinyl

CD

Sub Pop SP34b	US	2 extra tracks
Tupelo TUPCD6UK		

EPs
Blew

Discography

12" vinyl
Blew [31] / Love Buzz [27] / Been A Son [40] / Stain [41]
Tupelo TUPEP8   UK
CD
Blew [31] / Love Buzz [27] / Been A Son [40] / Stain [41]
Tupelo TUPCD8   UK

1990
Albums
Bleach
Cassette
Sub Pop SP34a   US
Tupelo TUPMC6   UK
CD
Sub Pop SP34b   US
Tupelo TUPCD6UK
Singles
Sliver
7" vinyl
Sliver [50] / Dive [39]
Sub Pop SP73   US   initial 3000 on blue vinyl
Sliver [50] / Dive [39]
Sub Pop SP73   US   various color vinyl

1991
Albums
Bleach
Cassette
Geffen GFLC19291   UK
LP
DGC/MCA 25002   Japan   with obi strip
CD
DGC/MCA MVCG93   Japan   with obi strip
Geffen GFLD1929   UK
Geffen GED24433   Australia
Nevermind
Cassette
Geffen DGCC 24425   US   promo without 'hidden' track
                                             Endless, Nameless [67]

239

Geffen DGCC 24425	US	without 'hidden' track Endless, Nameless [67]
Geffen DCCC 24425	US	
DGC GEC 24425	UK	
Geffen CC24425	Germany	
Geffen MVXZ12	Japan	

LP

Geffen DGC 24425	US	
DGC DGC 24425	UK	
DGC MVJG-25001	Japan	

CD

Geffen DGCD 24425	US	without 'hidden' track Endless, Nameless [67]
Geffen DGCD 24425	US	
DGC GED 24425	UK	
DGC MVCG-67	Japan	
GED DGCD24425	Germany	

EPs

Hormoaning

12" vinyl

Geffen GEF2171	Australia	5,000 copies - some on blue vinyl

Cassette

Geffen GEFC21711	Australia	5,000 copies

CD

Geffen GEFD21711	Australia	5,000 copies

Singles

Here She Comes Now

7" vinyl

Here She Comes Now [47] / Venus In Furs (by the Melvins)

Communion 23	US	various color vinyl

Molly's Lips

7" vinyl

Molly's Lips [L104] / Candy (by the Fluid)

Sub Pop SP97	US	4000 copies on green vinyl

Molly's Lips [L104] / Candy (by the Fluid)

Sub Pop SP97	US	2500 copies on black vinyl

240

On A Plain
On A Plain [57]
DGC CDPR04354   US   promo only

Sliver
7" vinyl
Sliver [50] / Dive [39]
Tupelo TUP25   UK   initial 2000 on green vinyl
12" vinyl
Sliver [50] / Dive [39] / About A Girl
Tupelo TUPEP25   UK   various color vinyl
CD
Sliver [50] / Dive [39] / About A Girl [L14] / Spank Thru [L5]
Tupelo TUPCD25   UK

Smells Like Teen Spirit
7" vinyl
Smells Like Teen Spirit [59] / Even In His Youth [42]
Geffen DGCCS7   US
Smells Like Teen Spirit [59] / Drain You [51]
Geffen DGC5   UK
12" vinyl
Smells Like Teen Spirit [59] / Even In His Youth [42] / Aneurysm [54]
Geffen DGCS 21673   US
Smells Like Teen Spirit [59]
Geffen PRO-A-4314   US   orange vinyl promo
Smells Like Teen Spirit [59] / Even In His Youth [42] / Aneurysm [54]
Geffen PRO-A-4314   US   yellow vinyl
Smells Like Teen Spirit [59] / Even In His Youth [42] / Aneurysm [54]
Geffen GET21712   Germany   picture disc
Smells Like Teen Spirit [59] / Drain You [51] / Even In His Youth [42]
Geffen DGCT5   UK
Smells Like Teen Spirit [59] / Drain You [51] / Aneurysm [54]
Geffen DGCTP5   UK   picture disc
Cassette
Smells Like Teen Spirit [59] / Even In His Youth [42]
Geffen DGCCS19050   US
Smells Like Teen Spirit [59] / Even In His Youth [42] / Aneurysm [54]
Geffen DGCSS21673   US

Smells Like Teen Spirit [59] / Drain You [51]
Geffen DGCS5   UK
CD
Smells Like Teen Spirit [59] / Even In His Youth [42] / Aneurysm [54]
Geffen DGCDS21673   US
Smells Like Teen Spirit [59]

DGC PROCD4308	US	promo with 'edit' and album versions

Smells Like Teen Spirit [59] / Drain You [51] / Even In His Youth [42] /
  Aneurysm [54]
Geffen DGCCD5   UK

1992
Albums
Bleach
Cassette

Sub Pop SP34a	US	remastered
Geffen GFLC19291	UK	remastered

LP

Waterfront DAMP114	1982	Australia	limited to 500 copies green vinyl/cloth bag

CD

Geffen GFLC19291	UK	remastered
Geffen MVCG-93	Japan	13 track album
Sub Pop SP34b	US	remastered

Incesticide
Cassette

DGC DGCC24504	US	
DGC DGCC1D24504	US	promo
MCA GEFC24504	Canada	promo
Geffen GEC24504	Germany	

LP

DGC DGC24504	US	blue vinyl
Geffen GEF24504	Holland	
DGC MVJG25003	Japan	

CD

DGC DGCD24504DJ	US	promo
DGC DGCD24504	US	

242

Geffen CGEFD24504	Canada	
Geffen GEFD24504	Australia	
Geffen GED24504	Germany	promo limited to 500 copies
MCA MVCG100	Japan	

Nevermind

LP

Geffen GEO236	Czech Republic	picture disc

EPs

Hormoaning

CD

Geffen MVCG17002	Japan	

Singles

Come As You Are

7" vinyl

Come As You Are [60] / Drain You [L51]

DGC DGCCS7	US	

Come As You Are [60] / Endless, Nameless [67]

DGC DGC7	UK	

Come As You Are [60] / Drain You [L51]

DGC GES19120	France	

Come As You Are [60] / Endless, Nameless [67]

DGC GES19065	Germany	

12" vinyl

Come As You Are [60]

DGC PROA4416	US	promo

Come As You Are [60] / School [L34] / Drain You [L51]

DGC DGCS21707	US	

Come As You Are [60] / Endless, Nameless [67] / School [L34]

DGC DGC7	UK	

Come As You Are [60] / Endless, Nameless [67] / School [L34]

DCC DGCTP7	UK	picture disc

Come As You Are [60] / Endless, Nameless [67] / Drain You [L51]

DGC GET21699	Germany	

Come As You Are [60] / Endless, Nameless [67] / Drain You [L51]

DGC GET21712	Germany	picture disc

Come As You Are [60] / Endless, Nameless [67] / Drain You [L51]
DGC GET21699   Australia
Cassette
Come As You Are [60] / School [L34] / Drain You [L51]
DGC DGCCS21707   US
Come As You Are [60] / Endless, Nameless [67]
DGC DGCCS19065   Australia
CD
Come As You Are [60]
DGC CDPRO4375   US   promo
Come As You Are [60] / School [L34] / Drain You [L51]
DGC DGCDS2I707   US
Come As You Are [60] / Endless, Nameless [67] / School [L34] / Drain You
  [L51]
DGC DGCTD7   UK

In Bloom
7" vinyl
In Bloom [48] / Polly [L11a]
Geffen GEF34   UK
12" vinyl
In Bloom [48] / Sliver [L50] / Polly [11a]
Geffen GFSTP34   UK   picture disc
Cassette
In Bloom [48] / Polly [L11a]
Geffen GFSC34   UK
In Bloom [48] / Polly [L11a]
Geffen GEFCS19097   Australia
CD
In Bloom [48]
DGC PR0CD44632   US   promo
In Bloom [48] / Sliver [L50] / Polly [11a]
Geffen GFSTD34   UK
In Bloom [48] / Sliver [L50] / Polly [11a]
Geffen GEFDM21760   Australia
In Bloom [48] / Sliver [L50] / Polly [11a]
Geffen MVCG13002   Japan

244

Lithium
12" vinyl
Lithium [45] / Been A Son [L40] / Curmudgeon [69]
DGC DGCS21815　　　　US
Lithium [45] / Been A Son [L40] / Curmudgeon [69]
DGC　DGCTP9　　　　UK　　　　picture disc
Lithium [45] / Been A Son [L40] / Curmudgeon [69]
DGC GET21815　　　　Germany
Cassette
Lithium [45] / Been A Son [L40] / Curmudgeon [69]
DGC DGCCS21815　　　　US
Lithium [45] / Been A Son [L40] / Curmudgeon [69]
DGC DGCCS19134　　　　Australia
CD
Lithium [45]
DGC CDPR04429　　　　US　　　　promo
Lithium [45] / Been A Son [L40] / Curmudgeon [69]
DGC DGCDM21815　　US
Lithium [45] / Been A Son [L40] / Curmudgeon [69] / D-7 [R100]
DGC DGCTD9　　　　UK
Spoken word
Nevermind: It's An Interview
Geffen PRO-CD 4382 CD　　US　　　　Interviews

1993
Albums
In Utero
Cassette
Geffen GEF/C 24607　　　US　　　promo
DGC DGCC24607　　　　US
Geffen GEFC24536　　　UK
Geffen GEFC24536　　　Australia
LP
DGC D6C24607　　　　US　　　clear vinyl
Geffen GEF24536　　　UK
Geffen GEF24536　　　Australia
DCC MVJG 25004　　　Japan

245

CD

DGC DGCD24607	US
Geffen GEFCD24536	UK
Geffen GEFD24536	Australia

Singles
All Apologies
7" vinyl
All Apologies [56] / Rape Me [71] / MV [77]

Geffen GFS66	UK

12" vinyl
All Apologies [56] / Rape Me [71] / MV [77]

Geffen GFST66	UK	with 2 art prints

Cassette
All Apologies [56] / Rape Me [71] / MV [77]

Geffen GFSC66	UK

All Apologies [56] / Rape Me [71] / MV [77]

Geffen GEFCS 21880	Australia

CD
All Apologies [56] / Rape Me [71] / MV [77]

Geffen GFSTD66	UK

All Apologies [56] / Rape Me [71] / MV [77]

Geffen GED21880	Germany

All Apologies [56] / Rape Me [71] / MV [77]

Geffen GED21897	France

All Apologies [56] / Rape Me [71] / MV [77]

Geffen GEFDM 21880	Australia

All Apologies [56] / Rape Me [71] / MV [77]

Geffen MVCG13011	Australia

Heart-Shaped Box
7" vinyl
Heart-Shaped Box [73] /Marigold [91]

Geffen GFS54	UK

Heart-Shaped Box [73] / Marigold [91]

Geffen GES19191	Germany	red vinyl

12" vinyl
Heart-Shaped Box [73] / Gallons Of Rubbing Alcohol Flow Through
   The Strip [79]

246

DGC PROA4558   US   promo
Heart-Shaped Box [73] / Milk It [76] / Marigold [91]
Geffen GFST54   UK
Cassette
Heart-Shaped Box [73] / Milk It [76] / Marigold [91]
Geffen GFSC54   UK
Heart-Shaped Box [73] / Milk It [76] / Marigold [91]
Geffen GEFD218449   Australia
CD
Heart-Shaped Box [73]
DGC PROCD4545   US   promo
Heart-Shaped Box [73]
DGC GED21849UK   promo
Heart-Shaped Box [73] / Milk It [76] / Marigold [91]
Geffen GFSTD54   UK
Heart-Shaped Box [73] / Milk It [76] / Marigold [91]
Geffen GEFCS19191   Australia
Heart-Shaped Box [73] / Milk It [76] / Marigold [91]
Geffen GED21856   France   card sleeve
Heart-Shaped Box [73] / Milk It [76] / Marigold [91]
Geffen MVCG13008   Japan

Oh, The Guilt
7" vinyl
Oh, The Guilt [55] / 'Puss' (by the Jesus Lizard)
Touch & Go TG83   US
Oh, The Guilt [55] / 'Puss' (by the Jesus Lizard)
Touch & Go TG83   UK   blue vinyl with poster
Oh, The Guilt [55] / 'Puss' (by the Jesus Lizard)
Touch & Go IV23   Australia   picture disc limited to
                                                      1500 copies
Cassette
Oh, The Guilt [55] / 'Puss' (by the Jesus Lizard)
Touch & Go TG83CS   US
CD
Oh, The Guilt [55] / 'Puss' (by the Jesus Lizard)
Touch & Go TG83CD   US

Oh, The Guilt [55] / 'Puss' (by the Jesus Lizard)
Touch & Go TG83CD   UK

Rape Me
CD
Rape Me [71] / All Apologies [56]
DGC NIRVA1   UK   promo

1994
Albums
In Utero
Cassette
DCC DGCC24705   US
CD
DCC DGCD24705   US

Live! Tonight! Sold Out!
Video
Geffen GEFV-39541   US   NTSC format
Geffen GEV-39541   UK   PAL format
MCA Victor MVLG-19   Japan   NTSC format
Laserdisc
Geffen GHV ID2772MS   US   NTSC format

MTV Unplugged In New York
Cassette
DGC DGCC24727   US
Geffen 090716   UK   promo
LP
DGC DGC24727   US
DGC DGC24727   US   white vinyl
Geffen GEF24727   France
Geffen GEF24727   Germany
Geffen GEF24727   Germany   white vinyl
MCA MVJG25005   Japan
CD
DGC DGCD24727   US
DGC DGCD24727DJ   US   promo
Geffen GED24727   UK
MCA MVCG163   Japan
DGC CDGCD24727   Canada

Discography

Singles
About A Girl
CD

About A Girl [U14] / Something In The Way [U63]
DGC PROCD4688A   US   promo
About A Girl [U14] / Something In The Way [U63]
Geffen GED21958   France
About A Girl [U14] / Something In The Way [U63]
Geffen GEDS003   Spain   promo
About A Girl [U14] / Something In The Way [U63]
Geffen GEFDS21958   Australia   promo 200 numbered
                                                    copies
About A Girl [U14] / Something In The Way [U63]
Geffen GEFDS2195   Australia

All Apologies
CD

All Apologies [U56]/All Apologies [56]
DGC PROCD4618   US   promo
All Apologies [56]
DCC PROCD4581   US   promo
All Apologies [56] / Rape Me [71]
DCC PROCCD4582   US   promo
All Apologies [56] / Rape Me [71] / MV [77]
MCA MVCG13011   Japan
All Apologies [U56]   Spain   promo

Lake Of Fire
CD

Lake Of Fire [U112] / Where Did You Sleep Last Night [U101]
Geffen PROCD4265   Australia   promo

Pennyroyal Tea
7" vinyl

Pennyroyal Tea [52a] / Where Did You Sleep Last Night [U101]
Geffen no cat. number   UK   test pressing limited
                                                    to10 copies
Cassette
Pennyroyal Tea [52a] / I Hate Myself And Want To Die [92] / Where
Did You Sleep Last Night [U101]

Geffen DGCC24705	Germany	

CD

Pennyroyal Tea [52a] / I Hate Myself And Want To Die [92] / Where
  Did You Sleep Last Night [U101]

Geffen DGCD24705	Germany	

Pennyroyal Tea [52a]

Geffen NIRPRO	UK	promo

Polly
CD
Polly [U11]

DGC GEDP022	France	promo

The Man Who Sold The World
CD
The Man Who Sold The World [U109]

DGC PROCD4704	US	promo

The Man Who Sold The World [U109]

DGC GEDS008	Spain	promo

Where Did You Sleep Last Night
CD
Where Did You Sleep Last Night [U101]

Geffen NIRVPRO1	UK	promo

Where Did You Sleep Last Night [U101]

Geffen NIRVPRO1	France	promo

Where Did You Sleep Last Night [U101]

Geffen PROCD4265	Australia	promo

1996
Albums
From The Muddy Banks Of The Wishkah
Cassette

DGC DGCC-A-25105	US	promo
DGC DGCC-25105	US	
Geffen GEC 25105	UK	

Double LP

DGC DGC2-25105	US	
Geffen GEF 25105(2)	UK	

CD

DGC DGCD-25105	US	
DGC DGCD-25105	US	promo
DGC CD ACETATE	US	promo
Geffen GED 25105	UK	
Geffen GED 25105	Australia	
Geffen GEFD-25105	Australia	
DGC DGCSD-25105	Canada	

In Utero
LP

Universal Music MVJG-25004	Japan

CD

Ultra Disc UDCD690	US	gold audiophile

Incesticide
LP

Geffen MVJG-25003	Japan

Live! Tonight! Sold Out!
DVD

Geffen 1709812 (NTSC)	Australia

Nevermind
LP

Mobile Fidelity Sound Lab MFSL 1-258	US	remastered

CD

Ultra Disc UDCD666	US	gold audiophile
Mobile Fidelity Sound Lab UDCD690	US	gold audiophile

Singles
Aneurysm
CD

Aneurysm [L54]

DCC	PROCD 1033	US	promo

Aneurysm [L54]

DCC	PROCD1033	UK	promo

Drain You
CD
Drain You [L51a]
DGC PROCD1070   US

Lithium
CD
Lithium [L45]
Geffen NIR 96010   Holland

Smells Like Teen Spirit
CD
Smells Like Teen Spirit [L59]
DGC/MCA F0010   France promo

1997
Albums
In Utero
CD
Mobile Fidelity Sound Lab UDCD690   US   gold

Nevermind
LP
Simply Vinyl SVLP 038   UK   180gm

1998
Albums
In Utero
LP
Simply Vinyl SVLP0048   UK   180g vinyl

MTV Unplugged In New York
LP
Simply Vinyl SVLP0053   UK   180g vinyl

Nevermind
LP
Simply Vinyl SVLP0038   UK   180g vinyl

Discography

2000
Albums
MTV Unplugged in New York
CD
Geffen GED24727   Brazil

2002
Albums
Bleach
LP
Sub Pop 9878700341   UK
CD
Rhino   5186561462   UK   20th Anniversary 25 track edition

Nirvana
Double LP
Universal 493523-1   UK
Geffen 493523-1   Europe
CD
DGC 0694935072   US
Geffen 493523-2   UK
Geffen UICY-1140   Japan
Geffen 493 523-2   Australia
Polydor Nirvana1#1   Spain   promo

Singles
You Know You're Right
CD
You Know You're Right [93]
DGC INTR-10853-2   US
You Know You're Right [93]
Universal   CD-R Acetate Japan
You Know You're Right [93]
Geffen PRO-CD-4835   France
You Know You're Right [93]
Geffen 01141-2   Mexico

2003
Albums
Bleach
CD

DGC WPCR-11525	Japan	
Geffen UICY2003	Japan	

From The Muddy Banks Of The Wishkah
Double LP

Geffen 425105-1	UK	remastered

In Utero
LP

DGC 4245361	US	Albini mix
Geffen 424516-1	UK	Albini mix

2004
Albums
Incesticide
CD

Geffen UICY-9719	Japan	

Nevermind
CD in 12" sleeve

Universal Music UICY-95014	Japan	limited edition

UMD

Eagle Vision EU300690	US	(All regions) for the Sony Playstation

With The Lights Out
3CD + DVD box set

Geffen B000372700	UK	PAL format
Geffen 602498648384	UK	PAL format
Geffen B0003727-00	US	NTSC format

Spoken Word
3 CD box set

Chrome Dreams BSCD6012 Collectors Box	UK	Interviews

Discography

2005
Albums
Nevermind
DVD

Eagle Vision EV30069-9	US	Classic Albums series NTSC format
Eagle Vision EREDV436UK	Classic Albums series	PAL format
Eagle Vision RV0296	Australia	Classic Albums series PAL format

Sliver: the best of the box
CD

Geffen B0005617-02	US
Geffen 602498867181	UK

2006
Albums
Live! Tonight! Sold Out!
DVD

Geffen B0007914-09	US	NTSC format

2007
Albums
From The Muddy Banks Of The Wishkah
CD

Universal Music UICY-93362	Japan	limited edition

In Utero
LP

Universal Music UICY-93360	Japan

Incesticide
CD

Geffen UICY-93359	Japan	limited edition

MTV Unplugged In New York
CD

Universal Music UICY-93361	Japan	limited edition

DVD

Geffen B0010263-09	US	NTSC format
Geffen 1750630	Australia	PAL format

Nevermind

LP

Universal Music UIJY 9009	Japan	200gm

CD

Universal Music UICY 93358	Japan	limited edition

2008

Albums

In Utero

LP

Geffen GEF 24536	Germany	180 gm

MTV Unplugged In New York

LP

DGC 720642442517	UK	
Geffen 0720642472712	UK	Back To Black series

SHM-CD

Universal Music	UICY-91062	Japan

2009

Albums

Bleach

LP

Sub Pop 034	US

Double LP

Sub Pop SP834	US	remastered
Sub Pop SP834	US	digipak

CD

Sub Pop 70834	UK	
Sub Pop 5051865614623	UK	remastered

In Utero

LP

Universal Music B00 12765-01	US	180gm

Discography

Live at Reading
Double LP
DGC BOO13538-01   US
CD
DGC 0625272036-7(6)   UK
CD + DVD
DGC B0013501-00   US   digipak
DGC 06025272037   UK
DGC 06252720347-3(7)   UK   PAL format
DGC 2720373   Australia   PAL format
SHM-CD/DVD
Geffen UICY-94346   Japan   NTSC format

MTV Unplugged In New York
LP
Geffen SVLP 053   UK
Universal Music BOO 12764-01 US   180gm
SHM-CD
Universal Music UICY - 94347 Japan

Nevermind
LP
Simply Vinyl SVLP 038   UK
Universal Music B001266-01 US   180gm

2010
Albums
Live At Reading
Double LP
Universal Music B1353801   UK   24 tracks

2011
Albums
From The Muddy Banks Of The Wishkah
SHM-CD
Universal Music UICY-7512   Japan

In Utero
SHM-CD
Universal Music UICY-5127   Japan

Incesticide
LP

Original Recordings Group	US	180gm
ORGM-1005		

SHM-CD

Universal Music UICY-75126	Japan

Live At The Paramount
DVD

Geffen 0602527779010	UK	PAL format

Blu-ray

Geffen B0015882-59	US	
DGC 0602527779003	UK	Blu-ray Multichannel

MTV Unplugged In New York
SHM-CD

Universal Music UICY-75128	Japan

Nevermind: 20th Anniversary edition
LP

Geffen 602527851983	UK	limited edition

Double LP

DGC B0015884-01	US

4xLP

Geffen 0602527779041	UK

CD

Geffen 602527851983	UK	limited edition
Geffen 0602527779089	UK	

Double CD

Geffen 0602527779034	UK
DGC 27777903	Australia

2CD+DVD

DGC B0015885-00	US

4CD + DVD

DGC B0015885-00	US
Geffen 0602527779058	UK

DVD

Eagle Vision EREDV436	Germany	Classic Albums series
		PAL format

258

Discography

Double SHM-CD
Universal Music UICY-15120   Japan
4xSHM-CD+DVD
Universal Music UICY-75124   Japan   box set

EPs
Hormoaning
12" vinyl
Geffen B0015411-01   UK & US   limited edition

Singles
Nevermind: The singles
4x10" vinyl box set
Geffen B0016231-01   US   4 singles from
Nevermind limited to
5000 copies

Disc 1: Smells Like Teen Spirit [59] / Drain You [51] / Even In His Youth [42] / Aneurysm [54]

Disc 2: Come As You Are [60] / Endless, Nameless [67] / School [L34] / Drain You [L51]

Disc 3: Lithium [45] / Been A Son [L40] / Curmudgeon [69] / D-7 (Live) [R100]

Disc 4: In Bloom [48] / Sliver [L50] / Polly [11a]

2012
Albums
Bleach
LP
Sub Pop SP034   US

Nirvana Tracks On Compilations

Sub Pop 200
contains the Nirvana track "Spank Thru" [5]

Sub Pop SP25 3LP 1989	US	5,000	limited edition
Sub Pop SP25b	CD	1990	US
Sup Pop SPCD71/238	CD	1990	Germany
Tupelo TUPCD 4/SP25	CD	1990	UK

Hard To Believe: A Kiss Covers Compilation
contains the Nirvana track "Do You Love Me" [38]

LP/2LP/CS/CD	1990

Kill Rock Stars
contains the Nirvana track "Beeswax" [21]

Kill Rock Stars KRS201	LP	1991	US
Kill Rock Stars KRS201	CD	1991	US

The Grunge Years
contains the Nirvana track "Dive" [39]

Sub Pop SP112a	Cassette	1991	US
Sub Pop SP112b	CD	1991	US
Sony SRCS5864	CD	1991	Japan

Heaven And Hell: A Tribute To The Velvet Underground
contains the Nirvana track "Here She Comes Now" [47]

Communion	20	LP	1991	US
Communion	20	Cassette	1991	US
Communion	20	CD	1991	US
Imaginary	Illusion 016	LP	1991	UK

The Fall OF DGC
contains the Nirvana tracks "In Bloom" [48] and "Come As You Are" [60]

DGC PRO-CD-4344	CD	1991	US

Eight Songs For Greg Sage And The Wipers
contains the Nirvana track "Return Of The Rat" [70]

Tim Kerr TK917010Trib2	4x7"	1993	US
4,000 on colored vinyl (10 different colors)			
Tim Kerr TK917010Trib2	4x7"	1993	US
6,000 on black vinyl			

Fourteen Songs For Greg Sage And The Wipers
contains the Nirvana track "Return Of The Rat" [70] Tim Kerr

TK91CD10Trib2	CD	1993	US

The Beavis And Butt-head Experience
contains the Nirvana track "I Hate Myself And Want To Die" [92]

Geffen GEF24613	LP	1993	UK	picture disc
Geffen GEFC24613	Cassette	1993	US	
Geffen GEBBD24613	CD	1993	Canada	
Geffen GEFD24613	CD	1993	US	

No Alternative
contains the Nirvana track "Sappy" [12]

Arista 18737-2	CD	1993	US
Arista 18737-4	Cassette	1993	US

DGC Rarities Volume 1
contains the Nirvana track "Pay To Play" [49]

DGC DGCC24704	Cassette	1994	US
DGC DGCD24704	CD	1994	US
DGC DGCBD24704	CD	1994	Canada

Home Alive
contains the Nirvana track "Radio Friendly Unit Shifter" [L58]

Epic E2C67486	2x Cassette	1996	US
Epic E2K67486	2x CD	1996	US

Fender 50th Anniversary Guitar Legends
contains the Nirvana track "Come As You Are" [60]

Pointblank 4208820	CD	1996	USA

Fifteen Minutes: A Tribute To The Velvet Underground
contains the Nirvana track "Here She Comes Now" [47]

Imaginary ILLCD047P	CD	1994	UK

Hype!
contains the Nirvana track "Negative Creep" [33]

Sub Pop SP378	4x7"	1996	US

The Birth Of Alternative Volume 1
contains the Nirvana tracks "Blew" [31], "Love Buzz" [27] and
"Where Did You Sleep Last Night" (Kurt Cobain and Krist Novoselic
play on this Mark Lanegan track)

Flashback R275293	CD	1998	US

The Birth Of Alternative Volume 2
contains the Nirvana track "About A Girl" [14] and "Down In The
Dark" (Kurt Cobain sings on this Mark Lanegan track)

Flashback R275294	CD	1998	US

Saturday Night Live: The Musical Performances, Volume 2
contains the Nirvana track "Rape Me" [T71a]

Dreamworks 205052	CD	1998	US
Dreamworks 4502062	CD	1998	UK

Terriyaki Asthma, Volume 1
CZ009 contains the Nirvana track "Mexican Seafood" [22]

C/Z Records 7" vinyl		1989	US

Nirvana Concert History

[R]   = a recording is available of this show
[V]   = there is a video available of this show

1987
March
7   House party, Raymond, WA [R]
-       Community World Theater, Tacoma, WA
-       GESSCO Hall, Olympia, WA

August
-       Olympia, WA

1988
January
23   Community World Theater, Tacoma, WA [R]
-       Tacoma, WA

March
19   Community Word Theater, Tacoma, WA

April
24   The Vogue, Seattle, WA
-       Evergreen State College, Olympia, WA
-       The Vogue, Seattle, WA
-       Evergreen State College, Olympia, WA

June
5   Central Tavern, Seattle, WA
-       Satyricon, Portland, OR
17   Hal Holmes Center, Ellensburg, WA
29   Moore Theater, Seattle, WA

July

3	The Vogue, Seattle, WA
3	Community World Theater, Tacoma, WA
10	Comet Tavern, Seattle, WA
30	Squid Row Tavern, Seattle, WA

August

29	The Vogue, Seattle, WA

October

30	Evergreen State College, Olympia, WA
31	Union Station, Seattle, WA

November

23	Speedy O'Tubbs Rhythmic Underground, Bellingham, WA

December

1	Hollywood Underground, Seattle, WA
21	Hoquiam Eagles Lodge, Hoquiam, WA [V] [R]
21	Pourhouse, Aberdeen, WA
28	Hollywood Underground, Seattle, WA [R]

1989

January

6	Satyricon, Portland, OR
21	Satyricon, Portland, OR

February

-	Evergreen State College, Olympia, WA
8	Community World Theater, Tacoma, WA
10	The Covered Wagon Saloon, San Francisco, CA
11	Marsugi's, San Jose, CA
-	Casbah, San Diego, CA
16	Freeborn Hall UC Davis, Davis, CA
17	Chatterbox, San Francisco, CA
-	The Vogue, Seattle, WA
25	University of Washington, Seattle, WA
-	Community Center, Ellensburg, WA

April

7	Annex Theater, Seattle, WA

264

14   Hal Holmes Center, Ellensburg, WA

15   Satyricon, Portland, OR

26   The Vogue, Seattle, WA

May

9   Central Tavern, Seattle, WA

26   Lindbloom Student Center, Auburn, WA [R]

June

9   Moore Theater, Seattle, WA [R]

16   Reko-Muse, Olympia, WA

21   The Vogue, Seattle, WA

22   The Covered Wagon Saloon, San Francisco, CA

23   Rhino Records, Westwood, CA [R] [V]

24   Al's Bar, Los Angeles, CA

25   Bogarts, Long Beach, CA

26   Sun Club, Tempe, AZ

27   Rockin' TP, Santa Fe, NM

30   Alfred's, San Antonio, TX

July

-         O'Cayz Corral, Madison, WI

6   Uptown Bar, Minneapolis, MN

7   Club Dreamerz, Chicago, IL

9   Sonic Temple, Wilkinsburg, PA

12   JC Dobbs, Philadelphia, PA [R]

13   Maxwell's, Hoboken, NJ [R] [V]

15   Green Street Station, Jamaica Plain, MA [R]

-         Newark, NJ

18   Pyramid Club, New York, NY [R] [V]

August

11   Hoquiam Eagles Lodge, Hoquiam, WA

12   Bellevue VFW Hall, Bellevue, WA

13   Center for the Performing Arts, Olympia, WA

26   Contemporary Arts Center, Seattle, WA [R]

September

-         St Louis, MO

-         Minneapolis, MN

9   Cabaret Metro, Chicago, IL
13   The Garage, Denver, CO
23   The Unicorn, Milwaukee, WI
26   The Vogue, Seattle, WA
30   Cabaret Metro, Chicago, IL [R] [V]

October
-      Frankie's Inner-City, Toledo, OH
3   Blind Pig, Ann Arbor, MI
6   Murphy's Pub, Cincinnati, OH [R]
7   The Outhouse, Lawrence, KS
8   Lift Tick Lounge, Omaha, NE [R]
11   The Garage, Denver, CO [R] [V]
24   Riverside, Newcastle, UK
25   Manchester Polytechnic, Manchester, UK
26   Duchess of York, Leeds, UK [R]
27   Student Union, SOAS, London, UK [R]
28   Portsmouth Polytechnic, Portsmouth, UK [R]
29   Edward's, Birmingham, UK [R]
30   Norwich Arts Centre, Norwich, UK [R]

November
1   Nighttown, Rotterdam, Netherlands [R]
2   Vera, Groningen, Netherlands
3   Tivoli, Utrecht, Netherlands [R] [V]
4   Gigant, Apeldoorn, Netherlands
5   Melkweg, Amsterdam, Netherlands [R]
7   B-52, Moenchengladbach, Germany [R]
8   Rose Club, Koln, Germany [R]
9   Bad, Hannover, Germany [R]
10   Enger Forum, Enger, Germany [R]
11   Ecstasy, Berlin, Germany [R]
12   Kulturzentrum, Oldenburg, Germany
13   Fabrik, Hamburg, Germany [R]
15   Schwimmbad, Heidelberg, Germany
16   Trust, Nurnberg, Germany [R]
17   Negativ, Frankfurt, Germany
18   Ku-Ba, Hanau, Germany [R]

19	Gammelsdort Circus, Gammelsdort, Germany
20	Kapu, Linz, Austria [R]
21	Petofihall, Budapest, Hungary
22	U4, Vienna, Austria
23	Forumstadtpark, Graz, Austria
24	Konkret, Hohenems, Austria
25	Fri-Son, Fribourg, Switzerland
26	Bloom, Mezzago, Italy [R] [V]
27	Piper Club, Rome, Italy [R]
28	Flog Auditorium, Firenze, Italy
29	UGDO, Geneva, Switzerland
30	Rote Fabrik, Zurich, Switzerland

December

1	MJC Farhenheit, Issy Les Molineaux, France [R]
2	Democrazy, Ghent, Belgium [R]
3	Astoria, London, UK [R]

1990
January

-	Olympia, WA
6	Hub East Ballroom, Seattle, WA [R]
13	Satyricon, Portland, OR
19	Rignall Hall, Olympia, WA
20	Legends, Tacoma, WA [R] [V]

February

9	Pine Street Theater, Portland, OR [R]
11	Cactus Club, San Jose, CA [R]
12	Cattle Club, Sacramento, CA [R] [V]
14	Rough Trade Records, San Francisco, CA
14	Kennel Club, San Francisco, CA [R]
15	Raji's, Hollywood, CA [R]
16	Bogart's, Long Beach, CA [R] [V]
18	Iguana's, Tijuana, Mexico [R]
19	Mason Jar, Phoenix, AZ [R] [V]

March

12	Town Pump, Vancouver, BC, Canada [R]

April

1	Cabaret Metro, Chicago, IL [R]
6	Club Underground, Madison, WI
9	7th Street Entry, Minneapolis, MN
10	Blind Pig, Ann Arbor, MI [R] [V]
14	Shorty's Underground, Cincinnati, OH
16	Lee's Palace, Toronto, ONT, Canada [R]
17	Foufounes Electriques, Montreal, PQ, Canada [R]
18	Man Ray's, Cambridge, MA
20	MIT, Cambridge, MA [R]
21	MIT, Boston, MA
24	Swartmore College, Swarthmore, PA
26	Pyramid Club, New York, NY [R]
27	Hampshire College. Amherst, MA
28	Maxwell's, Hoboken, NJ [R]
29	9:30 Club, Washington, DC [R]
30	JC Dobbs, Philadelphia, PA

May

1	Chapel Hill, NC
2	The Milestone, Charlotte, NC [R]
4	Ritz Theater, Tampa, FL [R]
5	Einstein-A-Go-Go, Jacksonville Beach, FL
6	Masquerade, Atlanta, GA [R]
8	Staches, Columbus, OH
11	Tulsa, OK
12	Emos, Houston, TX
13	Duffy's Tavern, Lincoln, NE [R]
17	Zoo, Boise, ID

August

13	Bogart's, Long Beach, CA
15	Roxy, Hollywood, CA
16	Calamity Jayne's Nashville Nevada, Las Vegas, NV
17	The Palladium, Hollywood, CA [R]
19	The Casbah, San Diego, CA [R]
20	Crest Theater, Sacramento, CA [R]
21	Fox Warfield Theater, San Francisco, CA

23   Melody Ballroom, Portland, OR
24   Moore Theater, Seattle, WA [R] [V]
25   New York Theater, Vancouver, BC, Canada

September
22   Motor Sports International and Garage, Seattle, WA [R]

November
25   The Off Ramp Café, Seattle, WA [R]

December
31   Satyricon, Portland, OR

1991
January
18   Evergreen State College, Olympia, WA [R]

March
2   The Bronx, Edmonton, AL, Canada
4   Westward Club, Calgary, AL, Canada
7   The Forge, Victoria, BC, Canada
8   Commodore Ballroom Vancouver, BC, Canada [R]

April
17   OK Hotel, Seattle, WA [R] [V]

May
29   Jabberjaw, Los Angeles, CA [R]

June
10   Gothic Theater, Denver, CO
11   Pompadour Rock & Roll Club, Salt Lake City, UT
13   Warfield Theater, San Francisco, CA [R]
14   The Palladium, Hollywood, CA [R]
15   Iguana's, Tijuana, MX
18   The Catalyst, Santa Cruz, CA [R]
19   Crest Theater, Sacramento, CA [R]
20   Melody Ballroom, Portland, OR [R]

August
15   Roxy Theater, Hollywood, CA

20	Sir Henry's Pub, Cork, Ireland [R]
21	The Top Hat, Dublin, Ireland
23	Reading Festival, Reading, UK [R] [V]
24	Monster of Spex Festival, Koln, Germany [R] [V]
25	Pukkelpop Festival, Hasselt, Belgium [R]
27	Bremen, Germany [R]
28	Halle, Germany
29	Longhorn, Stuttgart, Germany
30	Serenadenhof, Nurnberg, Germany

September

1	De Doelen, Rotterdam, Netherlands [R] [V]
16	Beehive Record Store, Seattle, WA
21	Foufounes Electriques, Montreal, PQ, Canada [R]
23	Axis Club, Boston, MA [R]
24	Axis Club, Boston, MA
25	Club Babyhead, Providence, RI [R]
26	The Moon, New Haven, CT [R] [V]
27	City Gardens, Trenton, NJ [R]
28	Tower Records, New York, NY [R]
28	Marquee Club, New York, NY
30	Graffiti's, Pittsburgh, PA

October

1	JC Dobbs, Philadelphia, PA [R]
2	9:30 Club, Washington, DC [R]
4	Cats Cradle, Chapel Hill, NC [R]
5	40 Watt Club, Athens, GA
6	Masquerade, Atlanta, GA [R] [V]
8	New Daisy Theater, Memphis, TN
9	Staches, Columbus, OH
10	The Empire, Cleveland, OH [R]
11	St. Andrew's Hall, Detroit, MI [R]
12	Cabaret Metro, Chicago, IL [R]
14	Let It Be Records, Minneapolis, MN [R]
14	First Avenue Club, Minneapolis, MN [R]
16	Mississippi Nights, St. Louis, MO
17	University of Kansas, Lawrence, KS

19	Trees Club, Dallas, TX [R] [V]
20	The Vatican, Houston, TX
21	Waterloo Records, Austin, TX [R]
21	Liberty Lunch, Austin, TX
23	After The Goldrush, Tempe, AZ [R]
24	Off The Record, San Diego, CA [R] [V]
24	Iguana's, Tijuana, MX
25	The Palace, Hollywood, CA [R] [V]
26	Warfield Theater, San Francisco, CA [R]
27	The Palace, Hollywood, CA [R]
28	The Palace, Los Angeles, CA
29	Fox Theater, Portland, OR [R]
30	Commodore Ballroom, Vancouver, BC, Canada
31	Paramount Theater, Seattle, WA [R]

November

4	Bierkeller, Bristol, UK [R]
5	Astoria, London, UK [R] [V]
6	Wulfrun Hall, Wolverhampton, UK [R]
10	Loft, Berlin, Germany [R]
11	Markthalle, Hamburg, Germany [R]
12	Batchkapp, Frankfurt, Germany
13	Nachtwerk, Munich, Germany [R] [V]
14	Vienna, Austria [R]
16	Teatro Verdi, Muggia, Italy [R]
17	Bloom, Mezzago, Italy
19	Il Castello, Rome, Italy, [V] [R]
20	Kryptonite, Baricella, Italy [R] [V]
23	Vooruit, Ghent, Belgium [R] [V]
25	Paradiso, Amsterdam, Netherlands [R] [V]
26	Bradford University, Bradford, UK [R]
27	The Hummingbird, Birmingham, UK [R] [V]
28	Sheffield University, Sheffield, UK [R]
29	Calton Road Studios, Edinburgh, UK [R]
30	University of Glasgow, Glasgow, UK [R]

December

1	Southern Bar, Edinburgh, UK

2   Mayfair, Newcastle, UK [R]
3   Rock City, Nottingham, UK [R] [V]
4   The Academy, Manchester, UK [R]
5   Kilburn National Ballroom, London, UK [R]
7   Salles Omnisport, Rennes, France [R]

Six shows scheduled between December 9 and 14 were cancelled in Norway, Sweden, Finland and Ireland.

27   Los Angeles Sports Arena Los Angeles, CA
28   Del Mar Fairgrounds, San Diego, CA [R]
29   ASU Activity Center, Tempe, AZ [R]
31   Cow Palace, San Francisco, CA [R]

1992

January

2   Salem Armory, Salem, OR [R]
24   Phoenician Club, Sydney, Australia [R]
25   Hodern Pavilion, Sydney, Australia [R]
26   Fisherman's Wharf, Gold Coast, Australia
27   Brisbane Festival Hall, Brisbane, Australia
28   Metro, Melbourne, Australia
30   Thebarton Theatre, Adelaide, Australia [R]
31   Palace, Melbourne, Australia [R] [V]

February

1   The Palace, Melbourne, Australia [R]
2   The Palace, Melbourne, Australia
5   ANU Bar, Canberra, Australia [R]
6   Coogee Bay Hotel, Sydney, Australia [R]
7   Coogee Bay Hotel, Sydney, Australia [R]
12   Logan Campbell Centre, Auckland, New Zealand
14   Kokusai Koryu Centre, Osaka, Japan [R]
16   Club Quattro, Nagoya, Japan [R]
17   Club Citta, Kawasaki, Japan
19   Nakano Sunpiaza, Tokyo, Japan [R]
21   Pink's Garage, Honolulu, HI
22   Pink's Garage, Honolulu, HI [R] [V]

Twenty-two shows scheduled between April 10 and May 10 were cancelled in the United States and Canada.

June

21	Point Depot, Dublin, Ireland [R][V]
22	King's Hall, Belfast, UK [R]
24	Le Zenith, Paris, France [R]
26	Roskilde Festival, Roskilde, Denmark [R] [V]
27	Ruisrock Festival, Turku, Finland [R] [V]
28	Kalvoya Festival, Oslo, Norway [R] [V]
30	Sjohistoriska Museum, Stockholm, Sweden [R]

July

2	Plaza de Toros de Valencia, Valencia, Spain
3	Palacio de los Deportes de la Comunidad de Madrid, Spain [R]

Four shows scheduled between July 4 and August 23 were cancelled in Spain and the United States.

August

30	Reading Festival, Reading, UK [R] [V]

September

10	Portland Meadows, Portland, OR [R]
11	Coliseum Arena, Seattle, WA [R]

October

3	Western Washington University, Bellingham, WA [R]
4	Crocodile Café, Seattle, WA [R]
28	The Palace, Los Angeles, CA
30	Velez Sarsfield Stadium, Buenos Aires, Argentina [R] [V]

Sixteen shows scheduled between November 3 and 25 were cancelled in the United States.

1993

January

16	Morumbi Stadium, Sao Paulo, Brazil [R] [V]
23	Praca da Apoteose Stadium, Rio de Janiero, Brazil [R]

April

9   Cow Palace, San Francisco, CA [R] [V]

July

23   Roseland Ballroom, New York, NY [R]

August

6   King Theater, Seattle, WA

September

8   Club Lingerie, Los Angeles, CA

October

18   Arizona State Fairgrounds, Phoenix, AZ [R]

19   Albuquerque Convention Center, Albuquerque, NM

21   Memorial Hall, Kansas City, KS [R]

22   Palmer Alumni Auditorium, Davenport, IA [R]

23   Aragon Ballroom, Chicago, IL [R]

25   Aragon Ballroom, Chicago, IL

26   Mecca Auditorium, Milwaukee, MI [R]

27   K-Wings Stadium, Kalamazoo, MI

29   Michigan State Fairgrounds Coliseum, Detroit, MI [R]

30   Hara Arena, Dayton, OH [R]

31   University of Akron, Akron, OH [R]

November

2   Verdun Auditorium, Montreal, PQ, Canada [R] [V]

4   Maple Leaf Gardens, Toronto, ONT, Canada [R] [V]

5   University of Buffalo, Buffalo, NY [R]

7   William and Mary Hall, Williamsburg, VA [R]

8   Drexel University, Philadelphia, PA [R]

9   Lehigh University, Bethlehem, PA [R] [V]

10   Civic Center, Springfield, MA [R]

12   Civic Center, Fitchburg, MA [R]

13   American University, Washington, DC [R]

14   New York Coliseum, New York, NY [R]

15   Roseland Ballroom, New York, NY [R]

26   Shrine Auditorium, Jacksonville, FL

27   Bayfront Park Amphitheater, St Petersburg, Miami, FL [R] [V]

28   Lakeland Civic Center, Lakeland, FL

29   The Omni, Atlanta, GA [R]

December
1   Boutwell Municipal Auditorium, Birmingham, AL
2   Civic Center, Tallahassee, FL [R]
3   Lakefront Arena, New Orleans, MO [R]
5   Fairpark Coliseum, Dallas, TX [R]
6   Astro Arena, Houston, TX
8   Oklahoma City, OK [R]
9   Ak-Sar-Ben Coliseum, Omaha, NE
10   Roy Wilkins Auditorium, St Paul, MN [R]
14   Salem Armory, Salem, OR [R]
15   University Pavilion, Boise, ID
16   Golden Spike Arena, Ogden, UT
18   The Coliseum, Denver, CO [R]
23   Arco Arena, Sacramento, CA
29   Sports Arena, San Diego, CA [R] [V]
30   Great Western Forum, Los Angeles, CA [R] [V]
31   Oakland Coliseum Arena, San Francisco, CA [R]

1994
January
1   Jackson County Expo Hall, Medford, OR
3   Pacific National Exhibition Forum, Vancouver, BC Canada
4   Pacific National Exhibition Forum, Vancouver, BC, Canada [R]
6   Spokane Coliseum, Spokane, WA [R]
7   Seattle Center Arena, Seattle, WA [R]
8   Seattle Center Arena, Seattle, WA

February
6   Pavilhao Dramatico, Cascais, Portugal [R] [V]
8   Pabellon de Deportes del Real Madrid, Madrid, Spain [R]
9   Palau Municipal dels Esports, Barcelona, Spain [R]
10   Palais des Sports, Toulouse, France
12   Zenith Omega, Toulon, France [R] [V]
14   Le Zenith, Paris, France [R]
16   Salle Omnisports, Rennes, France [R]
18   Le Summon, Grenoble, France [R]

19	Patinoires du Littoral, Neuchatel, Switzerland
21	Palasport, Modena, Italy [R] [V]
22	Palagacchio, Rome, Italy [R] [V]
24	Palatrussardi, Milan, Italy [R] [V]
25	Palatrussardi, Milan, Italy [R] [V]
27	Tivoli Hala, Ljubljana, Slovenia [R] [V]
28	Zurich, Switzerland

March

| 1 | Terminal 1, Munich, Germany [R] [V] |

Thirty-three shows scheduled between March 2 and May 10 were cancelled in Germany, the Czech Republic, Denmark, Norway, Sweden, Holland, Belgium, England, Scotland, Wales and Ireland.

Chart Positions
(Original releases only)
Singles

	UK	*US*
Love Buzz	No release	Did not chart
Blew	Did not chart	Did not chart
Sliver	Did not chart	Did not chart
Molly's Lips	No release	Did not chart
Smells Like Teen Spirit	7	6
Come As You Are	9	32
Lithium	11	64
In Bloom	28	No release
Heart-Shaped Box	5	No release
All Apologies	32	No release

Albums

	UK	*US*
Bleach	Did not chart	Did not chart
Nevermind	7	1
Incesticide	14	39
In Utero	1	1
Unplugged In New York	1	1
From The Muddy Banks Of The Wishkah	4	1
Nirvana	3	3
With The Lights Out	56	19
Sliver	56	21
Live at Reading	32	37

Bibliography

The following books were useful, to varying degrees, in researching the background for this book;

Arnold, Gina
On The Road To Nirvana
St. Martin's Press, New York, 1993

Azerrad, Michael
Come As You Are – The Story Of Nirvana
Virgin Books, London, 1993

Birkenstadt, Jim and Cross, Charles R.
Nevermind
Schirmer Books, New York, 1998

Brite, Poppy Z.
Courtney Love: The Real Story
Orion Books, London, 1998

Cobain, Kurt
Journals
Penguin Books, London, 2002

Crisafulli, Chuck
Nirvana - The Stories Behind The Songs
Omnibus Press, London, 1996

Cross, Charles R.
Heavier Than Heaven – The Biography Of Kurt Cobain
Hodder and Stoughton, London, 2001

Erlewine, Michael, et al (editors)
All Music Guide: Rock
Miller Freeman Books, San Francisco, 1997

Gambaccini, Paul, Rice, Jonathan and Rice, Tim
British Hit Albums
Guinness, London, 1994

Gambaccini, Paul, Rice, Jonathan and Rice, Tim
British Hit Singles
Guinness, London, 1995

George-Warren, Holly (editor)
Cobain – By The Editors Of Rolling Stone
Rolling Stone Press, New York, 1994

Halperin, Ian and Wallace, Max
Who Killed Kurt Cobain?
Blake Books, London, 2002

Hector, James
The Complete Guide To The Music Of Nirvana
Omnibus Press, London, 1998

Humphrey, Clark
Loser – The Real Seattle Music Story
Feral House, Portland, 1995

Kane, Jack (editor)
Rare Record Price Guide 2002
Parker Publishing, London, 2000

Kitts, Jeff, Tolinski, Brad and Steinblatt, Harold (editors)
Nirvana And The Grunge Revolution
Hal Leonard Corporation, Milwaukee, 1998

Lymkiln, Sarah (editor)
Nirvana Interviews
Tomal, UK, 2003

Rocco, John
The Nirvana Companion
Omnibus Press, New York, 1998

Sandford, Christopher
Kurt Cobain
Orion Books, London, 1995

uncredited
Nirvana – The Alternative CD & Vinyl Collectors Guide
Private publication, UK, 2000

Weisband, Eric and Marks, Craig
Alternative Record Guide
Vintage, New York, 1995

Wise, Nick
In Their Own Words – Kurt Cobain & Courtney Love
Omnibus Press, London, 1996

The following periodicals were also used in researching this book:

Alternative Press, Circus, Flipside, Goldmine, Guitar World, Kerrang!, Los Angeles Times, Melody Maker, Mojo, New Musical Express, New York Times, Pulse!, Q, Record Collector, Rolling Stone, Select, Spin, Sounds, The Advocate, The Guardian, The Rocket, Uncut and *Vox.*

Thanks & Acknowledgements

As usual this book was only made possible by the generous time donated by those with something interesting to say and those with information to share – it was my job to bring all of this together. Heartfelt thanks therefore goes out to the following, who literally made this book possible in many diverse ways and to many varying degrees! Thank you all

Asbjorn Anderson, Adam Andrews James Barber, Anton Brookes, Charles R. Cross, Jack Endino, Eric Erlandson, Gino Farabella, Charles Furth, Phil Godsell, Rasmus Holmen, Chris Jacobs (at Sub Pop), Barrett Jones, Carolyn Jovanovic, Robert Lang, Courtney Love, Michael Miesel, Paul Murphy, Mike O'Connell at Helter Skelter, Doug Olsen, Charles Peterson, Graham Palmer, Scream Studios, Wendi Wills (at Bad Animals).

In memory of Sean Body

– for making it all possible in the first place.

Index

The index does not cover the preliminary pages (i–xiii) or the discography.